Ian Allan
PUBLISHING

LONDON'S HOSPITAL FOR THE MAD

First published 2009

ISBN 978 0 7110 3387 0

© Paul Chambers 2009

Published by Ian Allan Publishing

an imprint of Ian Allan Publishing Ltd, Hersham, Surrey, KT12 4RG
Printed in England by Ian Allan Printing Ltd, Hersham, Surrey, KT12 4RG

Code: 0909/B

Visit the Ian Allan Publishing website at www.ianallanpublishing.com

LONDON'S HOSPITAL FOR THE MAD

PAUL CHAMBERS

In Memoriam Matris

Contents

Acknowledgements

Creating this book was a complicated and lengthy affair that was greatly facilitated by the assistance and support of a number of individuals. I am grateful to Ilona Jasiewicz and Ian Drury for drawing my attention to Bedlam, and to Nick Grant of Ian Allan Ltd for seeing the book's potential. The staff at Ian Allan, especially Nick Grant and Mark Beynon, have offered much encouragement and have made the editing and production process run smoothly. My agents, Mandy Little, Sugra Zaman and Isabel Atherton (of Watson, Little Ltd), all had a hand in the sometimes protracted business of promoting this manuscript, and I am thankful that they were able to bear the strain with their usual good humour.

I am particularly grateful to the staff at the following institutions and companies who assisted me during the research phase and who, without exception, answered all my enquiries with diligence and patience: Bethlem Royal Hospital, Archives and Museum (Kent); Bodleian Library (Oxford); British Library (St Pancras); British Newspaper Library (Colindale); Cambridge University Library; Cruciform Library (University College Hospital); D. M. S. Watson Science Library (University College London); Family Records Centre (Islington); Hertfordshire Library Services; Institute for Historical Research (London); Society of Genealogists Library (London); The Welcome Library (London) and The National Archives: Public Record Office (Kew).

As ever, I received (apparently unlimited) moral support from my family and friends but especially my wife Rachel and daughter Eleanor. While I was writing this book my mother contracted a terminal illness and I shall remain forever in debt to the staff at Jersey Hospice Care (especially Margaret McGovern) for their help and assistance during what was a difficult time.

Author's Note

When planning this book I was keen to understand why a centuries-old institution like Bedlam Hospital should continue to conjure up visions of chaos, disorder and abuse in the modern world. I wanted to discover when and how Bedlam had obtained its poor reputation and, above all, whether the many lurid stories of neglect, brutality and mismanagement had any basis in fact. As my research progressed it became clear that for an extended period of time during the eighteenth and nineteenth centuries most aspects of Bedlam's dubious reputation were well-deserved. However, it was also evident that behind the examples of abuse that are often quoted in history books, there is a subtler, more intricate story that reveals the hospital to be as much a victim of the prejudice, ignorance and corruption of outsiders as of its own internal mismanagement. Beneath the lurid tales of violence, rape and murder is a compelling story in which Bedlam is placed at the centre of power struggles, political conspiracies and financial corruption. The hospital frequently found itself unable to control events; instead it was forced to react to the actions of others, and all too often it was the patients and inmates that suffered as a consequence. These public and private battles did not just affect Bedlam but rippled outwards into the wider 'trade in madness' that once thrived in Britain.

It is this turbulent part of Bedlam's story that fascinates me, not least because it offers an insight into how British society transformed from the community-based treatments of the mentally ill in the seventeenth century to the routine institutionalising of the insane in Hanoverian and Victorian eras. At all times Bedlam was the centre of attention, it being the ascribed authority on the diagnosis and treatment of mental illness, and yet it was also in direct competition with other charitable and private 'madhouses' that were keen to exploit Bedlam's reputation and its wealthier fee-paying patients. Thus, although this book covers the whole of Bedlam's history, from its foundation in 1247 to the present day, the prime focus is on the period between about

1728 and 1855 when four generations of the Monro family had a controlling interest in the hospital. Not uncoincidentally, it was during this turbulent period that the allegations of abuse and corruption were at their peak and when society's attitude towards madness in general was highly polarised.

It should be noted that while aspects of the story told here are appearing in print for the first time, this is a work of popular non-fiction and as such it cannot compete with the many fine textbooks that cover Bedlam's history and that of mental illness in general (see the Bibliography). My aim is to keep the story flowing smoothly, so the main body of the text is largely devoid of complex explanations and overlong discussions. Those seeking further information on individual topics or events should consult the Endnotes, where individual entries list my sources, expand on certain points and provide suggestions for further reading.

Prologue

In the autumn of 1699 the diarist, raconteur and flamboyant wig-wearer Edward 'Ned' Ward adopted the guise of a London tourist and went in search of 'the common vanities and follies of mankind'. Ward possessed a gigantic ego, a low boredom threshold and preferred always to be the centre of attention, all traits that made him somewhat tedious to be with. Those long-suffering friends on whom he imposed himself were forced to convey him about London in search of people and places that might whet his journalistic appetite. One particularly fraught day started with a visit to Gresham College, better known to Londoners as 'Maggot-mongers Hall' because of its display of stuffed and pickled bodies, both animal and human. Here there were rows and rows of dead birds, snakes, fish, monkeys and other horrors such as pickled foetuses and preserved human genitals. Most visitors found the sight compelling but it was not long before Ward grew bored and asked for a change of scene. 'And so,' wrote Ward, 'glutted with the sight of those rusty relics and philosophical toys, we determin'd to steer our course towards Bedlam.'

At this time Bedlam, or Bethlem Hospital as it is more properly titled, was a large mental asylum located at Moorfields in the heart of London's emerging business district. As well as being England's oldest and only charitable madhouse, Bedlam was also a tourist attraction. Viewed from the street outside, the hospital's imposing palatial architecture and landscaped gardens were a source of marvel, but for the cost of a single penny it was possible for the public to pass through Bedlam's ornate gates and have free access both to its grounds and to its lunatic wards. A visit to the 'madman's college' was high on the list of must-see London sights and Ned Ward, like so many of the capital's other tourists, thrilled at the prospect. As their carriage drew nearer to Moorfields, Ward and his host debated the merit of London having so large and ornate a hospital reserved solely for 'mad folks'.

Is it not surprising, asked Ward, that so much charitable money should have been spent on 'so costly a college for such a crack-brained society'? His host agreed: 'This ostentatious piece of vanity is but a monument of the City of London's shame and dishonour, instead of its glory.' This sentiment expressed, the two gentlemen paid their penny and walked through Bethlem's gates to the courtyard within. To Ward the experience saw him cross a threshold from normality into a separate and far more terrifying world.

> 'We heard such a rattling of chains, drumming of doors, ranting, holloaing, singing and rattling, that I could think of nothing but Don Quevedo's vision where the damn'd broke loose, and put Hell in an uproar.'

Ward was unnerved by this racket but nonetheless followed its origin to one of Bethlem's ground-floor galleries, which housed the patients' cells. It was here that the paying public could see and converse with Bethlem Hospital's star attractions: its 'crack-brained' inmates or, as many preferred to call them, Bedlamites.

Ward initially found the Bedlamites to be amusing and he took delight in taunting and teasing them, safe in the knowledge that there was a locked cell door between him and the object of his bullying. One of the first Bedlamites encountered by Ward claimed to be in command of an army of eagles but complained bitterly that there was little wine to be had inside the hospital. Ward addressed the fellow, saying: 'If you are a Prince of the Air, why don't you command the Man in the Moon to give you some?'

'The Man in the Moon's a sorry rascal,' replied the earnest Bedlamite. 'I sent to him for a dozen bottles but t'other day, and he swore his cellar had been dry this six months.'

Getting a rise from Bethlem's inmates was considered good sport and the practice was not discouraged by the hospital's staff. They were, after all, 'mad folks' whose shame, emotional feelings and ability to rationalise had long since been rendered obsolete by their insanity. Even so, most Bedlamites did not enjoy being verbally assaulted and would try to dissuade people from approaching their cells. Ward, for example, had a mouthful of bread and cheese sprayed at him by a dishevelled man who objected to being stared at, while another woman, who could only be viewed via a small peephole in her cell door, delighted in embarrassing her onlookers. When a young girl asked her how old she was, the woman replied, 'I am old enough to have hair where you have none!' The young girl fled down the corridor in embarrassment.

Over the course of a couple of hours Ward was witness to a full variety of Bedlam's inmates. At one end of the scale was a learned musician from St John's College, Cambridge, whose chronic bouts of depression had led to his incarceration ('a fiddling fellow with so many crotchets in his head that he crack'd his brains,' observed Ward); at the other extreme was a raving man who smelled of urine and ran round his cells clapping his hands and shouting 'halloo, halloo, halloo…'

Perhaps the most interesting Bedlamite he encountered was a man who claimed to have been sent to the hospital for being a vocal anti-monarchist. On hearing this Ward accused the man of treason, to which the inmate replied: 'Truth is persecuted everywhere abroad, and flies hither for sanctuary, where she sits as safe as a knave in a church, or a whore in a nunnery. I can use her as I please and that's more than you dare do. I can tell great men such bold truths as they don't love to hear, without the danger of a whipping post.' The man was quite correct. So long as he was classified as mad, he was free to express his anti-establishment views without fear of repercussion. Should he ever be declared sane and released then these same views would more than likely land him in prison or the pillory.

Lunchtime was approaching and, although Ward had derived much pleasure from the 'frantic humours and rambling ejaculations of the mad folks', his stomach was telling him it was time to move on. Ward asked his host to take him from the hospital and instead to escort him to the nearest pie shop.

'All I can say of Bedlam is this,' wrote Ward in his journal. 'It is an alms-house for madmen, a showing-room for whores, a sure market for lechers, a dry walk for loiterers.'

Ward had endured enough misery and madness for one day and desired a more enlivening experience; in consequence his host took him to the Royal Exchange, which, to Ward's delight, was home to bands of European exhibitionists including a crowd of 'mincing Italians' with 'effeminate waists and buttocks like a Flanders mare'. Being somewhat of a dandy himself, this gaiety suited Ward far better than the turmoil of Bethlem Hospital, whose inmates had been an uncomfortable reminder of the human persona's fragility.[1]

PART ONE

Bedlam in the Making

1

Humble Beginnings

Bethlem Hospital is one of the world's first infirmaries and is certainly the oldest mental institution in Britain. At the time of Ned Ward's 1699 visitation, Bethlem had already been in existence for four and half centuries and was London's second most famous landmark after St Paul's Cathedral. The original Bethlem was founded in 1247 when a wealthy political figure named Simon FitzMary donated a piece of land to the Bishop of Bethlehem with the express aim of establishing a dependency house for paupers. FitzMary's endowment was located on the northeastern fringe of the City of London in Bishopsgate Ward, an area that he thought was ideally suited to the needs of a charitable hospital. The Bishop of Bethlehem complied with FitzMary's wishes and founded the Prior of St Mary of Bethlehem, a religious order devoted to healing sick paupers. The small establishment was soon being referred to as Bethlehem Hospital, a name which in time was itself abbreviated to just 'Bethlem'.

Bethlem Hospital was continually short of money but somehow it always managed to scrape by and was, by the 1380s, being referred to by Londoners as 'Bedelem', a nickname that afterwards became a byword for all things chaotic.[2] There are so many gaps in Bethlem's early records that it is not known exactly when its monks began to accept patients whose symptoms stemmed from mental illness rather than physical injury or disease. One sixteenth-century rumour tells of how an unnamed medieval King of England had become so fed up with the distraught and lunatic people milling about outside his palace that he 'caused them to be removed further off to Bethlem'. This tale is probably apocryphal but it is known that by 1403 lunatic patients formed a majority of Bethlem's clients, making it London's only dedicated mental hospital, a status that it would retain for several centuries afterwards.[3]

The hospital's Bishopsgate plot was, at less than 2 acres, small and simply laid out. The site consisted of a rectangular walled courtyard in the middle of which sat a chapel. Opposite this, and pushed up against courtyard's north wall, were Bethlem's main buildings. These were a compact affair and, even after some post-medieval rebuilding, the plain, single-storey edifice contained only a dozen or so cells for its patients; appended to these were a kitchen, staff accommodation and an exercise yard.

Bethlem may not have been the largest of London's hospitals, but it was certainly the most famous. Londoners had a fascination with anything that was bizarre or unusual, so were quite aware of the City's only mental hospital; they commonly referred to it in everyday language and used it as a backdrop in their plays and poetry. Jacobean playwrights, including Shakespeare, made regular reference to Bethlem and its inmates, usually to underline a character's descent into madness or as a dramatic setting. In the 1605 play *The Honest Whore (Part One)*, various characters at times find themselves despatched to Bedlam after being driven mad by their spouses. Fortunately the hospital always managed to effect a cure and all ends well, although the playwright's final scene, set inside the hospital itself, reminds the audience that: 'Wives with weak husbands that vex them long, in Bedlam they must dwell, else dwell them long.'

Aside from an amusing talking point and a threat for errant husbands and wives, the hospital was also a tourist attraction. In 1669, for example, the diarist Samuel Pepys glibly records that: 'All the afternoon I at the Office while the young people went to see Bedlam.' Pepys took Bedlam for granted and rarely troubled himself to visit; this was probably true of most Londoners who, like Ned Ward's host, may only have visited the hospital when guests were in town. There were, however, some Londoners who took a very keen interest in Bethlem indeed, but not as a tourist attraction: they appreciated that the hospital was of great political significance and that those who exercised control over it had much to gain.[4]

Bethlem's management structure was unusual and was the cause of many of its later problems, including the accusations of physical and sexual abuse, corruption and even murder. When founded, it had been administered as a religious hospital, but at around the time of the Black Death its management became the subject of dispute between the Church, the King and the Corporation of London (the political authority that governs the City of London). From 1504 the Corporation of London made periodic bids to control Bethlem, but it continued to operate in a quasi-independent fashion, treading a fine line between the desires of the Church and the King.

It was King Henry VIII who brought an abrupt end to Church control over Bethlem when, in 1536, he ended the monastic tradition in England and Wales by ordering the dissolution of all religious houses including their hospitals. Property that had belonged to the Church was taken by the Crown and afterwards administered by the State or parcelled up and sold off as private land. Bethlem was seized by the King but, instead of being decommissioned, the fate of some other London hospitals, it was allowed to retain its function as a charitable mental institution, possibly because it was the only such facility in England. With Bethlem no longer in Church hands, the Corporation of London renewed its campaign and pressed the King to give it overall control; the idea was resisted until January 1547 when the 'custody, order and governance' of Bethlem was transferred to the Court of Aldermen, an elected body within the Corporation of London. The King died two weeks later but he had not relinquished total authority and made it clear that, while the Court of Aldermen was in charge of Bethlem's management, the Crown retained the right to intervene whenever it felt necessary.

For a time the Court of Aldermen tried running Bethlem single-handedly, but the results were far from satisfactory. By 1574 the Aldermen recognised that they had neither the time nor the experience to run a charitable mental hospital and consequently Bethlem's management was handed over to nearby Bridewell Hospital, an institution that acted as a place of punishment for 'lewd women' and which, like Bedlam, had long been part of London's urban folklore as a place to be both admired and feared.

Incorporating Bethlem into Bridewell's management structure (which was also shared by Christ's and St Thomas's hospitals) was a logical and sensible move on the part of the Aldermen. Bridewell was run by a Court of forty-two Governors who oversaw the work of the hospital's senior officers and administrative staff. Placing Bethlem under the control of these Governors was to be a pivotal moment in its history, the effect of which would be felt for centuries afterwards in both positive and negative terms.

It was the quality of Bethlem's Governors and the decisions that they took which helped to define the outside world's view of the hospital; yet becoming a Governor for Bridewell and Bethlem (as they were jointly known) was not at all difficult. A would-be Governor needed only to make a donation (usually at least £50) into the coffers of either hospital, after which his application to join the Court of Governors would almost certainly be met with approval. The majority of Governors treated the job as an honorary position, leaving the hard work to a handful of keen individuals who, together with the hospitals' senior officers, would manage the finances and take all necessary management decisions. Around four times a year the Court of Governors would meet to hear any reports and to vote on matters affecting the hospitals' management. Once a year, usually in April, a Grand Court of all the Governors (although often fewer than half would attend) was convened to, among other things, confirm senior staff appointments. As we shall see later, a Grand Court could also be raised at any time during periods of emergency or crisis.

In the early days of Bethlem's accession to Bridewell, most of the Governors had a connection with Bethlem's controlling body, the Corporation of London. Many were Aldermen, former mayors or senior members of the various mercantile guilds and livery companies that operated within the City of London (these were associations that would license and control various crafts and trades). As time progressed, this narrow pool broadened to include MPs, members of the landed gentry and well-to-do professionals such as doctors, lawyers and artists. (Both the writer Jonathan Swift and the artist William Hogarth, who is responsible for the most famous graphical depiction of the hospital as part of his 'Rake's Progress' series, were

Bridewell and Bethlem Governors.) Being a Bridewell and Bethlem Governor was something out of the ordinary and the position brought with it a certain degree of influence, especially among the political and mercantile classes.

Even though the Court of Governors was drawn largely from the City of London's governing body, it frequently proved itself to be independently minded; it often resisted the bullying tactics used by the Court of Aldermen and, more rarely, the King's Privy Council. However, the tripartite split of power between the City, Crown and Governors was unsatisfactory and led to occasional but serious conflicts of interest, especially when it came to the question as to who had the right to admit lunatic patients into Bethlem.

The importance of Bethlem as a political prize was entirely related to it being the only dedicated mental hospital in England, yet its buildings, which were all located on the original 1247 site, could only hold around forty inmates. In comparison to the population of London, which was around 250,000 in 1600, this appears to be a startling under-provision of mental health care, but there were times when fewer than half of these cells were occupied.[5]

This is not to imply that there was a lack of potential mental health patients in the London area – far from it. Every residential street had people who were labelled as being 'distracted', 'idiotic', 'mad' or 'lunatic', but instead of institutionalising them it was traditional for families to treat their insane relations within the community. In practice this meant that those who were considered to be simple, insane or melancholic would be cared for using the family home. Even violent and irrational lunatics were kept within the home, but they were often manacled to prevent them causing trouble in neighbourhoods at large although some were allowed to run free. Around 1628 one doctor records treating one Goodwife Jackson, a woman who had spent twelve years running barefoot up and down the streets with her dress torn and her hair wildly loose; periodically she would 'lye down and pull up her cloaths to everyone', causing much disgust locally. Miss Jackson was only put forward for treatment after she became obsessed with a local man who was himself placed in prison, causing the madwoman to lash out at people in frustration and to destroy private and public property. Jackson was allowed to behave like this for eighteen months before a doctor was called in to help restore her mental faculties. Such treatment within the community was the norm and it was left to Jackson's family to ensure that she was kept under control whether by restraint or medicine.[6]

Those who had no family to care for them often ended up as 'vagrant lunatics', a class of homeless people with mental health issues whose only means of support came from begging. In Shakespeare's day vagrant lunatics were referred to as Tom O'Bedlams in the mistaken belief that they had once been inmates at the hospital. Much pity was shown towards the Tom O'Bedlams, most of whom were considered to be harmless or even entertaining. In time this class of ragged wanderers played up to their stereotype and developed a sort of costume that immediately set them apart from other beggars.

'The Tom O'Bedlam', wrote Randle Holme in the 1680s, 'has a long staff and a cow or ox horn by his side. His cloathing [is] fantastic and ridiculous for, being a madman, he is madly decked and dressed all over in ribbons, feathers, cuttings of cloth and what not, to make him seem a mad man or one distracted.'

Dressed in this manner the Tom O'Bedlam would go from door to door begging money, food or drink (the latter being placed in the cow horn). Another account tells of how, on being cast from Bethlem Hospital, a Tom O'Bedlam would have an iron ring fastened round his arm, which he could not remove and was a symbol of his madness. In fact, most Tom O'Bedlams had been nowhere near a doctor, let alone a hospital, but they inspired affection and sympathy from many people and feature in a number of plays and poems, including Shakespeare's King Lear. Their bizarre dress and mannerisms would occasionally be adopted by 'Abram men', who were sane beggars looking for a better source of income.[7]

This reliance on domestic care and public charity lessened the need for specialist mental facilities and, as a consequence, only the severest cases would be considered for Bethlem Hospital, and even then admission was by no means guaranteed. The Governors' strict policy held that they would admit to Bethlem only those people who were 'raving and furious, and capable of cure, or if not, yet are likely to do mischief to themselves or others, and are poor, and cannot otherwise be provided for.' Those who were adjudged to be 'melancholic or idiots and judged not capable of cure' were routinely turned away. However, although the Governors professed only to be interested in severe (but ultimately curable) charitable cases, there was more than one means by which a patient could be admitted to the hospital, and this is where trouble frequently arose between Bethlem's three controlling bodies.[8]

The majority of Bedlam's inmates were pauper lunatics whose behaviour had caused their parish authorities or, more rarely, a local magistrate to recommend them to the hospital. Once a week a meeting would be held during which the cases of potential new admissions would be presented to one of Bethlem's senior officers and any attending Governors. If an individual was deemed to be sufficiently mad, but also potentially curable, a warrant would be issued and the person admitted. However, those who sponsored the patient (usually their relations or their local parish) had to agree to provide a sum of money for their bedding, food and upkeep and also agree to remove the person should they be cured or diagnosed as an 'incurable lunatic'.

It was by this means that Bethlem received the majority of its inmates, but the hospital's other political overseers, the Court of Aldermen, also had the power to admit patients, a privilege that was sometimes subject to abuse. It was, for example, not uncommon to find an Alderman trying to get his wife admitted as a lunatic so that he could conduct an affair with a lover or spend her inheritance. Periodic censuses frequently brought such unfortunate patients to light and saw them quickly released back onto the streets. Stories of false imprisonment in Bedlam were exploited and enhanced by playwrights and led to a widespread fear of being unjustly locked up in the hospital; it seems, however, that very few sane people ended up as patients.

Those falsely admitted were often released by the Governors, who had the power to overrule admissions made via the Aldermen. Unfortunately the same was not true for those patients sent to the hospital via the King's Privy Council, the body that advised the monarch and retained a role in Bethlem's management. Being unable to veto the Privy Council, the Governors were occasionally forced to watch as apparently sane people were admitted to Bedlam as lunatics on the grounds that they were vocal opponents of the monarchy. One such victim of the Privy Council's displeasure was Richard

Stafford, a zealous Jacobite who became one the first Bedlam patients to develop a celebrity status.

Stafford had been a young London lawyer when, in 1689, he witnessed the removal of the pro-Catholic James II from the British throne in favour of his Protestant daughter Mary. As an ardent Jacobite, Stafford reacted to this so-called 'Glorious Revolution' by publishing various short pamphlets that attacked Queen Mary and the House of Commons. This behaviour twice led to Stafford's arrest and, finally, to his forced removal from London to Gloucestershire, but this did nothing to dampen his enthusiasm. In the autumn of 1691 Stafford was caught handing out defamatory leaflets outside the Queen's court in Kensington. He found himself in custody again but this time his enemies were determined to take him off the streets once and for all. On the evidence available, obtaining a lengthy gaol sentence for the Jacobite would have been problematic, so the Privy Council instead looked towards its power of admission to Bethlem Hospital.

In his published pamphlets Stafford frequently claimed that his Jacobite sympathies were not so much his own viewpoint but in fact belonged to the spirit of God who had chosen to speak to the world through him. 'I speak nothing of myself,' wrote Stafford, 'but from His [ie God's] Word only.' On the strength of this apparent claim to be a prophet, the Privy Council were able to declare Stafford a madman even though he showed few other diagnostic signs of insanity. Despite protests from Stafford, the Privy Council despatched him to Bethlem on a warrant that declared him to be 'distracted', a contemporary description for someone considered to be 'utterly mad'. For good measure they also noted that Stafford had proved 'very troublesome to their Majesties at Kensington by dispersing books and pamphlets full of Enthusiasm and Sedition'.

The warrant sealed Stafford's fate and ensured that he would remain in Bethlem until shortly before his death, aged just forty, in 1703. This is not to say that Stafford's views were tempered by his imprisonment; in fact they became more vociferous and, because he was considered mad, he was free to express them to whoever chose to listen. As an eloquent and opinionated man, Stafford became one of Bethlem's star attractions and was high on the tourists' list of 'must-see' inmates. It is probable that the nameless polemic who told Ned Ward that Bethlem was the safest place to expound his anti-monarchist views was actually Stafford (see the Prologue). A couple of years before Ward's visit, the Speaker at the House of Commons had requested that Stafford be denied access to a pen or paper to stop him writing politically charged letters to MPs, but incarceration had done nothing to diminish to his views.[9]

Blatant abuse of the admissions system caused Bethlem's Governors to bristle with rage, and throughout the seventeenth century there were infrequent purges that saw those whom they regarded 'as not to be kept' discharged back into the community. Even so, many politically contentious cases, which included Stafford, had to remain within Bethlem awaiting 'his majesty's pleasure' which, in most cases, meant spending the rest of their lives as a certified lunatic. Fortunately such patients were always a minority, and even genuinely afflicted inmates usually enjoyed a relatively brief stay with only a very few being incarcerated for a year or more. But it was not just the admissions procedure that led to tension between Bethlem's three ruling bodies: there was also the matter of its hierarchy of officers and staff and, in particular, who was responsible for making individual staff appointments.[10]

On joining with Bridewell Hospital, Bethlem acquired not only its Court of Governors but also its three senior officers, namely the same President, Treasurer and Auditor-General. The Corporation of London usually sought to fill these positions from within its own ranks: the role of President, largely ceremonial, would be given to an ex-Lord Mayor, while the Treasurer and Auditor-General, who took care of the accounts and thus formed the real hub of power, were invariably members of the Court of Aldermen. In charge of the paperwork for both institutions was the Clerk, a responsible and well-paid job that required secretarial ability and long hours. The need for such skills meant that the post of Clerk was less subject to patronage and could be filled by outsiders; on falling vacant, the post would attract dozens of applications from people in all stations of life.

Below the level of Clerk, Bridewell and Bethlem had separate officers and staff who were charged with the day-to-day running of each institution. These positions were also subject to political wrangling, none more so than the Keeper, Bethlem's most senior residential officer, who, following the merger with Bridewell, reported directly to the Clerk and the Court of Governors but whose sphere of influence did not extend beyond the hospital's walls.

The Keeper was the man in charge of managing the hospital's staff and ensuring that all ran smoothly with regard to cleanliness, food provision, maintenance, patient care, etc. He had no control over Bethlem's budget (that was the task of the Treasurer) but did have the right to raise money by renting out certain properties of Bethlem's and by charging the patients (or, more usually, their relations or parish of origin) for linen, bedding, food, medicines and other services. As with many aspects of Bethlem's management, the boundaries between the responsibility of the Keeper, Governors and Treasurer were blurred. Some Keepers took advantage of this confusion by pocketing the money they collected and by appointing their friends and relations as members of staff. Perhaps most surprising of all was that the Keeper did not need to offer any form of routine medical care to his inmates, even though they were incarcerated within a building that described itself as a hospital. This is not to say that there was no medical care at all: if someone was deemed to be seriously ill or injured, a doctor would be brought in to deal with them, but for those who were judged to be in good health there was little or no treatment. Although Bethlem advertised itself to its benefactors as a place where the insane could be cured, those inside the system were offered few practical therapies that could coax them back to sanity. It was at this point that Bethlem's generally well-organised hierarchy fell apart, for while there were rules and conventions dictating most aspects of the hospital's management, there was no policy concerning the medical treatment of the inmates. Indeed, if the glimpsed descriptions we have of the hospital's patients are generally indicative, then some people would have been lucky to come out in one piece, let alone cured.[11]

2

Crooke's Revolution

As far back as 1403 Bethlem had a reputation for offering treatment that was deemed to be 'wretched indeed'. An inventory from that year shows that there were six lunatics in residence (plus three sane patients) and that the hospital also owned six sets of chains and locks. This coincidence of numbers has led to the assumption that Bethlem's medieval inmates were routinely chained up, a theory that is supported by the hospital also owning four sets of manacles and two pairs of stocks. Reports from this time forwards make scattered references to patients having been routinely restrained with chains and of their being regularly beaten. There is, for example, a reference to a sixteenth-century patient whose 'leg is so ulcerated that it is thought it must be cut off', and another who complained that 'her foote was rotten'. It is little wonder that Londoners lived in dread at the prospect of being sent to Bedlam.[12]

The need for a more formalised system of health care did not go unnoticed, but the infighting between Bethlem's Governors, the Aldermen and the Crown led to an impasse on the issue. At the heart of the problem was the refusal of successive Keepers to take an interest in the idea of employing a permanent visiting physician or doctor, perhaps because of the expense this would incur, or because it would erode some of the Keeper's sphere of influence at the hospital. This problem was compounded by a near permanent battle between the Governors and the Court of Aldermen over who had the right to appoint the Keeper. The Aldermen saw the post as a political prize and would routinely offer it to merchants and tradesmen associated with the Corporation of London. Most of their appointees were drapers, cloth-workers or grocers with little or no relevant experience for the job. Richard Minnes, who was appointed Keeper in 1561, got the job for having been the Mayor's porter. The Governors repeatedly tried to exert their own influence over the post, including at least one attempt to get a sitting Keeper sacked, but to little avail. It took a rather strange turn of events to effect a change in this status quo.

The man responsible for creating a minor revolution within Bethlem was Helkiah Crooke, an unusual and controversial character who had been a continual source of irritation and embarrassment to London's medical community. Crooke was born in 1576 to a middling Suffolk family whose relative poverty meant that he had to enter Cambridge University as a pauper student on a scholarship. It is conceivable that Crooke's embarrassment at his humble origins may account for some of his later behaviour, especially his obsession with money. Following seven years of study, Crooke emerged with an MD in 1604 and began to practise medicine in London, where he was regarded with caution by many.

In 1610 Crooke's application to the Royal College of Physicians was rejected when, during his entry interview, he accused a colleague of malpractice. It seems that even at this early stage Crooke had a reputation for rudeness, bullying and slander. 'After actions at law', recorded the Royal College in its files, 'and other charges against him, and not a few charges of unwarranted interference, [Crooke] was advised to behave himself and have more regard for authority.' It was to be another two years before the College of Physicians begrudgingly accepted Crooke's application, but his behaviour did not moderate. The College authorities received many complaints from Crooke's patients and were embarrassed at the number of law suits enacted against him, but, perhaps most irritating of all, he was continually in arrears with his fees despite running an apparently prosperous business.[13]

Crooke's reputation as a trouble-maker was sealed in 1615 following the publication of *Microcosmographia*, an illustrated collection of mostly European anatomical papers that he had translated from Latin into English. The book was much needed and sold well, but many surgeons felt that Crooke, being a physician, had no place writing about anatomy and, furthermore, that by writing in English he was popularising a topic that had hitherto been the preserve of an academic elite. There was further outrage from both academics and the Church when it was discovered that *Microcosmographia* included images depicting the human reproductive organs in all their glory. Crooke was threatened with damnation unless he withdrew the offending images, and the President of the College of Physicians even promised to burn every copy he could find, but the author was unapologetic and the work went through many editions both during his life and afterwards, helping to raise his profile. At some point during this turbulent career Crooke had become acquainted with the Royal Court of King James I, although probably not as one of the monarch's personal physicians, as is claimed in *Microcosmographia*. This connection was to prove invaluable to Crooke during his next battle, which, in 1618, was launched against Thomas Jenner, the then Keeper of Bethlem Hospital.

What inspired Crooke to attack Jenner remains unknown; it may have been a genuine concern over conditions at Bethlem but, given his track record, it seems more likely that he had spotted an opportunity to further his own ambition. Jenner was accused by Crooke of being unfit for the job because he held no medical qualifications (although no previous Keepers had either) and because of alleged 'irregularities' committed while in office. Perhaps through his court connections, Crooke was able to get a Royal Commission into Jenner's behaviour, which concluded that the position of Keeper should be handed to Helkiah Crooke who was a 'faithful and skilful man'.

The King was in overall charge at Bethlem, so, in April 1619, the Court of Governors voted for Crooke to become Bethlem's new Keeper. He was the first person in the post to hold a medical qualification, although, as one biographer noted, Crooke was 'sadly lacking in certain other desirable qualifications'. The Governors were aware that they were employing somebody who possessed many flaws: Crooke was made to swear that he would be subservient to the Governors' will and that he would hand over any donations, bequests and other charitable money directly to them.

Crooke's time as Keeper was predictably controversial and within months the new Keeper was being investigated over a number of financial irregularities as well as an accusation of impropriety against a female patient. The Court of Aldermen, and even the Lord Mayor, were kept busy by continual complaints made both by Crooke and by the Governors. This state of tension continued for some years until, in 1628, Crooke began to campaign for Bethlem to be given financial independence from Bridewell. Following a threat by Crooke to petition Parliament on the matter, it was agreed that from 1630 onwards the two hospitals would keep separate accounts, a move that led him to demand increased funding for his pauper patients.

In February 1631 a committee of Bridewell Governors made an inspection of Bethlem, possibly at the insistence of Crooke who was keen to drive home his message that the hospital was seriously underfunded. Among other things, the Governors discovered that the hospital was operating with almost no food in its kitchens, a situation that was causing starvation amongst those pauper inmates who could not afford to buy in supplies from outside. As Crooke had hoped, the inspection achieved an increase in funding, but the slovenly conditions drew the attention of the Privy Council who, after some years of inactivity, decided that it was time for the King to step in and settle the acrimonious dispute between the Aldermen, Governors and Crooke.

The Privy Council ordered an increase in the allowances given to the pauper lunatics and demanded that the King be provided with copies of all the accounts relating to Bethlem since 1547. For a short while matters looked to be moving in Crooke's favour, especially when the Privy Council requested additional financial details from the Court of Aldermen, but the Keeper may have overestimated his influence within the Royal Court. Crooke had been a favourite of King James I but his successor, Charles I, was a very different monarch and did not much like the look of the way in which Bedlam was being run.

In 1632 the King announced that there would be a Royal Commission into Bethlem Hospital, which would include the various accusations and complaints that had been lodged by and about its Keeper. The findings were damning and highlighted some very odd bookkeeping practices, which suggested that Crooke had been creaming money from the accounts for himself. These were not small sums; it was estimated that the Keeper had been reaping annually roughly twice the amount it would have cost to fund the entire hospital in the days when his predecessor Thomas Jenner had held the post. In October 1632 a further Royal Commission was established, which uncovered evidence that the errant Keeper had been falsifying accounts and stealing charitable donations (including selling gifts made specifically for the upkeep of pauper lunatics), and had at one time or another managed to break every single one of the hospital's rules.

The effect was visible for all to see. According to the Royal Commission, Crooke's financial allowance was 'double to that which other hospitals have, yet the poor are in none of them so ill ordered and provided for, as in this: and that he doth nothing at all towards their cure ... how fit the said Doctor may be held to be further trusted with the government of the said Hospital, and how worthy to carry away the greatest part of the renew thereof besides what he otherwise exacteth, We most humbly submit to your Lordship's grave wisdom and judgement.'[14]

Although Bethlem was receiving sizeable sums of money, conditions inside were filthy with little in the way of food, medical help or basic comforts for the majority of inmates. It was a situation that could not be allowed to continue and, on 24 May 1633, Crooke was dismissed from his post.

Crooke's fourteen-year stint at Bethlem left the hospital in a worse state than he had found it, yet the self-serving and embezzling Keeper inadvertently managed to bring about some changes that would in time be of great benefit. Immediately following his dismissal his joint role as Keeper and Physician was separated, ensuring that, following centuries of ad hoc medical care, Bethlem would for ever afterwards have a non-residential Physician on the staff who would (in theory) make regular visits and attend to the inmates' needs. Shortly afterwards the medical staff was enlarged to include a non-residential Surgeon (to tend to physical afflictions and wounds) and a residential Apothecary (to prepare and dispense drugs). Having a team of dedicated medical officers can be attributed to Crooke's time as Keeper and it appears that Crooke may also have been the first person to employ a Steward and a Matron at Bethlem. This created a whole new hierarchy of staff at the hospital whose job it was to look after the building and its patients. From Crooke's time onwards these were the ordinary workers who kept the hospital running on a daily basis and who acted as a bridge between the patients and the Governors.

The Steward was in general charge of routine administration and acted like a clerk, dealing with the paperwork, accounts, finances, admissions and discharges as well as staff management. Below the Steward came the Porter, another administrative post that included more hands-on duties such as keeping tabs on food stocks and the coming and going of staff and visitors. The Matron was usually the Porter's wife and the person who was in charge of the domestic staff (cooks, cleaners, laundresses, etc) and also oversaw the female patients, ensuring that they were not taken advantage of by the staff or other inmates. Right at the bottom of the pile were the 'basketmen', a term coined in Crooke's time, and maidservants, whose role was to do all the manual work such as the cooking and serving of food, cleaning the cells and washing clothes and patients, as well as helping move patients about or, on occasion, restraining them.

As well as reorganising the staff, Crooke's other legacy to Bethlem came as a consequence of the amount of strife he had caused the City of London authorities. The Court of Aldermen had endured fourteen years of Crooke's complaints and accusations and, perhaps prompted by the Privy Council, they agreed to relinquish their right to the appointment of Bethlem's Keeper and to control its finances. These responsibilities were instead handed to the Bridewell Governors, giving them effective control of the hospital's management, something that they had been requesting for decades. This was a significant step down the road to making Bethlem an independent institution.

Crooke did not accept his sacking with grace and for years afterwards complained of being unfairly dismissed and, of all things, being owed money by the Governors. With his reputation in tatters, the Royal College of Physicians paid Crooke £5 on condition that he renounced his Fellowship; he did so and afterwards withdrew from the medical trade, to the relief of many. He died in 1648 and was buried in Clerkenwell, London.[15]

The turbulence of Crooke's reign saw Bethlem start to break away from its post-medieval roots, but the hospital was about to face a new challenge: after centuries as England's only mental asylum, it was to find itself in competition with a new generation of commercial, often brutal, asylums.

3

The New Bedlam

During the mid-seventeenth century the flow of London society was disrupted by the English Civil War and afterwards by the uncertainty created by Oliver Cromwell's Commonwealth era. By the time King Charles II was restored to the throne in 1660 the land over which he was to preside had undergone many changes. Great leaps had been made in the fields of commerce, law, science and technology, the effects of which were to drag English society inexorably away from the religion-dominated philosophy of the post-medieval era and towards what would afterwards be termed the ages of Reason and Enlightenment.

Nowhere were these changes more keenly felt than in London, a City that had suffered much during the Civil War but which had recovered to grow physically and economically, albeit with the occasional blip. In the decade following the Restoration of King Charles II, London was ravaged first by the Plague of 1665 and, a year later, by the Great Fire, which by some miracle did not touch Bethlem but did severely damage nearby Bridewell Hospital. In the years following the Fire, England's population began to grow rapidly, but London was expanding faster still. The City had found wealth through England's foreign colonies, which in turn attracted country folk who came to town in search of jobs and adventure. The influx of cash caused a property boom that saw residential London expand far beyond the City walls along the Thames into Westminster. Here there was space enough to construct the large houses and roads desired by the nouveau riche traders and brokers. The result was to create a second urban centre, the so-called 'West End', which was frequented by London's new tier of wealthy elite and their servants. However, this new-found wealth and social mobility came at a price.

The expansion of London brought with it a slow dissolution of the community spirit that had hitherto pervaded its parishes and boroughs. As work patterns, job titles and the availability of accommodation changed, so did the dynamics of family life. Work hours increased, as did the distance people had to travel to work, while, conversely, pressure of space led to the indiscriminate building of low-cost housing, which swallowed up what were once discrete villages into the urban sprawl of Greater London.

A noticeable effect from all this change was a breakdown in the cohesiveness of family life. A lack of housing space, pressure of work and an increased cost of living meant that that many families became unable, or were unwilling, to play host to their lunatic and melancholic relations. This intolerance of lunatics was reflected in the wider community where concerns about beggars and vagabonds led to a succession of poor laws and settlement acts designed to curtail the activities of vagrants. These laws affected the Tom O'Bedlams, the colourful lunatic vagrants that had been a common sight in Shakespearean England. Many Tom O'Bedlams were rounded up by magistrates and either moved on or placed in correctional facilities or workhouses: by around 1660 the Tom O'Bedlams had entirely disappeared from the English landscape.[16]

This change in society's attitude towards the insane was mirrored by the medical profession, whose view of the treatment of madness had also shifted. Instead of recommending community-based care, many doctors advised institutionalising insane patients. This attitude is highlighted by the esteemed physician and anatomist Thomas Willis who, in around 1669, recommended that the insane be not only locked up but also brutalised back to good health. The cure of madness, wrote Willis:

'...requires threatenings, bonds, or strokes as well as physic [ie medication]. For the madmen being placed in [a] house convenient for the business, must be handled both by the physician, and also by the servants that are prudent, that he may in some manner be kept in, either by warnings, chidings, or punishments inflicted on him, to his duty, or his behaviour, or manners. And indeed for the curing of mad people, there is nothing more effectual or necessary than their reverence or standing in awe of such as they think their tormentors. For by this means, the corporeal soul being in some measure depressed and restrained, is compell'd to remit its pride and fierceness; and so afterwards by degrees grow more mild, and return in order; wherefore, furious madmen are sooner, and certainly cured by punishment and hard usage, in a strait room, than by physick or medicines.'[17]

Willis's belief that the mad should be thrashed back to health was even then controversial, but his view that the insane were better off inside purposeful establishments was a generally held idea. Consequently, there quickly arose the need for institutions that could house and take care of society's 'mad folks', many of whom had been abandoned to their fate by their families. Bethlem remained the only charitable mental hospital in England, but it could accommodate only a couple of dozen patients and its admission procedure was so strict that it was of little use to most people. It was therefore left to an emerging class of English entrepreneurs to find a market-led solution to the problem of London's lack of mental health accommodation; thus, from around 1660 onwards, the first 'private madhouses' opened their doors to the public.

As their name implies, private madhouses were commercially run mental asylums that would, for a fee, take in those who were considered to be 'troubled in mind, melancholic, mopish or distracted'. In an age of emerging capitalist principle, the private madhouse was a natural solution to a situation where demand for asylum places was outstripping supply. It was not, however, necessarily the perfect solution; as we shall see later, the unregulated nature of private madhouses led to widespread abuse in both admissions procedures and the general environment within these asylums. Also, not everyone could afford the luxury of housing their mad relations in a private madhouse, and there were many types of lunatic that the private madhouses would not touch, such as those who were prone to violence or who were criminally minded. This left a sizeable number of unwanted lunatics whose home parishes and relations could not find accommodation.

The Governors at Bethlem found themselves swamped with applications for admission, but the hospital was impossibly small and its buildings were falling into disrepair. In January 1674 the matter of Bethlem's unsuitability was discussed by its Court of Governors. They concluded that 'the Hospitall House of Bethlem is very old weake and ruinous and too small and straight for keepeing the greater number of Lunatikes as are therein att present and more are often needful to be sent thither.'[18]

This pronouncement was swiftly followed with an application by the Governors to King Charles (who remained Bethlem's ultimate authority), which requested his approval for a new and much larger hospital to be built somewhere within the City of London. At the same time the President of the Governors, Sir William Turner, approached the eminent architect and scientist Robert Hooke, who, together with Sir Christopher Wren, had been responsible for reconstructing large parts of London following the Great Fire of 1666. Hooke and Turner were already well known to each other and had helped rebuild the fire-damaged Bridewell Hospital. Hooke was pleased to be approached about the Bethlem project and, after discussing the matter further with Turner, agreed to work on it.

By the time of Hooke's appointment the Governors had already decided that the Bishopsgate site, on which Bethlem had stood since 1247, was unsuitable for their planned new building. At just over an acre, the plot was too small to house a sizeable hospital and its location, at the end of a narrow lane behind several blocks of residential housing, too inconvenient. Both Hooke and the Governors had ambitious plans for the new hospital that required a large plot of land in a highly visible part of London. Their scouts had identified a plot of several acres in the fashionable district of Moorfields, which had the advantage of being sizeable, accessible and yet also entirely within the confines of the City of London. Moorfields was at this time relatively undeveloped, and retained large tracts of open ground to the north of the proposed Bethlem site. This would give the Bedlamites a commanding view of London and, conversely, give Londoners a commanding view of the new hospital.

Hooke started work on planning a building to fit the rectangular dimensions of the plot and, in July 1674, he presented the Governors with two different designs. Both were for a 'New House for Lunatikes intended to be erected betweene Moorgate and the Posterne next London Wall where there will be ground enough for One Hundred and Twenty Roomes for the Lunatikes and Officers being about Fower Hundred and Twenty foote long.'[19] Within weeks the Governors had agreed on which design to use and had provided a draft budget of around £17,000. With the finances in place and the necessary permission having been obtained, work on the new hospital began in April 1675.[20]

Progress was very rapid and just over a year later, on 29 August 1676, the hospital building was declared finished and ready for habitation. For a while the speed of the new Bethlem's construction became part of London folklore, with many claiming, incorrectly, that it had taken less than a year to build. In truth the entire project took just over two and half years, but even so this remained a remarkably quick turnaround and led some to suspect that the builders had cut corners. There was some truth in this, but it would be another century before the Governors would discover the scale of the new hospital's shortcomings. In the meantime 'New Bedlam' was heralded as an outstanding and bold example of modern architecture. King Charles, who visited the building shortly after its opening, agreed, declaring that Hooke had given Londoners a magnificent new landmark to admire.

The new Bethlem Hospital building was vastly bigger than its predecessor and was actually larger than its designer had intended. Instead of being 480 feet long, as originally proposed by Hooke, the building was 540 feet and, with four storeys, stood more than 60 feet high. Its wide symmetrical design was purposefully ostentatious and planned to inspire awe and admiration in those that viewed it. Hooke's design had been influenced by the Parisian Chateau de Tuilleries, but when Louis XIV learned that his palace had been the model for a madhouse, he was much offended. In revenge Louis is said to have used the plans of St James's Palace when constructing an 'inferior office' in Paris.[21]

Adding to the palatial effect were landscaped gardens, intricately laid out in front of the hospital, and a low front wall that separated Bethlem from the public road, ensuring that Londoners had a good view of the hospital. It is little wonder that on first seeing the new Bethlem building Ned Ward believed it to be the Lord Mayor's Palace, saying that 'he could not imagine so stately a structure could be design'd for any quality inferior.'[22]

Bethlem may have looked impressive, but inside its ornate walls the building still had to function as a viable mental institution. To this end the main building, which was located at the centre of the structure, housed the officers' and administrative rooms while running off it on each side were wings that held the lengthy corridors forming the central galleries on the ground and first floors. The galleries housed the patients' cells, with each corridor holding around thirty-eight occupants. The top storey contained the attic rooms that housed either staff or some of the less boisterous patients. The exercise yards and windows into the inmates' cells were placed behind the main building so as not to interrupt the public's view of the front entrance.

From the day of its opening the new Bethlem was a fully functioning hospital; only one feature of the new building presented an immediate problem, the positioning of the male and female wards. Hooke had placed the female patients in the gallery on the first floor with the males on the ground floor, but this proved inconvenient and the arrangement was changed so that the men were placed in the east wing of the building and the women in the west. However, having male and female patients on the same floor presented a risk of violence, rape and unwanted pregnancies. It was initially suggested that solid iron gates should be placed between the two wings, so as to create a physical barrier between the male and female galleries, but this was strongly resisted by Bethlem's Governors. They were concerned not to disrupt Hooke's original design and declared that gates 'will obscure the Grandeur and Prospect of the said Galleryes'. An experiment using wooden gates was abandoned in 1676 because, as the Governors had feared, they did indeed spoil visitors' views of the lunatics in their cells; instead the Governors ordered that the inmates be prevented from mixing by ordering them not to wander along the galleries unaccompanied. The danger associated with this policy was exposed in 1681 when two of the female inmates, Mary Loveland and Esther Smyth, were discovered to be six and three months pregnant respectively. The culprit fathers were quickly uncovered, but they turned out not to be male patients, as had been suspected, but two of the 'basketmen' (male servants) who had gained access to the women's cells. The men were dismissed and afterwards two locks were added to the women's cell doors, with one key being held only by the Matron. It was not until 1689 that iron grills were installed between the male and female wards.[23]

Even as it was being built, the people of London could see that the new Bethlem was going to be something special. Only a few weeks after the opening ceremony one poet wrote of Hooke's design: 'So brave, so Neat, so Sweet it does appear/Makes one Half-Madd to be a Lodger there.'[24] Soon every guide and survey of London contained a description of the new Bethlem, encouraging their readers to view the building for themselves.

'The noble edifice is finely situated,' wrote one guide. 'The middle, and ends, project a little, and are well ornamented; and, rising above the rest of the building, have each a flat roof, with a handsome balustrade of stone, in the centre of which is an elegant turret; that in the middle is adorned with a clock, and three dials, a gilt ball and a vane on top. The entrance is grand … it encloses a range of gardens, wherein such of the lunatics as are well enough to be suffered to go about, are allowed to walk, and enjoy the benefits of the fresh air. The inside chiefly consists of two galleries, one over the other, which cross the wings, and are 193 yards long, 13 feet high, and sixteen feet broad (without including the cells for patients which are 12 feet deep).'[25]

One feature that received particular attention was the sculpture that sat atop Bethlem's front gates greeting visitors as they passed into the gardens beyond. It depicted two shaven-headed, male Bedlamites positioned in a semi-reclined position. The left-hand man sported a loincloth and had a doleful look on his face: he represented 'melancholy', a person caught in throes of depression, tormented by the misery of his own thoughts. (It is alleged that the model for 'Melancholy' was Daniel, the one-time porter to Oliver Cromwell, who was alleged to be 7 feet 6 inches tall and much famed as a prophet.) The right-hand figure, whose inspiration is unknown, was naked save for a chain that ran between his two manacled wrists; his body was taut and his head twisted at an angle. This was a portrait of 'raving madness', another affliction displayed by Bedlamites. Both 'Melancholy' and 'Raving Madness' were fashioned by the Danish artist Caius Gabriel Cibber, and were considered to be 'esteemed pieces of exquisite sculptor', noted for their life-like nature.[26]

The statues became a landmark in their own right, but some Londoners feared them and lived in terror of being forcibly dragged through Bethlem's ornate gates to become a patient there. One such was Alexander Cruden, who, on finding that he was being taken to a madhouse, pleaded with his captors: 'Oh! What are you going to do with me? I bless God, I am not mad. Are you going to carry me to Bethlehem? How great is this affliction! This is the way to put an end to all my usefulness in the world, and to expose me to the highest degree! Oh! What shall I do? God help me!'[27]

On that occasion Cruden did not end up in Bethlem, but plenty of others did and, once there, they found themselves in the hands of its mad doctors whose job it was to offer a cure to all the hospital's patients.

4

Mad Doctors

The new Bedlam at Moorfields was a far bigger establishment than the old hospital at Bishopsgate, and on opening it had enough cells to hold 120 patients in comparison to its former limit of around 40. This greater capacity should have been matched by a significant increase in staffing levels, but finances were tight and only a handful of new 'basketmen' and laundry maids were employed. One area where the pressure from an increased number of inmates was felt most acutely was in the medical department, which, despite a threefold increase in the number of patients, remained in the hands of just three senior officers – the Physician, Surgeon and Apothecary – all of whom had to tend to Bridewell's inmates as well.

The three medical officers held a great deal of power between them, especially the Physician and Surgeon, who were non-residential and employed as visiting consultants. Although the Governors were in charge of the hospital's management, very few ever troubled themselves to visit its galleries and so had little idea as to what conditions were like for the inmates. It was the job of the medical officers to keep an eye on the patients, not just to make sure that they were healthy, but also to spot any instances of abuse or neglect. This had the effect of placing Bethlem's medical officers in charge of the hospital's general policy towards the treatment of its patients and made them responsible for developing care regimes that would include innovations that could help Bethlem keep pace with changing ideas and attitudes towards the issue of mental health.

It was Helkiah Crooke who had introduced the concept of medical officers, but he had skewed the balance of power to ensure that it was the Physician who held the greatest sway within the hospital. Many of Bethlem's future troubles would stem from its medical officers, and especially its physicians, whose idiosyncratic approach towards the job would, in time, see the hospital become embroiled in a number of highly conspicuous scandals.

By the time of Crooke's departure in 1633 the post of Bethlem Physician had become so politically important that whenever it became vacant the post would be the subject of intense rivalry and interference from outside bodies. The three Physicians that followed Crooke were Othewell Meveral, Thomas Nurse and Thomas Allen, two of whom (Meveral and Nurse) were appointed following interference by the Privy Council, who wanted to see former palace physicians working at Bethlem. These three medics did not usher in many changes at Bethlem (although Allen did refuse permission for outside doctors to perform the country's first blood transfusion 'upon some mad person at Bedlam'), but they did contrive to make the post of Physician an extremely lucrative one by exploiting the blossoming trade of 'mad doctoring'.

The term 'mad doctor' was slang for any physician or MD who chose to trouble himself with the plight of insane and melancholic patients. The trade in mad doctoring came about as a direct consequence of the booming private madhouse industry, whose establishments were usually owned and managed by individuals with no medical experience whatsoever. To compensate for this, madhouse managers would retain the services of a professional medic who would be paid to visit the premises regularly (usually once a week) to check on any new arrivals and to attend to existing patients. The visiting mad doctor's expenses would be paid for by the patient's sponsors (usually a relative) and, at around a guinea a time, it was easy money.

Many medics set themselves up as mad doctors but most had little or no experience of handling lunatic patients. In fact, the only medics in the country who regularly tended to the insane were the Bethlem Physicians; their status as official mad doctors enabled them to command high fees from those madhouses that wanted to use their services, but they also took separate commissions from rich individuals who wanted their mad relations privately tended to. Eventually all of Bethlem's Physicians would enter the mad trade in a more direct way by opening their own upmarket private madhouses, which would deal solely with rich clients.

The Governors were well aware of these outside commissions and, in the case of Thomas Allen, suspected that wealthy patients were being diverted away from Bethlem and into his own private practice. There was little that the Governors could do to stop this from happening; the post of Physician was non-residential, poorly paid and part-time, which meant that the incumbent had to continue with his private practice in order to make ends meet. This the Physicians were certainly able to do, with both Meveral and Allen being worth several hundred pounds apiece on their deaths.[28]

The prestige and earning potential that came with the job of Physician ensured that when Thomas Allen died in 1684 there was no shortage of potential applicants. However, the King's will still prevailed over the wishes of either the Governors and the Aldermen, so the post went to Edward Tyson, a respected anatomist with a passion for human autopsy and a reputation for always mumbling his words. Tyson came into the post only a short while after the move to Moorfields and was inspired to make several important changes to Bethlem's medical regime including the addition of nursing care for inmates, follow-up care for ex-patients and the establishment of a medical dispensary within the hospital. On the down side (at least as far as many of the inmates were concerned) was Tyson's introduction of enforced 'therapeutic' cold baths, which were universally loathed by patients.[29]

The use of cold bathing (also known as psychrolouisia and hydrotherapy) as a therapy was virtually unknown until around 1700, when the physician Sir John Floyer noticed that some of the 'peasantry' in his native town of Lichfield would bathe in natural springs as a remedy for various illnesses. Based on his observations, Floyer became convinced that cold bathing had genuine medical benefits and, after discovering that it had been popular with ancient Greek and Roman doctors, he started to inflict the practice on his patients. The results so amazed Floyer that in 1702 he published a book promoting cold bathing as a near universal cure and, perhaps more importantly, as an alternative to some of the more brutal medical practices such as bleeding. The book was an instant success and quickly went through several editions; after lying dormant since the Middle Ages, cold bathing was back in use with a vengeance.

Floyer claimed that cold baths were a cure for many types of disease, including mental illness, but that they could also act as a general health preservative. Cold baths, wrote Floyer, prolong life because they 'act much on the spirits, and preserve them from evaporation, and render them strong and vigorous ... but cold baths do much more strengthen all the nervous parts, and stop the evacuation of humours, and that also helps the circulation, in which life itself chiefly consists.'[30]

With recommendations like this, it is no wonder that physicians like Edward Tyson adopted the practice. Although unpopular with patients, cold bathing remained in use at Bedlam for over a century. Some time afterwards a facility for adding hot water to the baths was introduced, although this may have only been used to warm up patients who were so cold that they had lost all sensation in their arms and legs.

'In the heat of the weather,' wrote one commentator in 1734, 'a bathing place, to cool and wash them in, is of great service in curing their lunacy, and is easily made an hot bath for restoring their limbs when numb'd, or cleaning and preserving them from scurvy, or other cutaneous distempers.'[31]

Some of Tyson's contemporaries complained that his persona was as cold as the baths that he recommended, but to counter this there are several references to his having been 'famous for his kindness to lunatics'. He was certainly interested in their brains and was prone to dissect any Bedlamite who had the misfortune to die at the hospital, although he does not seem to have used these studies to throw light on the origins of the patients' madness. In fact, the majority of Tyson's published works concern his fascination with the natural world including, most famously, his dissection of a chimpanzee, an animal that he deemed responsible for reports of 'pygmie' humans in Africa and elsewhere.[32]

It was during Tyson's tenure that the tension between Bethlem's governing authorities finally reached boiling point. The three-way spilt between the Governors, Court of Aldermen and the King's Privy Council had long been inconvenient, but the move to Moorfields had served to exasperate matters. The new building required a bigger budget, which brought with it a greater administrative burden, and considerably higher maintenance bills. To make up the considerable shortfall between its regular income (from rent and investments) and its outgoings, Bethlem was reliant on the money it received from its patients' sponsors. A patient who could not afford to sponsor himself or herself (or did not have someone else who could do so) would typically have his or her costs paid for by the local parish authority. These costs varied and the weekly charge could be as little as a few pence or as much as 5 shillings, depending on the individual's financial circumstances. This would cover the cost of a patient's board and lodging but did not stretch to other sundries such as staff wages and routine maintenance. However, there were regular instances where the sponsoring parish defaulted on its payments or where they refused to pay for medical, clothing and other costs run up by the patient. In such instances the Bethlem authorities would invariably foot the bill themselves (the unacceptable alternative being to turn the inmate out into the street), all of which meant that 'pauper lunatics' acted as a drain on the hospital's finances.

Of more desire to Bethlem were those inmates who had private sponsors (usually their relations but sometimes friends or commercial organisations) who could be charged higher rates and were less likely to default. For many years Bethlem's budget was reliant on offsetting the loss-making pauper lunatics against the more lucrative privately sponsored ones, a situation that typically left the hospital's annual budget with a shortfall of a third that had to be fulfilled by charitable donations. This careful balancing of wealthy patients against paupers was upset by the arrival of the private madhouses, whose prices undercut Bethlem's by a considerable margin. The private madhouses were a cost-effective alternative to Bethlem with the added attraction of a 'no questions asked' admissions policy. Why waste time and energy on Bethlem's strict admissions procedure when the local madhouse would usually take in an inmate without fuss or, in many cases, without even bothering to check whether they were insane?

Private madhouses proved to be especially attractive to better-off families who were looking for a permanent place to house a distracted relative. The madhouses would often accept cases that Bethlem would refuse to admit, such as those suffering from depression (melancholia) or those who were judged to be incurably mad; by the 1690s Bethlem found itself unable to compete in the madhouse marketplace and saw its proportion of wealthy patients shrink while that of the financially draining pauper lunatics increased dramatically.

The Governors spotted this problem early on and chose to answer it by making their charitable income more secure and predictable. They decided to steer the hospital's income away from cash donations, which were difficult to obtain and irregular, towards money that could be derived from commercial interests and investments. They were assisted by the landmark status of Bethlem's Moorfields building, which had led to an increase in wealthy benefactors, many of whom wanted to be associated with the magnificent edifice. However, rather than accept cash, the Governors asked their donors to provide them with gifts or legacies that offered long-term financial benefits, such as property, which could be rented out, and government bonds, which provided an annual cash income. Even when large cash donations were received, the Governors often used them to buy land or other secure investments; Bethlem even began to lend money to London's businesses community and livery companies, benefiting from the annual rates of interest that it would charge.

Over the space of many years this policy turned Bethlem from being an insecure charitable hospital into an organisation that approached financial self-sufficiency. The confidence that this financial independence provided inspired Bethlem's Governors to make a renewed claim for independence from the City of London and the Royal Court.

These calls for autonomy were not heeded until the 1690s when the Governors were incrementally given greater control over Bethlem's management and its appointments procedure. By the turn of the eighteenth century Bethlem was not only financially self-sufficient, but was also operated in a mostly (though not entirely) autonomous fashion by the Governors, with the Court of Alderman and the Privy Council having elected to play a largely ceremonial role.

This autonomy was put into good effect following the death of Edward Tyson in 1708, which left the post of Physician vacant for the first time in nearly a quarter of a century. With the Aldermen and Royal Household no longer interfering in staff appointments, the Governors took steps to advertise and organise a proper election for their next Physician. Several candidates applied and probably included Dr John Branthwait, a London physician who had done little to distinguish himself in the field of medicine, and Dr John Woodward, a highly controversial figure who was noted for his rudeness and ability to resort to the sword to settle his arguments. Woodward was quickly excluded from the running, as was Branthwait, who came second to the eventual winning candidate, a man named Dr Richard Hale. On learning of John Woodward's defeat by Hale, one of his critics is alleged to have said that 'they might as well elected him a patient, had he sense enough to have been mad'.[33]

Dr Richard Hale had much in common with his predecessors, being both Oxford University-educated and possessing an academic background in human anatomy. Hale was a former colleague of Edward Tyson (a connection that doubtless helped), but had only been an MD for seven years and had hitherto shown little interest in the treatment of insane patients. Nonetheless, the appointment was made and it was to turn Hale from a little-known medic into a rich and famous mad doctor. Within weeks of his appointment he had gained admission into the Royal College of Physicians, and within months was being regarded as the foremost mad doctor in England, despite his inexperience. He was soon elected as a Fellow of the Royal Society and began to supplement his meagre Bethlem wages with a lucrative involvement in the private mad doctoring business. By the time of his death, twenty years later, Hale was reputed to be worth £100,000 (about £10 million today).[34]

Richard Hale's appointment did not just benefit his bank balance; the new Physician also brought many positive changes to Bethlem. On a personal level, he is said to have been a genial man who sought to work with his colleagues, rather than trying to get the better of them. He performed his duties efficiently and standardised the admission procedure so that the assessment of potential patients would take place without fail each week on a Saturday morning. Hale developed a particular interest in those patients who had been diagnosed as incurably insane and as such were automatically excluded from admission to Bethlem so as not to clog up the cells with long-term inmates. For the same reason 'incurable lunatics', as they were commonly called, were often barred from the better private madhouses as well.

Disturbed by this, Hale campaigned for the Governors to build a new ward solely for incurable pauper lunatics whose enlargement in society 'would be dangerous and who have no friends able to bear the expenses of confinement'. With the hospital on a sound financial footing, the request was eventually granted, but Hale's poor health meant that the new facility was opened only a matter of weeks before his death in September 1728. Hale did not get to experience the benefits of his campaigning, but he did bequeath £500 to Bethlem's incurable patients and would doubtless have been delighted when, a few years later, the hospital opened a second ward solely for incurable female lunatics.[35]

5

Dr Hale and Mrs Clerke

It was during Richard Hale's incumbency at Bethlem that some of the failings associated with the mad doctoring trade began to be aired in public. Of especial concern were persistent stories about perfectly sane people who had been falsely locked up in a private madhouse. The majority of such cases concerned families who were anxious to take control of a relative's finances by getting them certified as insane. Lunatics had few legal rights and their next of kin could apply for power of attorney over their affairs, a situation that allowed greedy relations to get their hands on a person's property and cash while they were still alive. Like many social fears, the number of such rumours was not matched by reality, but it did make wealthy people nervous of their scheming relations and, conversely, made the job of the mad doctors that much more difficult. These pitfalls are highlighted by Dr Hale himself, who had the personal misfortune to become embroiled in a dispute over the alleged madness of a wealthy heiress named Sarah Clerke (sometimes spelt Clark or Clerk). The case coincided with an expansion in London's fledgling media industry and received much publicity in both newspapers and pamphlets, thus providing us with one of the earliest detailed accounts of the tribulations of a suspected lunatic in Hanoverian society. It also starkly demonstrates the dangers that awaited those Bethlem Physicians who chose to involve themselves in the trade of mad doctoring.

On 1 January 1717 Sarah Clerke returned to her London town house after spending the autumn on a recuperative break in Bath. She was visited by her brothers, Edward and Arthur Turnor, who found her to be sleepy but otherwise quite well. Over the next few days Mrs Clerke started to behave out of sorts and would be at times very sleepy, then afterwards become hyperactive, talking non-stop for several hours at a time. Her brothers were concerned and called in a doctor who prescribed a tonic for her, but Mrs Clerke refused to take it, claiming that her family was trying to poison her. Clerke's paranoia escalated so that within days she had accused the maid and footman of putting ground glass in her food and drink; she also displayed signs of irresponsibility with regard to money.

Towards the end of January Edward and Arthur Turnor believed that their sister had become 'distracted' (ie mad) and that professional help was needed. Dr John Freind and Dr Richard Mead, two eminent London physicians, attended Mrs Clerke but she was uncooperative. It was Dr Mead who suggested that there was only one person who could help her now: Dr Richard Hale, the famous mad doctor from Bethlem.

By this stage, news of Mrs Clerke's plight had begun to circulate around London's coffee-houses. Rumour had it that she was mad and that 'one of the doctors she had with her was the Physician of Bedlam'. Being associated with Bedlam in any way, shape or form was not good for an individual's reputation, especially if they were a person of means. These rumours prompted some of Mrs Clerke's friends to rally around her, advising that she refuse all medicines offered by Hale and telling her that 'she was as well as ever was in her life'. Mrs Clerke was, however, far from right and, although she had brief periods of lucidity, her 'distraction' was becoming worse.

On 13 February, for example, she 'talked much of her purity, and of her being as unspotted, and as far from the knowledge of man as the Virgin Mary.' Her brother Edward gently pointed out to that 'she was ten years married and lay nightly with her husband.' Mrs Clerke chose not to reply. The day afterwards Dr Hale ordered that, for her own safety and that of her household, Mrs Clerke be confined to her bedroom. Dr Hale duly arrived with an apothecary's journeyman and two nurses; Clerke was downstairs and attempts were made to persuade her to go to her room voluntarily. She refused, so the four men bodily lifted her (or dragged, according to Clerke's friends) up the stairs to her chamber, locking the door behind them. The rumours in the coffee-houses now held that Mrs Clerke was being held prisoner by her brothers so that they could get control over finances and estate. This so concerned Clerke's friends that they applied to a judge to have Mrs Clerke released.[36]

On 21 February Drs Mead and Freind were called to give an account of their behaviour in court. The eminent Dr Freind claimed that Mrs Clerke's moods would come and go and that 'though she had her intervals of sense, 'twas no more than the maddest person in Bedlam had'. Freind spoke on behalf of himself, Mead and Dr Hale when he told the judge that they 'were men of a profession, and not of a trade' and that they managed their patients with judgement and prudence.

On hearing this, the judge found himself being harangued by Clerke's supporters and, under duress, ordered that the Turnor brothers should allow access to their sister by her friends provided that they were accompanied by a physician. In the coming days chaos ensued as Mrs Clerke's friends continually visited her, bringing with them a variety of physicians; on one occasion Dr Hale was very surprised to find himself surrounded by several women, all berating him for having ordered the confinement.

At the heart of this melee was one Lady Katharine Jones, who had been unable to accept Mrs Clerke's madness and who, furthermore, believed the many untruths that her deluded friend was telling her. The judge requested that all the concerned parties be brought before him again on 27 February, but Lady Jones and several others became concerned that any decision made by the judge might not go in their favour. A rumour was spread about that Mrs Clerke was to be murdered the day before her case was to be heard; this prompted a local constable and several other parish officials to break into Clerke's house, smashing the front door and several windows. They were going to break down the door to her bedroom when a maid opened it. Inside were Mrs Clerke and Dr Hale, sitting peaceably by the fireside. The pair had been chatting when the mob interceded, but Hale was not in the least bit fazed; he addressed the constable and his men, telling them that Clerke was 'much better than at any time since he visited her and likely to be well soon, if she was not discomposed afresh by this ruffle and surprise'. The mob ignored him and seized Mrs Clerke, removing her from the building to the nearby house of a female friend.[37]

The next day, Mrs Clerke's case was heard in court, which saw, among others, both Dr Hale and Mrs Clerke give evidence. Hale declared that 'Mrs Clerke was better by what medicines she had already taken, and doubted not but in some time she might have been well recovered [had she not been] carried away.' There was great excitement in court when Mrs Clerke was called forward and asked to take the stand. Far from sounding mad, Clerke gave an excellent account of her adventures from the moment of her having gone to visit Bath the previous October. She was so impressive that at one point the judge interrupted to tell her that 'she had a very good memory, and spoke very distinctly'. This was all bad news for the Turnor brothers, who had to listen as their sister shredded their reputations in public.

Her most startling claim was that she had been 'dragged up by the arms to her chamber, and hauled and pulled, and that when she was brought she was tied in her bed, and an iron thrust into her mouth which had a great round knob upon it, which hurt her lips.' She claimed to have been bound and gagged, to have had medicines forced down her throat, to have been beaten and starved and to have had her money stolen from her. It must have been quite a show for, after Mrs Clerke had finished, the judge refused to hear any more testimonies and, despite protest from Edward Turnor, set her at her liberty, although he did appoint two hitherto unknown doctors to attend to her. It was suggested that Dr Hale continue to visit Mrs Clerke but he refused, the implication being that he would not work with the court-appointed physicians.

Following the trial an anonymous pamphlet appeared, entitled 'Mrs Clerke Case', which portrayed the Turnor brothers as money-making, sadistic, self-serving maniacs bent on locking up their sister so that they could spend her money. Dr Hale was accused of being compliant with the Turnors' alleged plan by taking cash in return for giving a false diagnosis of madness. The scandal this caused was extraordinary and prompted the Turnor brothers to publish a pamphlet in reply. This provided many affidavits that backed up their case, and ended with a stout defence of Dr Hale, whom they called 'the most famous of his brethren'. The brothers even suspected that the anonymous author of 'Mrs Clerke's Case' was a rival physician of Hale who was trying to 'cast a blot upon his reputation'.[38]

Poor Dr Hale had become the inadvertent victim of a family feud, but he managed to come out of the affair with his reputation unscathed. As far as we know he did not require Mrs Clerke to be forcibly restrained or to take physical treatments such as Edward Tyson's cold baths. Most importantly, this affair gives the impression that Hale was a genial, conscientious doctor who, a decade after his arrival at Bedlam, was already by far and away the country's premier mad doctor. It is little wonder that he was in demand with his private patients and, in truth, situations such as the one he experienced with Mrs Clerke cannot have been that uncommon.

On 28 September 1728 Doctor Richard Hale died suddenly of a stroke. He was only fifty-eight and there was much shock at his passing. An obituary said of him that, while he had been Bethlem Physician, 'his indefatigable care, join'd to his sound learning and skill in his profession, was attended with such success, as deservedly raised him a great name, and at the same time, conducted to him innumerable patients of that most miserable sort, who apply for the recovery of their lost reason'.[39]

Hale had been Bridewell and Bethlem Physician for just two decades and many of his contemporaries had not expected to see the post fall vacant for some years yet. Given the ability of a Bethlem Physician to generate personal wealth, it is little wonder that when the Governors invited applications for the job they were overwhelmed with submissions. In September 1728 a shortlist of seven names was released, most of which were of renowned medics with a good track record of working in large institutions.

The list included such medical luminaries as Sir Richard Manningham, William Rutty, Richard Tyson and Charles Hale, all well known and respected. The Governors, however, had a reputation for ignoring obvious candidates in favour of an outside runner and, following three rounds of voting, they elected to the job an unknown candidate named James Monro. The announcement, made in October 1728, was greeted with amazement in some quarters, for although Monro was a proficient medic, he was not considered the most able nor the best qualified of the candidates. Some of his rivals were not only more experienced but had also spent many years preparing themselves for the post.[40]

Take Richard Tyson, who was already Physician to St Bartholomew's

Hospital, a post for which Monro had unsuccessfully applied three years earlier. At thirty-eight years old, Tyson was the same age as Monro but had a string of additional qualifications and responsibilities, including many posts within the Royal College of Physicians. He even had family connections to Bethlem (he was the nephew of both Edward Tyson and Richard Hale), a factor that had played a part in the appointment of previous staff. The majority of the other candidates were also better qualified and already held Fellowships of the Royal College of Physicians and/or the Royal Society, as well as, in some instances, being Physicians to other hospitals.

James Monro, on the other hand, was chiefly known for his involvement in the first trials for a smallpox vaccine and also for being the son of the Reverend Alexander Monro, a divinity professor and former Principal of Edinburgh University. He was not even a member of the Royal College of Surgeons; this honour was to come about two months later, in December 1728, almost certainly as a consequence of his appointment as Bethlem's Physician. He was also controversial for another reason: his Scottish father had been a vocal supporter of the deposed King James II. Many believed it likely that the new Physician would hold many of his father's political views and sympathies, although there was no actual evidence of this. In fact, Monro was very anglicised and had not only adopted the Anglican faith but had also chosen Oxford University for his education and afterwards had opened a medical practice in Greenwich. Although some of Monro's detractors continued to refer to him as being a Jacobite, there is nothing to back up this label.[41]

Dr James Monro took up the post of Bedlam's Physician on 9 October 1728 and immediately benefited by inheriting one of Dr Hale's wealthy private clients. What the Governors' expectations were when they employed Monro is anybody's guess, but as a young candidate it may have been hoped that he would, like Dr Hale, bring innovative medical practices to Bethlem, perhaps trying out new drugs and therapies or devising better curative regimes. At the very least it must have been hoped that, like the two previous holders of the post, he would keep abreast of current thinking and treatment in the field of mental health, ensuring that Bethlem was employing the latest curative techniques.[42]

If such things were expected of James Monro, the Governors were to be sorely disappointed. His appointment was to mark the start of a bleak era in the history of Bethlem, which would see its medical practices questioned and its name repeatedly dragged through the mud. Furthermore, James would be the first of a succession of four Monros to hold the post of Physician, creating a dynasty that would last for more than 125 years and, in the process, almost totally destroy Bethlem's reputation.

PART TWO

The Monro Era

6

The Start of a Dynasty

In October 1728 James Monro became the Physician of a hospital that had physically changed little since its move to Moorfields over half a century earlier. Bethlem and its gardens retained the same intricate layout, and it was still regarded as one of the capital's most handsome buildings, attracting thousands of tourists annually. Within the hospital itself there had also been little change to its management and administrative structure, which was rigidly hierarchical and subject to occasional political rivalry. Although he was the new boy, Monro did not seek merely to take his place within this hierarchy but instead set about fashioning himself a personal empire.

By the time of Monro's appointment the position of Bethlem Physician had been in existence for more than a century and, thanks largely to changes made by Tyson and Hale, the role was now well defined. Dr Monro was given a job description that required him to make at least two hospital visitations a week, during which he had to assess the medical needs of any newly admitted patients as well as those of the resident inmates. He was also required to attend on a Saturday morning when applications from new patients were considered and where any patients adjudged to be cured would be discharged.

Within the hospital James Monro was expected to work closely with the Apothecary, whose job it was to formulate and dispense medicines to patients. The Apothecary post was residential, so he attended the hospital on a more regular basis than the Physician and was generally available for consultation on most days. For this reason it was actually the Apothecary that made a majority of routine medical decisions within the hospital, so much so that the

Physician would often simply have to check up on his handiwork. The same was true of Bethlem's non-residential Surgeon, who also relied on the Apothecary to direct him towards any patients who had wounds, ulcers and other physical defects. At the time of Monro's arrival the Apothecary was William Elderton, about whom little is known, and who continued to serve until 1751 when he was dismissed for allegedly neglecting his duties. The Surgeon was John Wheeler, whose work was overshadowed by that of Monro, although he did once claim to have 'annually blooded about a thousand in and out patients' in both Bridewell and Bethlem.[43]

Between them the Physician, Surgeon and Apothecary had total control over Bethlem's medical regime, but their work was not carefully managed by the Governors and there were instances when, for some reason or another, one or more of the officers would be absent for lengthy periods, often without having arranged any replacement cover. What the patients did for medical care during times like these is not clear, but they were probably left in the hands of Bethlem's Steward, who had no formal medical training at all.

The prime objective of Bethlem's medical regime was to restore its lunatic inmates to full sanity so that they could be discharged back into the community. Devising curative medical regimes was the sole provenance of the Physician, but in the days of James Monro there was very little understanding as to the causes of mental illness. Monro regarded all forms of mental ill-health as varieties of a single disorder; thus he would treat every lunatic in the same manner, whether they were depressive, manic or paranoid. His single curative catch-all medical regime would be meted out to each patient regardless of the symptoms. It involved some very unpleasant courses of treatment that would leave some inmates physically and emotionally crippled following weeks of enforced bleeding, vomiting and diarrhoea.

Monro was notoriously uncommunicative about his medical practice, but there is a written record of his modus operandi that was left by the Methodist preacher John Wesley. In 1740 Wesley was approached by a Mrs Shaw whose son Peter had exhibited signs of mental distress and, as a result, had been sent to see Monro as a private patient. Monro told Peter to put out his tongue. Wesley records what happened next:

'Then without asking any questions, he told his mother: "Choose your apothecary, and I will prescribe." According to his prescription they, the next day, bloodied him largely, confined him to a dark room, and put a strong blister on each of his arms, and another all over his head. But he was still as "mad" as before, praying and singing, or giving thanks continually; of which having laboured to cure him for six weeks in vain, though he was now so weak he could not stand alone, his mother dismissed the doctor and apothecary, and let him beside himself in peace.'[44]

These were the hallmarks of James Monro's curative regime: a cursory diagnosis followed by a prescription of bleeding, vomiting and laxatives, regardless of whether the patient was suffering from 'atrabilarious humours' (ie depression), 'raving madness' (ie aggressive and/or violent) or some other form of mental disorder. This somewhat unpleasant treatment was actually far from original and was almost identical to cures that had been in use a century earlier during the time of Helkiah Crooke. Monro, and other mad doctors, saw no need to update their methods, but the contemporary textbooks reveal just how brutal such regimes could be. Take, for example, the case of Mrs Miller, a melancholic who was brought to the physician Daniel Oxenbridge for treatment.

'I bled her plentifully in the cephalic vein,' wrote Dr Oxenbridge, 'on the arms, in both feet, in the forehead, under the tongue and by leeches to the haemorrhoid vein. I made her drink much cider made fresh in the house.'

Like the majority of his contemporaries, Dr Oxenbridge did not view madness as a disease of the brain but instead one of the body, which could be cured using strong medicines to purge the body of its 'melancholic humours'. Every few days Oxenbridge administered Mrs Miller herbal potions designed to induce violent vomiting fits or a sudden evacuation of the bowels: 'I either bled her or vomited her strongly, or purged her. This strong vomit did much good. I gave her posit-ale [infused with the herb hellebore]; with this she would vomit twelve times, and purge two or three times downward; at other times, as her strength would bear, I purged her with harmech.'

To Oxenbridge's surprise, Mrs Miller's depression showed no signs of abating, so he moved on to a final phase of treatment. 'I shaved all the hair off her head and to her head I apply'd the warm lungs of lambs, sheep, young whelps and pigeons alive. When the weather grew hot I bathed all her body in a bath of lukewarm water alone, and sometimes herbs as afore were boiled in it, where she continued an hour, two or three, and four sometimes.' According to Oxenbridge, this did the trick and the unfortunate Mrs Miller was adjudged by him to have been cured.[45]

Admittedly, Monro probably drew the line at administering warm lambs' lungs to a patient's head but, together with the other mad doctors of his day, he used bleeding, purgatives and vomits to cure his patients as well as caustic substances that would burn and blister the skin. His predecessors at Bethlem used similar techniques, but Monro would seem to have applied these medicines with more regularity and for longer periods of time. He also seems not to have kept a close eye on his patients' progress, leaving the Apothecary to continue prescribing medicines for people who had become physically weakened through blood loss and malnutrition brought on by continual purgatives. Such treatment of the insane was not considered controversial at the time and the few protesters against it, who included John Wesley, went mostly unheeded, but this would not be the case for ever.

Descriptions of the inside of Bethlem are rare but we can see exactly the sort of environment that was operating within the hospital at the time of Monro's appointment from a timely account provided by an anonymous pamphleteer who bribed the Keeper to give him a personally conducted tour of the lunatic galleries. Unlike the rubber-necked writings of Ned Ward, who had briefly toured Bethlem a quarter of a century earlier, the pamphleteer's interest lay not in teasing the inmates but instead in trying to understand what had brought them to Bedlam in the first place.

The Keeper began the pamphleteer's tour in the ground floor east gallery, which looked to him like 'some Royal Palace, into which the doors of about fifty chambers open themselves in regular order'. This was the wing that contained Bedlam's non-violent male patients, the first of whom engaged him with some lines of poetry that were so impressive that the pamphleteer believed the inmate to be sane. The Keeper cautioned him against such thoughts. 'To believe that men in Bedlam are in their wits, and those in Newgate [Prison] are in their right, would render a man suspected either in his wisdom or morals.'

As the pamphleteer's tour progressed he was surprised to find that many of the cells did not contain the screaming madmen for which Bedlam was legendary, but instead housed lucid, intelligent men, some of whom were graduates of Oxford and Cambridge universities.

One Oxford scholar, who wore only a nightgown, was asked what he thought of the hospital. 'We know so very little of each other', replied the melancholic academic, 'that I cannot satisfy you so particularly. But my private opinion is that we are in another world where the inhabitants demean themselves as if this place were the antipodes of cleanliness and reason; or that this is the resting place of demons, who have charge of our souls, to carry 'em from orb to orb, partly to put us on new trials, and partly to awaken our lethargic souls to a sense of their conditions.'

The misery continued as the pamphleteer witnessed further expressions of woe and despair from other learned inmates including a clergyman and a lovelorn surgeon. The mood lightened with the arrival of a hearty Irishman who had been locked away after apparently becoming infatuated with the thighs of a country girl living in Shannon. 'Oh! The richest thighs that ever a mortal viewed,' he explained, and thereafter burst into song:

Upon a dunghill sat my own true love,
Much fairer she, than any rook or crow;
To scratch her arse I did pull off my glove,
Where scabs, in clusters thick as grapes did grow.
Says I to her, my dear, what is the matter?
Nothing, my love, said she, but harmless nature.
Your harmless nature, then, and you, be damned!
Pox take your arse! I've all beshit my hand!

The pamphleteer assumed the ditty to have been given in jest and laughed out loud. This produced a strong reaction from the Irishman who had given the song in earnest. 'Is it not reasonable for a man to love a woman for good thighs than good eyes?' he asked angrily.

The tour had thus far revealed a world full of melancholic men, few of whom exhibited the sort of raving behaviour that he had been led to expect. That changed when the Keeper took his guest across to the west wing where the women were housed. The gallery was outwardly similar to that of the men although it was observed that there were more chamber pots and some pieces of looking glass. The behaviour of the female inmates was, however, much more animated than that of the men, so much so that many of them could only be safely viewed through peepholes in their cell doors. Despite being cautioned by the Keeper, the awaiting sights were truly shocking.

'Looking in at a cranny,' recalled the pamphleteer, 'I saw a vigorous girl gasping, with her tongue half out of her mouth, her eyes half shut, a clammy sweat on her forehead and in a posture somewhat indecent, wiping her taper fingers with her inmost linen veil. What shall I say? I was heartily ashamed of this, but the next sight was somewhat worse. It was of a grave matron who was probing the profundity of her matrix with the stem of a tobacco pipe which, perhaps, was more for curiosity than lechery.'

The pamphleteer was greatly troubled at this overt display of female sexuality. 'Unless they were to be manacled,' commented the Keeper, 'there is no other course to prevent their giving way to these furors; for no physic or abstinence prescribed to them could.'

Fortunately other female inmates were less animated and, like their male counterparts, seemed to suffer from varying degrees of depression, usually brought about by ill-fated love affairs. The pamphleteer listened to several tales from women who had been seduced and then abandoned by men, but he quickly grew tired of these and asked to be taken to see the upstairs wards, which were inhabited by Bedlam's star attractions: the ranters and the raving mad.

In respect of their ability to rant and rave, the inmates did not disappoint the pamphleteer, but he found them impossible to talk with. These were

Bedlam's long-term patients, many of whom had spent years locked inside their cells. They were used to being stared at and, much to the pamphleteer's disappointment, were by and large unable to converse with him in the same semi-lucid manner as the lesser lunatics on the floor below. Instead, they subjected him to a barrage of semi-coherent nonsense, verbally living out their fantasies and completely oblivious to the hopelessness of their situation.

One thing that is apparent from this visit is the poor state in which these raving men were being kept. One middle-aged gentleman was dressed in clothes that were 'ragged and threadbare', while a few cells further on was the sorry sight of a man with 'no other bedding but straw' who sat in his cell shivering beneath a blanket; the pamphleteer was quick to observe that the man had been chained to the bed with manacles. On seeing that he had visitors, the physically restrained inmate started to shout out blasphemous verses that so upset the pamphleteer that he prematurely ended his visit to Bethlem and quite literally fled from the hospital: 'I was glad to breathe the free air again,' he observed.[46]

Unlike many of his contemporaries, whose visits to Bedlam were made with the aim of gawping at or provoking the inmates, this voyeur appears to have had a genuine (if somewhat cursory) interest in the inmates and the origins of their distress. His description is revealing, especially in the light of some of later abuses at the hospital, but it also says something about the way in which Bethlem had repositioned itself within the commercial marketplace of mad doctoring.

For a long while Bethlem had been losing its wealthier admissions to the cheaper private madhouses, leaving it with a predominance of pauper lunatics. The pamphleteer's visit, together with analyses made of the hospital's admissions records, reveal that Bethlem was no longer just home to the poor and disposed. A noticeable number of the people encountered by the pamphleteer were either educated (some to graduate level) or had at one time held a trade or a position of trust. In addition to the university scholars, clergymen and poets he encountered there were several businessmen together with a parson's widow and a French schoolmistress.

After years of expansion, the number of pauper inmates in Bethlem was shrinking in proportion to patients from the 'middling' classes. This is no coincidence, but was a result of the Governors' reaction to the financial troubles that had manifested themselves during Edward Tyson's reign as Physician. In the course of restructuring Bethlem's finances the Governors had decided to compete with the private madhouses by reducing their charges for independently supported patients from a high of 8 shillings a week (around £50 today) to just 2s 6d (£16 today). They also dispensed with many of the supplementary charges made for food, medicines and other sundries, leaving inmates with a duty to pay for only their clothes, bedding and surgical procedures. The new cut-price Bedlam began to attract an increasing number of privately supported patients who proceeded to take up cells that had previously been occupied by paupers living on parish welfare.

Following James Monro's employment as Physician, further changes were made that raised the cost of the security bond payable by new patients to an eye-watering 10 shillings; this was directly intended to put off parish authorities from submitting their pauper lunatics. This was no covert action – the Governors explicitly stated that they would prefer to admit lunatics with private sponsors in the place of those who were paupers. All this helped Bethlem to balance its budget and may even have generated a profit, but it was a subversion of the hospital's charitable aim of caring for society's dispossessed and disadvantaged lunatics. It was a general reflection of the way in which care of the mentally ill was being seen less as a form of charity, and more as a means of making money; and there was nobody who would make more money out of it than the Monro family.[47]

7

A Rival Across the Road

Bethlem's Physicians had a tradition of dying rich, usually through the extortionate fees they charged their private patients, but James Monro was to take the practice to new heights. Monro shows little sign of having been interested in the academic study of madness and even less concerned with adopting or devising new techniques for its cure. Most of Bethlem's Physicians had, in one form or another, published scientific papers detailing aspects of their patients behaviour and anatomy. This was not true of Monro who, in his entire career, only published the transcript of one speech, given to the Royal College of Physicians in 1737, which offers almost no insight into his thoughts about madness or its treatment. One biographer writes of him that 'his lack of commitment to broadening knowledge and debate about madness, as well as his uncritical espousal of traditional evacuative medicaments, were to meet with posthumous censure.'[48]

Rather than pursue an academic path that might result in a better understanding and treatment of the insane, Monro set about using his position within Bethlem to garner a clientele of private patients and private madhouses to which he could act as official mad doctor. In this way he built up an astounding personal fortune and a reputation as the foremost living authority on mental health matters, although, as already stated, there is scant evidence of the extent of his understanding of madness.

Monro also gathered a reputation for having an atrocious bedside manner and was accused of being rude and dismissive with a level of arrogance that eventually became legendary. Rather than taking pride in his medical skills, he revelled in his status as the country's premier mad doctor, in his personal wealth and his social standing. It would appear that his patients, rather then being objects of pity, were viewed as the means to enhancing his wealth: they were an inconvenient side effect of being a Physician.

Many of Monro's worst qualities were revealed in a series of booklets published by the Scottish religious zealot Alexander Cruden, who was for a short while incarcerated in a private madhouse under Monro's care. Typically, the Bedlam Physician made only a cursory examination of Cruden before ordering him to be bled, vomited and purged. (In fact, Cruden claims that Monro's initial diagnosis was made six days before the two men actually met.) There is even evidence that Monro may have conspired with the madhouse owner to given him power of attorney over Cruden's affairs and later of trying to get him admitted to Bethlem. However, Cruden was able to escape from the madhouse and later attempted to bring a lawsuit against Monro (amongst others) for false imprisonment. For a while it looked as though this might succeed until Cruden's eccentric behaviour in court so irritated the judge that he cut the case short by finding in favour of Monro.

'Dr Monro is always on the severe side of the question [of madness] with the respect to the poor patients,' said Cruden, 'and I have always observed this to be so. On this and some other accounts, if I wanted a physician then Monro should be the last man I would choose.'[49]

Any criticisms of James Monro's abilities as a medic were ignored by Bethlem's Governors; he remained in his post and, like his predecessors, held an ambition of working at the hospital until the day of his death. However, by 1751 his advancing age (he was seventy-one years old) was making the thrice weekly visits to the hospital and his committee duties increasingly difficult to manage. Rather than struggle on alone, Monro suggested that it might be opportune for Bethlem to employ a second Physician who could act as his apprentice. Such a move was unprecedented but the Governors agreed and on 21 June 1751 Bethlem Hospital elected a young assistant to work alongside the ageing Physician; but the choice of candidate was controversial. The new Physician's name was John Monro, the incumbent's eldest son.

Nepotism was commonplace in Hanoverian Britain, and in many professions it was whom you knew, not what you knew, that would help define a career path. The appointment of John Monro might not have been to everyone's liking, but nor did it appear controversial or, indeed, entirely illogical. James Monro was considered to be the country's foremost mad doctor, whose methods were rarely questioned and whose social connections had provided Bethlem with valuable publicity and money. Monro had performed his duties admirably, at least as far as the Governors were concerned, so why risk employing an unknown quantity when his son John was ready and willing to accept the job? Also, the new assistant Physician was hardly lacking in medical experience.

At the time of his appointment John Monro was thirty-five years old and admirably qualified to take over from his father. Following his graduation from Oxford University in 1740, Monro was elected as a Radcliffe travelling fellow, a post that his father allegedly obtained for him through his friendship with Prime Minister Sir Robert Walpole. The fellowship required Monro to practise medicine in different European countries, the aim being to gain experience of different regimes; he consequently spent a decade as a travelling doctor, although, like his father, he preferred treating the wealthy elite to the needy poor. His stay in Rome at the time of the Jacobite rebellion in England reopened old accusations that Monro, like his grandfather, was a supporter of the Scottish cause. Robert Walpole's waggish son Horace labelled John 'a Jacobite abroad' and noted that he was spending a good deal of time in the company of a pretender to the Italian throne. 'If Monro has any skill in quacking madmen, his art may perhaps be of service in the Pretender's court,' wrote Walpole.[50]

It was in 1748 that John, perhaps at the bequest of his father, began to display an ambition for the post of Bethlem Physician. A donation to the hospital earned him a Governorship and, although still periodically living abroad, he began attending committee meetings, which ensured that other Governors were familiar with his face, name and medical experience. It is little wonder that he was first in line for the post of joint Physician and, with his father's health beginning to fail, it must have been evident that it would not be long before he would be Bethlem's sole Physician. As a prerequisite to this, John was made a candidate of the Royal College of Physicians in June 1752 and shortly afterwards, on 4 November, his father passed away. James

Monro had died a rich man, much of which was a direct result of his having been Bethlem's Physician. His sons did well from the estate but it is sad to note that James's married daughters did not see much of their father's fortune; they received just a guinea each in the will, their father explaining that 'I do not expect to die in circumstances able to do more'.[51]

John Monro stood in awe of his father and adopted not just his job at Bethlem and his private patients, but also his style of medical practice. A patient who had been under the care of James Monro would have noticed almost no difference after John's accession as Physician; they would still have received the same herbal vomits and purgatives and the same venous bleeding and caustic blistering regardless of their symptoms.

At the time of John's arrival in Bethlem only a handful of people had ever questioned whether these methods were the best and kindest means of treating the victims of mental illness. In 1746, for example, a pseudonymous author argued against 'large scale bleeding and purging' and, to drive home his point, dedicated his pamphlet to James Monro 'to contribute towards making your daily fatigues less troublesome to you'. A more serious attempt at arguing against 'blisters, seatons, cupping, scarifying and all other punishments of like kind' was made in 1750 by Lewis Southcomb, but this too fell on deaf ears (probably because Southcomb was a country clergyman whose lack of medical qualifications held little sway against the Monro family's reputation). Both these objections aimed themselves at Bethlem because, as the foremost and most famous madhouse in Europe, the practices of its Physicians tended to be adopted by other mad doctors. Few Physicians were prepared to stand up and argue against Bethlem's Physicians in public about the suitability of their regime; to do so was to risk being ostracised by Monro's friends and colleagues. To make a dent against a Bethlem Physician would require someone who was not only an intellectual heavyweight but also experienced in the treatment of lunatics. Dr William Battie was just such a person and he would be one of the few people to give the Monro family a run for their money.[52]

William Battie was comparable to John Monro in terms of age, intellect and medical experience. He had originally studied law before, on inheriting a small fortune, turning his attention to medicine. For some years he ran a successful practice in Uxbridge, Middlesex, where, according to a fellow medic, 'he is one who has taken great pains to be well qualified in his Profession'. In 1738 Battie became a Fellow of the Royal College of Physicians and afterwards was very active within the organisation; it was around this time that his interest in the treatment of insanity arose. The initial cause of this fascination remains unknown, but his aspirations of being a madhouse physician faced a number of serious obstacles.[53]

Most mad doctors did not welcome competition from outsiders and, except for family members, would not take on apprentices, a practice that prevented medical students from obtaining any experience with treating mental illness. With no connections in the madhouse business, William Battie started to circumvent these restrictions by associating himself with Bethlem. In 1742 he bought himself a Governorship and started to play an active role in the hospital's management by attending the majority of committee meetings, especially those where a big decision was to be taken. He was anxious to understand the nature of lunacy and its remedy, but the more he learned about the treatments in use at Bethlem, the more concerned Battie became that its patients were not being cured but were instead being physically abused.

The event that was to mark a change both in the fortune of Dr Battie and the way in which Bethlem was viewed by others came on 17 June 1750 when a group of six medics and merchants met in the King's Arms Tavern in London's Exchange Alley. They were convinced that the City was not serving its mentally ill residents (or their relations) in a proper fashion and had gathered to discuss the plight of London's pauper lunatics. Much of the blame for this could be pinned on Bethlem Hospital, which, in their view, was self-serving, conservative and bureaucratic. By the end of the evening the six men had an agreed solution to this problem: they would build a new charitable lunatic hospital for London's pauper lunatics that would be in direct competition with Bethlem but also purposefully different in its operation and outlook.

Soon afterwards a prospectus was released whose message was perfectly clear: current mental health provision, especially that of Bethlem, was failing, and the solution was to create an entirely new kind of charitable asylum of a type never before witnessed in London:

'Notwithstanding that this Metropolis does already abound with Hospitals and Infirmaries, calculated for the relief of almost every distemper attending the poor; yet it is much to be wished that this sort of charity could be extended one step farther, by encouraging a design to establish an Hospital for the immediate reception and cure of Poor Lunatics.

'We have already the hospital of Bethlem, a noble and extensive charity from which the public have as much benefit as can be reasonably expected; but it is well known that this hospital is incapable of receiving and maintaining a great number of melancholy objects of this sort who apply for relief; and that this is a truth we appeal to every Governor of that house and to every person who has had occasion to apply for the admission of a patient into it, the compassing of which is generally the work of several weeks, and indeed unavoidably so from the great numbers upon the list. Such, therefore, as cannot be received must either want the proper and necessary means of cure, or it must be procured for them at an expense which people in mean circumstance cannot bear.

'The usefulness and necessity of hospitals for poor lunatics is evident, for there is no disease to which human nature is subject so terrible in its appearances or so fatal in its consequences; those who are melancholy often do violence to themselves, and those who are raving, to others, and too often to their nearest relations and friends, the only persons who can be expected to take the trouble of these unhappy objects upon them.

'The law has made no particular provision for lunatics, and it must be allowed that the common parish work-houses (the inhabitants whereof are mostly aged and infirm people) are very unfit places for the reception of such ungovernable and mischievous persons, who necessarily require separate apartments.

'Persons afflicted with other diseases are admitted without delay into one or other of our hospitals, but persons afflicted with this worst of all diseases are not admitted into any hospital but Bethlem (probably on account of the safety of the other patients), a small limited number into Mr Guy's only excepted.

'Would it not, therefore, be a most useful and necessary charity to establish a Hospital where such unhappy persons may be immediately admitted, and have the proper means of cure early administered to them, which are found most effectual when the patients are under the management of strangers, and by which many fatal accidents may be prevented.

'If we may judge of the probability of success in this undertaking, by the great spirit of charity and generosity that has lately attended the setting on foot some other hospitals, it may be fairly concluded that whenever a proper scheme for this purpose is offered to the public it will meet with suitable encouragement.'[54]

The concerns expressed in the prospectus persuaded others to come into the open. Within days the original committee found themselves inundated with offers of cash and support; no fewer than six apothecaries came forward to offer their services, as did many dignitaries and merchants from the City of London. The prospectus also pricked the interest of William Battie, who decided to align himself with the new hospital; he must have made quite an impression because, in October 1750, he was appointed Physician to the planned, but still non-existent, facility. Events moved quickly; by November a suitable site had been found – an old cannon works (known as The Foundry) in Upper Moorfields, which, as luck would have it, directly faced Bethlem Hospital. The physical opposition of the two buildings mirrored the differences in their approach to mental health, a point that was not missed by many commentators.

The new institution was formally called St Luke's Hospital (after the parish in which it resided) and progress proved to be remarkably swift. On 30 July 1751, just over a year after the inaugural meeting, St Luke's was in a position to accept its first patients, who were placed under the care of William Battie. From that day forward Bethlem and St Luke's were rival institutions in all respects, a situation that had arisen because of a need for an increased capacity in lunatic provision within London but also by the determination of Battie and others behind the St Luke's project to provide a therapeutic alternative to the violent methods practiced by James Monro and his son John.[55]

This rivalry even stretched to the design of the St Luke's building, which had been engineered by Charles Dance the Elder to rile the officials at Bethlem. 'This hospital,' wrote one commentator of St Luke's, 'is a neat and very plain structure at the North end of Moorfields. Nothing here is expended on ornament; and we only see a building of considerable length plastered over and whitened with windows on which no decoration has been bestowed.'[56]

This simplicity was meant to reflect St Luke's charitable nature and its high moral aims, but it also contrasted sharply with the sprawling ornate buildings of Bethlem and its highly manicured gardens. The message was clear: in contrast to Bethlem, which had a reputation for overindulging its management and wealthy patrons, St Luke's was a no-nonsense utilitarian institution designed primarily to serve its inmates, not its staff and governors.

This posturing by St Luke's was no publicity stunt; it really was a different kind of lunatic asylum. There was no admission to the general public, which meant that the inmates could receive their treatment in private, away from the taunts of gawping visitors. There was also no cherry-picking of wealthy or curable patients, as occurred at Bethlem; instead those referred to St Luke's would be admitted 'without favour or partiality'. Perhaps the greatest differences between Bethlem and St Luke's came with the latter's refusal to use violent medicines and its willingness to open itself to inspection by its patrons and supporters, and, most importantly of all, it initiated an apprenticeship scheme that allowed medical students to gain hands-on experience with insane patients.

St Luke's Hospital had been operational for just over a year when John Monro became Bethlem's sole Physician. Those in charge at St Luke's, and especially their Physician William Battie, must have wondered whether their stated opposition to Bethlem would affect John Monro. However, if they were hoping that Bedlam's new Physician would be the instigator of progression within Bethlem, they were to be seriously disappointed.

If Bethlem's Governors had sought continuity by the appointment of John Monro, they must have been delighted with their choice. The transition from father to son occurred so smoothly that there were probably a few inmates who did not even notice that their Physician had changed appearance. Like his father, John made regular visits to the hospital and personally vetted those seeking admission, but he certainly did not believe that Bethlem was an institution in need of reform.

William Battie was well placed to follow any changes taking place at Bethlem as he remained a Governor and continued to attend meetings regularly. It must have quickly been apparent that Monro had no intention of changing the status quo. Other than expanding Bethlem's infirmary in 1753, Monro's first few years in the job are notable for a lack of innovation. As time progressed Battie was frustrated to see that, despite his conservatism, John Monro was being hailed as Britain's premier mad doctor (as once his father had been). St Luke's Hospital was not short of financial subscribers nor of potential inmates (by 1753 it had fifty-seven residential patients), but it was suffering from a shortage of influence within the medical world. Battie blamed just one person for this – John Monro – and in 1757 his anger boiled over.[57]

For years Battie had been formulating his own views about the causes of madness and the best means of treating it. These came not just from his experience at St Luke's but also with his own private madhouse at Woods Close, which he bought in 1754. His ideas had already been partially aired in a series of lectures he gave to the Royal College of Physicians, but the resultant publication was in Latin and did not attract much attention. To gain a wider audience Battie began to pen a lengthy, populist essay (in English) that outlined his theories on madness while simultaneously deriding those of others. The resultant publication, entitled A Treatise on Madness, reached the bookstalls in December 1757, its stated aim being to introduce 'more gentlemen of the Faculty to the study and practice of one of the most important branches of physick'.[58]

A Treatise on Madness did not pull its punches and consequently caused a great stir among members of the medical community. On the first page Battie made sure that his reader was under no illusion as to how little regard he had for his contemporaries' views on insanity. The opening sentence reads: 'Madness, though a terrible and at present a very frequent calamity, is perhaps as little understood as any that ever afflicted mankind.' He then goes on to apportion blame:

> 'Our defect of knowledge in this matter is, I am afraid, in a great measure owing to a defect of proper communication: and the difficulties attending the care of lunaticks have at least perpetuated by their being entrusted to empiricks, or at best to a few select physicians, most of whom thought it advisable to keep the cases as well as the patients to themselves. By which means it has unavoidably happened that in this instance experience, the parent of medical science, has profited little, and every practitioner at his first engaging in the cure of lunacy has had nothing but his own natural sense and sagacity to trust to.'[59]

Battie was speaking from personal experience; his desire to become a mad doctor had been hampered by the system operated by James Monro and his colleagues. With Bethlem and other asylums routinely denying access to their inmates and with their medics refusing to publish details of the cases they were treating, there was no way for a medic to learn anything of the nature of mental health or its treatment. This secretive and conservative attitude had led to stagnation, with doctors relying on outdated views of madness and old-fashioned cures that were of little material benefit. Battie's solution was simple: scrap all existing thinking about the definition, causes and treatment of madness and begin again from scratch.

> 'In order that we may fix a clear and determinate meaning to the word madness; we must for some time at least quit the schools of philosophy, and content ourselves with a vulgar apprehension of things; we must reject not only every supposed cause of madness, but also every symptom which does not necessarily belong to it, and retain no one phenomenon but what is essential, that is without which the word madness becomes nugatory and conveys no idea whatever: or, in other words, no definition of madness can be safe, which does not, with regard at least to some particular symptoms, determine what it is not, as well as what it is.'[60]

The eighty pages that follow provide a new and radical assessment of the entire field of madness that was utterly contrary to every belief that most doctors held dear, including the Monros. Battie's chief assertion was that madness is not a single disease (as most then believed) but a multiplicity of disorders, some of which had nothing to do with insanity at all. Rather than subdividing madness into melancholia and lunacy, as asylums such as Bethlem had been doing for generations, Battie offered up a more refined definition based on his belief that insanity was related to the body's sensory system. Most forms of madness, he wrote, could be related to 'deluded judgement' caused by either anxiety ('too lively a perception of objects') or insensibility ('too little and too languid a perception of things'). In relating madness to an individual's mental interpretation of the outside world through their senses, Battie was anchoring insanity within the physiology of the brain. He proposed that there were two main types of insanity. 'Original madness' was caused by an 'internal disorder of the nervous substance', where the person's behaviour cannot be produced by external stimulation; such original madness may be due to a physical trauma to the head (such as an accident) or to hereditary disorders or disease. 'Consequential madness', on the other hand, could be triggered by (or could be related to) the external excitement of the senses; it could result from a vast array of different sensory stimulants including intoxicating drugs, overwork, childbirth, etc.

Battie's environmental causes ran contrary to contemporary thinking, which held that madness was very much a self-contained disorder related to an individual's inability to make meaningful judgements. This difference in thinking led Battie to believe that the conventional treatment being meted out to the insane was not just wrong, but was actually barbaric. This was the most controversial part of his thesis.

Battie suggested that 'original madness' (caused by tumours, hereditary disorders, etc) was incurable and could not be helped by 'the science of physick in its present imperfect state'. Consequential madness, on the other hand, was curable, not by the use of the medicines being prescribed by John Monro and others but instead by the careful management of an inmate's environment.

'Madness then, considered as delusive sensation unconnected with any other symptom, requires the patients being removed from all objects that act forcibly upon the nerves, and excite too lively a perception of things, more especially from such objects as are the known causes of his disorder; for the same reason as rest is recommended to bodies fatigued, and are not attempted to walk when the ankles are strained.'[61]

In practice this meant removing the patient from his home and, in some cases, from his family and placing him in a space that was clean, had fresh air, simple food and offered 'amusements not too engaging nor too long continued'. By providing such a stress-free existence, the inmate will gradually return to his senses without the need for violent medication. It was on this last point that Battie chose to express his greatest displeasure.

'Although frequently taken for one species of disorder, nevertheless, when thoroughly examined, it discovers as much variety with respect to its causes and circumstances as any distemper whatever. Madness, therefore, like most other morbid cases, rejects all general methods, e.g. bleeding, blisters, caustics, rough cathartics, the gums and faetid antihysterics, opium, mineral waters, cold baths, and vomits.'

Ordinary medical men know little about madness, wrote Battie, but they may have some knowledge of purges and vomits; if, however, they were ever to see the effects of these medicines it 'would soon make him wish he had never heard of them.'[62]

This was controversial stuff. Battie was telling the world that almost every mad doctor then in practice was prescribing cures to his patients that were not just ineffective, but were actually inflicting physical damage on them. It is little wonder that Battie's ideas received a hostile reaction.

There was no doubt in the minds of most medics that the prime target of Battie's A Treatise on Madness was the late James Monro, whom he blamed for turning the use of purges and vomits into the standard treatment for the insane. In 1751 Battie had complained of Dr Monro senior's monopoly over the issue of madness by commenting that the subject had been 'already too long confined (almost) to a single person'.

However, in deriding James Monro, Battie also belittled his son John, who had adopted his father's practices and beliefs totally and in an unswerving manner. Indeed, the bond between James Monro and his son was so strong that John once said of his father: 'You were second to none in the other parts of medicine but in this one, you were easily the leader.' It was inevitable that John Monro would have something to say about Battie's radical publication and his slur upon his father's legacy.[63]

By making his views public, William Battie was inviting his critics to respond in kind and, four months later, John Monro did just this with the publication of a pamphlet entitled Remarks on Dr Battie's Treatise on Madness. This was the first publication by a member of Bethlem's medical staff for a generation, but Monro did not wish to expound his own theories on madness – he was more concerned with assassinating the character and reputation of his rival.

'My own inclination would never have led me to appear in print,' wrote Monro in the introduction, 'but it was thought necessary for me, in my situation, to say something in answer to the undeserved censures, which Dr Battie has thrown upon my predecessors.'[64]

Monro chose to structure his pamphlet in an identical fashion to Battie's A Treatise on Madness, rebutting his individual observations, theories and evidence on a measure-for-measure basis. Despite professing an alleged reluctance to appear in print, Monro took a certain amount of delight in the severity of his reply. He certainly did not hold back on his criticisms of Battie, and on many occasions resorted to sarcasm and mild abuse. There is scarcely a single point in Battie's Treatise with which Monro does not take issue, from the definition of madness through to his presumed causes and cures. Monro took Battie's words and subjected them to criticism and ridicule, but whereas Battie illustrated his ideas using contemporary studies, especially of the brain, Monro chose to answer his critic using generalisations, quotes from older works (sometimes centuries old) and, on more than one occasion, with abuse and nit-picking.

For example, in answer to Battie's criticism of a lack of publications made by Bethlem physicians, Monro rather patronisingly observes that he and his predecessors 'thought it disingenuous to perplex mankind with points that must forever remain dark, intricate and uncertain'. He also undermines several of Battie's general considerations with comic sarcasm; one such case is an imaginary scene involving a doctor's consultation in which Monro uses Battie's theories (given below) to placate a patient:

'Pray doctor what is the cause of my anxiety?'

'Why sir, it may be owing to the too great or too long continued force of external objects or to the ill-conditioned state of the nerve...'

'Dear Doctor, I thank you, just my case; you have hit it exactly, but after this agonising impatience wears off, I am as it were in a kind of insensibility, from whence proceeds that?'

'That sir, nothing could be easier to be accounted for...'[65]

This playground taunting is present throughout and gives the impression that Monro thought of himself as being so superior to Battie that he need not answer him in detail. Only in a couple of places does this smug attitude break down; the first of these is when Monro defends his father's reputation and the second when he answers Battie's criticisms of his prescribed cures for madness.

On the matter of his father, whom Battie called an 'eminent practitioner', Monro gives an emotional defence, saying that 'he was infinitely superior to such a newspaper compliment; to say that he understood this distemper [ie madness] beyond any of his contemporaries, is very little praise... He was a man of admirable discernment, and treated this disease with an address that will not soon be equalled. He knew very well that, that the management requisite for it was never to be learned, but from observation; he was honest and sincere, and though no man was ever more communicative, upon points of real use, he never thought of reading lectures, on a subject that can be understood no otherwise than by personal observation; physick he honoured as a profession, but he despised it as a trade; however partial I may be to his memory, his friends acknowledge this to be true, and his enemies will not venture to deny it.'[66]

His second impassioned defence comes over his treasured medical cures for lunacy. 'I will venture to say, that the most adequate and constant cure it is by evacuation; which can alone be determined by the constitution of the patient and the judgement of the physician... I never saw or heard of the bad effect of vomits, in my practice; nor can I suppose any mischief to happen, but from their being injudiciously administered; or when they are given too strong, or the person who orders them is too much afraid of the lancet.'[67]

Monro's superior attitude is perhaps best exemplified by the quote from Horatio that he placed on the title page, which reads 'O major tandem parcas insane minori' ('O greater madman, pray have mercy on a lesser one'); this witticism caused much mirth and for years afterwards the St Luke's Physician was known to his rivals as Major Battie rather than by his correct title of Doctor. Monro ends by commenting that it was up to the reader to decide whether it is he or Battie that has the upper hand on this issue, although, naturally, he supposed himself to be the more correct; the majority of his contemporaries agreed with him.[68]

On reviewing the two pamphlets, Tobias Smollett commented that both doctors were 'very eminent in their profession' but that they were 'rivals in fame, and hitherto the contest is conducted with spirit and decorum, free from personal abuse and abounding with matter of real utility.' That said, he favoured the Bethlem Physician's point of view, commenting that 'if Dr. Battie has reflected on the late Dr. Monro [ie James], the son has vindicated him with spirit.'[69]

This favouring of Monro's defence of his father's practices over Battie's new ideas was the generally held view. 'I've gained little from Battie on madness,' wrote anatomist Albrecht von Haller in 1759. 'It's purely conjectural, without a trace of empirical reality.'[70] Indeed, for the next half-century doctors and psychologists continued to give more weight to Monro's ideas than to Battie's, which were viewed as being out of step with modern thinking. However, it was also commonly recommended that both pamphlets should be viewed as a single work. Matthew Ballie, a physician to King

George III, certainly thought so when, in 1810, he requested copies of 'Dr. Battie's Treatise and the old Dr. Monro's remarks upon that treatise'.[71]

Even modern authors cannot agree on the significance of this debate. Some view the two doctors in polarised terms, with Battie being a progressive practitioner in contrast to Monro's regressive, conservative stance. Others argue that the two mad doctors were not so far from one another as their writings might imply and that both men were operating within institutions that were inhumane but in differing ways. It is, however, generally agreed that this exchange of ideas marks a fundamental moment in the history of psychiatry and was, in general terms, responsible for alerting the medical world at large to society's changing attitudes towards the issue of mental health. Following centuries of ignorance, both Bethlem and the private madhouses would henceforward find themselves the subject of public scrutiny – and some people did not like what they were seeing.[72]

8

A Change in Attitude

The years following Battie and Monro's spat did not see any measurable criticism being levelled against either Bethlem or St Luke's, but there was a rise in complaints against the private madhouses. These institutions had a collective bad reputation that stretched back decades: the first known prosecution of a mad doctor for false imprisonment and maltreatment was in 1714 while, in 1728, Daniel Defoe called these institutions 'the height of barbarity' and demanded that they be licensed. They were thereafter regularly accused of kidnap, beatings and other abusive practices, but such charges had been widely ignored. However, an increase in newspaper readership and the expansion of Britain's middle classes led to a greater awareness of the problem and created a determination by some to do something about it.[73]

The first articles and letters criticising the private madhouses began to appear shortly after Drs Battie and Monro had published their respective pamphlets, but it was the case of one Mrs Hawley that was to draw political attention to the plight of inmates within London's private madhouses.

Mrs Hawley was a London woman who had endured a troubled relationship with both her husband and mother and, from what we know of her past, seems to have been estranged from them. On 5 September 1762 Mrs Hawley was surprised to receive an 'affectionate letter' from her husband inviting her to a party at Turnham Green. Mrs Hawley was suspicious and consulted with a friend of hers, Mr La Fortune, who promised to enquire should she not return from the party. Their suspicions were confirmed when, later that day, Mrs Hawley was kidnapped by her mother and husband and taken to Turlington's private madhouse in Chelsea. There she 'kneeled down and exhorted the keeper to let her go. He refused her on the authority of her mother who directed him to keep her confined, that she be kept up night and day in a chamber locked and barricaded and refused the use of a pen or paper. No notices were allowed to be carried to any relation or friend and she was never visited by her mother nor desired to take any medicines whatever.'[74]

Fortunately Mr La Fortune made good his promise and, after finding no sign of Mrs Hawley at her house, searched the capital's madhouses until he found her. La Fortune applied to Lord Mansfield at the King's Bench court for a writ of habeas corpus, which would require the court to determine whether or not Mrs Hawley had been lawfully imprisoned. Mansfield refused the writ on account of La Fortune not being a direct relation, but he did order that a Marlborough Street surgeon named Dr Riddle visit Mrs Hawley to determine her state of mind.

At first the madhouse refused Dr Riddle entry, claiming that Mrs Hawley wasn't resident there, but as the doctor argued with the Keeper, Hawley called out from her cell window, attracting his attention. The pair spoke long enough for Riddle to decide that Mrs Hawley was perfectly sane. He said as much to Lord Mansfield who, on 4 October, issued the desired writ of habeas corpus that instructed Turlington to release Mrs Hawley. Perhaps because of the involvement of Lord Mansfield, who was an eminent and famous judge, this case came to the attention of the MP Thomas Townsend, who had a long-standing interest in the madhouse industry and believed that it was in need of reform. Townsend used Mrs Hawley's case to persuade his colleagues that this was an issue that needed closer examination. Duly, on 27 January 1763 a Committee of MPs was appointed to inquire into the state of the private madhouses.

During the course of the next month the parliamentary Committee examined four cases of false imprisonment (including Mrs Hawley's) that were alleged to have taken place at two madhouses, Mr Turlington's at Chelsea and Mr Miles's at Hoxton. All four cases (one of which was later dismissed as being a genuine case of insanity) involved women who had been forcibly admitted to the madhouses by their relations. Incensed by what they heard, Mr Turlington was summoned before the Committee and asked to explain his madhouse's policies.

'I leave the admission of patients to my manager, Mr King,' Turlington told the MPs.

'What instructions do you give to Mr King?'

'The rule is general,' replied Turlington. 'He is to admit all persons that are brought there.'

Further questioning revealed that Mr King had no medical training and, furthermore, that no physicians ever attended the madhouse. Under pressure, Turlington also admitted that he sometimes took sane people as 'lodgers' who would, like the insane folks, be confined to the asylum. The cost to relatives was £20 to £60 a year, depending on what level of care and diet they required.

Mr King also came before the Committee and testified that he was formerly in the wool trade; he confessed to having admitted Mrs Hawley as a lunatic 'on account of her drunkenness'. This upset the MPs further.

'Upon what authority do you admit people charged only with drunkenness into a house of confinement kept only for lunatics?' they demanded.

'Upon the authority of the persons who bring them to us,' King confessed. He then admitted that during the six years he had worked at the madhouse he had never encountered a genuine lunatic. Uproar followed.

'Have you ever refused any persons who have been brought, upon any pretence whatsoever, provided they could pay for their board?'

'No,' answered King frankly.

With Mrs Hawley's case in mind, the Committee proposed the following scenario to Mr King. 'If two strangers should come to your house, one calling herself the mother of the other, and charging her daughter with drunkenness, would you confine the daughter, upon the representation of this woman calling herself the mother, even though she was a stranger to you and the daughter herself was apparently sober at the time?'

'I certainly would!'

The apparent use of private madhouses as convenient places to dispose of unwanted wives and other relations greatly troubled Townsend and his parliamentary Committee; in order to obtain 'every degree of assistance and information' on the subject they requested that Drs Monro and Battie come before them to give evidence.

Since their exchange of words five years previously, both Monro and Battie had held their tongues and, instead of criticising each other, had concentrated on furthering their respective reputations. Despite opposing ideas on the nature of madness, Battie and Monro were both held in high regard and were described by the Committee as being 'two very eminent physicians, distinguished by their knowledge and their practice in cases of lunacy'.

Both Battie and Monro were themselves the owners of private madhouses but neither had ever expressed any desire to see them come under any form of regulation. We can be reasonably certain that Monro, a conservative, would have been against the idea, but even the reformist-minded Battie had been quiet on the issue. However, on being questioned by the MPs, both men acted to type, revealing the gulf that lay between them.

Battie was first before the MPs and immediately agreed that better regulation was needed and the sooner the better. Admission procedures for madhouses were, he argued, too loose and left in the hands of people 'not competent' to diagnose cases of lunacy. He suggested that 'frequent visitation is necessary for the inspection of the lodging, diet, cleanliness and treatment' of inmates. This emphasis on the patients' diet and surroundings coincided with his stated belief that environment, not medicine, was the key to curing the insane.

Dr Monro also agreed that admission procedures were lax, and even cited some examples where he had discovered sane people who had been forcibly locked up in madhouses. He agreed that there should be regulations that covered who could own a madhouse and their admissions procedures, but he stopped short of requesting the sort of inspection regimes that Battie had put forward. At heart Monro did not welcome the idea of inspections and he held a deep-seated fear that any regulations brought in for private madhouses would eventually be applied to charitable hospitals such as Bedlam. Given that there were people such as Battie calling for changes in the care of the insane, the last thing Monro wanted was other people telling him how he should be treating his patients.

The two physicians were at least agreed on the need for control over admissions, and on 22 February the Committee produce its report, which concluded that 'the present state of the private madhouses in this kingdom require the interposition of the legislature'. The House of Commons agreed and resolved to have a Bill brought in that would provide such a regulatory regime for private madhouses. Campaigners such as Battie may have believed that they had won a small victory, but as time passed, with no action, it became obvious that the promised Bill was not going to materialise and that the status quo would remain.[75]

Quite why the legislation was abandoned is not known. Some claim it was due to opposition from the College of Surgeons, which may have been tasked with regulating the madhouses; others that it was opposition from MPs, lawyers or influential people from within the madhouse industry, possibly including John Monro who, we may suspect, was not unhappy at the Committee's lack of action.[76]

The fact that MPs were troubling themselves in this matter was symptomatic of an increasing uneasiness about the whole issue of lunacy. This disquiet had also been expressed in a growing number of court cases bought about by aggrieved asylum inmates who believed themselves to have been compos mentis when locked up. Battie and Monro had been involved as expert witnesses in several such cases and, shortly after the 1763 Committee inquiry, the two gentlemen were to be brought together by a Mr Wood, who pressed charges against Monro for alleged false imprisonment at Mile's Madhouse at Hoxton.

This case also came before Lord Mansfield at the King's Bench, but Monro's lawyer had a great deal of difficulty in making Mr Wood appear in any way insane. Despite a 'severe examination', Mr Wood put on a magnificent performance and appeared to be perfectly rational. For a while Monro's reputation looked to be in trouble, but Lord Mansfield, who had dealt with a number of cases involving lunatics, retained some suspicions and asked that Dr Battie be brought in to make his own examination of Wood. This cannot have pleased Monro, especially when Battie started applying his theories concerning deluded imagination to Mr Wood. After a cursory examination, Battie instructed his lordship to ask Wood what had become of the princess with whom he had corresponded using cherry-juice. It was a masterstroke for, as Mansfield recalls in his own words:

'Wood answered that there was nothing at all in that, because having been (as everybody knew) imprisoned in a high tower, and being debarred the use of ink, he had no other means of correspondence but by writing his letters in cherry-juice and throwing them into the river which surrounded the tower, where the Princess retrieved them in a boat. There existed, of course, no tower, no imprisonment, no writing in cherry-juice, no boat; but the whole was the inveterate phantom of a morbid imagination. I immediately directed Dr Monro to be acquitted.'[77]

One might have thought that Monro would have been grateful to Battie for saving his skin, but if this were true then he had a strange way of showing it. Three years later it was Battie who found himself in court accused of falsely imprisoning a woman named Hannah Mackenzie, whom he had certified as mad some time previously. John Monro was brought in to examine Mackenzie but did Battie no favours whatsoever when he declared her to be perfectly sane. Battie was forced to admit that she may have recovered her senses since his original pronouncement; fortunately the judge chose to believe him.

The publicity afforded to cases of alleged false imprisonment (none of which directly involved either Bethlem or St Luke's) was having a subtle but noticeable effect on the Governors at Bethlem. They sensed that London's intelligentsia were becoming more aware of social issues and that their opinion of insane people was shifting away from one of fear, curiosity and ridicule towards pity and concern for their treatment and conditions of confinement. This was not yet organised enough to be called a reform movement, but Bethlem was financially reliant on the benevolence of its wealthy patrons and was forced to make small changes so as to appear to be keeping up with the times. Improvements were made to the hospital's cleanliness and its staff were banned from accepting tips and other gratuities, both from patients and visitors, but the greatest change forced upon Bethlem concerned its policy on visitors and came about following a dramatic series of events.

The admittance of visitors to Bethlem had been a standard practice for centuries, and a trip to the hospital was high on the things-to-see list of London tourists as well as some locals. The diaries of many historical Londoners record a visit to Bedlam, including such famous luminaries as Horace Walpole and Dr Johnson, who, according to his biographer James Boswell, had 'his attention arrested by a man who was very furious, and who, while beating his straw, supposed it to be William Duke of Cumberland, whom he was punishing for his cruelties in Scotland.'[78]

When Bethlem had been on its old site at Bishopsgate, the admission of paying visitors had been used as a means of raising much-needed cash and of keeping the hospital in the public eye. When the new Bethlem Hospital was erected at Moorfields it was hoped that the ornate building and landscaped gardens would continue to attract fee-paying visitors. They did, and in such large numbers that, by the time of John Monro's employment, the hospital was attracting thousand of sightseers a year. Exactly how many passed through the gates is a matter of dispute; one modern estimate places the figure at 96,000, but this is probably too high; more realistic is the 1753 correspondent who reckoned that at any one time during Easter week the hospital building held around a hundred people. Allowing for the fact that visitor numbers were seasonal (the summer months, weekends and holidays being prime times), this suggests that the number of visitors per year would have been in the low tens of thousands.[79]

During the reign of James Monro, visitors would typically pay a penny for admission, which raised around £300 a year in cash (about £40,000 today). This figure grew slightly in the opening years of John Monro's tenure, peaking in 1763 at around £450 (£60,000 today), but by this time the income from visitors was no longer considered essential. In 1676, when the Moorfields Bethlem opened its doors, tourist income was vital to the hospital's well-being, but shortly afterwards the radical change in financing obtained by the Governors, who favoured steady income over small donations, meant that the few hundred pounds raised at the gates was insignificant compared to the money being brought in by the hospital's investments and by its wealthy benefactors. In 1763, for example, Charles Savage left £1,500 each to Bethlem, Bridewell and St Luke's hospitals, and in

1765 Jeremiah Marlow left £500 each to Bethlem and St Luke's, while many others left sums that, when added together, amounted to a small fortune. With their money no longer essential to the hospital, the visitors had become more trouble than they were worth.[80]

Those who chose to visit Bethlem did so in order to see the 'mad folks', but their attitude and behaviour sometimes left a lot to be desired. It was thought good sport to taunt and tease the inmates physically and verbally, with visitors crowding around individual cells, shouting abuse. Other patients would be plied with drink, sexually taunted or, if the 'basketmen' were absent, physically assaulted. As a consequence much of the mayhem associated with Bethlem resulted, not from the ravings of its patients, but instead from the shouts, taunts and laughter of visitors. This was tolerated for a long time because it was believed that lunatics were so emotionally debased that goading them had little measurable effect, but by the era of William Battie and John Monro many in the educated classes had come to frown upon the actions of the visitors. The view of a young woman visiting Bedlam in 1750 illustrates this change in attitude:

'I was at a loss to account for the behaviour of the generality of people who were looking at these melancholy objects. Instead of the concern I think unavoidable at such a sight, a sort of mirth appeared on their countenances; and the distemper'd fancies of the miserable patients most unaccountably provoked mirth and loud laughter in the unthinking auditors; and the many hideous roaring, and the wild motions of others, seemed equally entertaining to them. Nay, so shamefully inhuman were some, among whom (I am sorry to say it!) were several of my own sex, as to endeavour to provoke the patients into rage, to make them sport.'[81]

William Battie had long been uneasy about the practice of exhibiting lunatics to the public and had banned not only paying visitors from St Luke's Hospital, but sometimes also the inmates' relations. He believed that isolating patients from anything that might excite or upset them was essential to their cure, and wrote that: 'The visits therefore of affecting friends as well as enemies, and the impertinent curiosity of those who think it pastime to converse with madmen and to play upon their passions, ought strictly to be forbidden.'[82]

Monro did not see the harm in exhibiting his inmates and probably, like his forebear Richard Hale, regarded 'jollity and merriment and even a band of music' as conducive to the patients' well-being. When Battie confronted Monro about Bethlem's policy on visitors, he sidestepped the issue by ignoring the general public and instead talking about the patients' relations whose attendance 'should be submitted to the judgement of the physician'. However, within Bethlem money talked, with most of its staff, for a fee, being willing to conduct people around the hospital's restricted areas, while its grounds and main galleries remained open to any paying person off the street. This general admissions policy was not just leading to the abuse of inmates; it was also seriously affecting Bethlem's reputation.[83]

Soon after its opening, the Moorfields building became notorious as a red light venue. 'Mistresses were to be had of all ranks, qualities, colours, prices and sizes,' wrote Ned Ward in 1700, 'from the velvet scarf to the Scotch plaid petticoat. Every fresh comer was engaged in an amour; tho' they came in single, they went out in pairs. Any stranger may purchase a purge for his reins at a small expense, and may have a pox by chance flung into the bargain.' This situation still existed half a century later when a London woman wrote of Bethlem: 'I have been told this dreadful place is often used for the resort of lewd persons to meet and make assignments.'[84]

Not that this stopped the visitors from coming. To judge by the annual takings at the gate, the early 1760s saw a steady increase in visitor numbers even though (or perhaps because) this was also a period of growing disquiet about madhouses and the treatment of lunatics. The behaviour of visitors did not improve, and overcrowding during holiday periods started to cause problems. Matters reached a head in the Christmas holiday of 1763 when the crowd's exuberance tipped over into disorder; trouble broke out in the hospital's galleries (always a focal point for badly behaved individuals) leading to a riot that appears to have involved both visitors and inmates. The scale of the problem was such that, following similar riots at the Easter and Whitsuntide holidays, the hospital assigned to each gallery four constables who, together with 'four stout fellows', were to 'suppress any riots or disorders that might happen'. Bedlam had long been used as a metaphor for all things chaotic, and it appeared that the hospital was starting to act out its own mythical reputation.[85]

Rather than ban visitors altogether, further attempts were made at marshalling them, with the staff under instruction to enforce an old rule that banned 'lewd or disorderly persons, nor any boys or girls, that they think are apprentices, and come there to idle away their time.'[86] The measures had only a limited effect: visitor numbers remained high and their behaviour continued to be rowdy. With all other measures having failed, in April 1766 the Governors took the decision to ban visitors during holiday times, thus bringing to an end a centuries-old London tradition.

Perhaps because of these restrictions, but doubtless also because of disgust felt by some at Bethlem's open visiting policy, tourist numbers started to drop. In 1763 annual takings at the gate had been £450; by 1769 they had dropped to £150, and in November 1770 Bethlem's Apothecary recommended ending the indiscriminate visiting policy in favour of admission by ticket only. The Governors agreed, but John Monro may not have approved of this decision, for while William Battie was present at the meetings where these restrictions were enacted, the Bethlem Physician was curiously absent.[87]

This clampdown did not see an abatement in people's desire to visit Bethlem, and those who were well connected enough could still gain admission by use of tickets provided by Governors and others attached to the hospital. This was certainly the case with Dr Samuel Johnson, who made an apparently unremarkable visit in 1775. To stem the flow altogether, successive restrictions were applied until it was decreed that 'no persons whatsoever, except Governors, or those in company with a Governor, or the Physician, be permitted to view the Hospital and patients, except on Mondays and Wednesdays from ten o'clock till twelve, and then only by virtue of a ticket, signed by one of the Governors, or the Physician but no person under sixteen years of age, or who has been discharged as incurable, can be admitted to see the patients.' This did the trick, and by the 1780s weekly visitor numbers were down to just a handful, with the gate money amounting to only a few pounds annually.[88]

An embargo on visitors was generally welcomed by the Governors (as well as by social commentators), but in the long term it did not necessarily help those housed within the hospital. For centuries many areas of Bethlem had been subject to inspection by anyone who could afford the entry price; this ranged from the lowest in society to medics, MPs and the landed gentry. The curtailing of visitors placed the hospital and its galleries behind closed doors, out of sight of all save those who could get permission from either the Governors or the Physician. This excluded the well-meaning visitors as well as the undesirable ones, leaving the possibility that, without the public to scrutinise them, standards within Bethlem might slip. Unlike St Luke's, the Governors of Bethlem had not seen fit to put in place an independent inspection regime; instead it had opened a book wherein visitors could 'enter complaints of neglect or misconduct and suggest reforms'. The inmates of Bethlem had been cut off from the outside world and while, in theory, the few reforms made in the 1770s and '80s should have improved their lot, in fact their plight was about to get a whole lot worse.

9

Cash Crisis

The failure of Parliament to act on the unsavoury findings of its 1763 Select Committee had been a welcome outcome for many private madhouse owners as it allowed them to carry on trading without undue external interference. Inevitably this meant that instances of physical abuse and false imprisonment continued to occur, usually with the compliance of the madhouse staff. The delicate nature of many of these cases and the ambiguity of the law meant that while some sane patients, like Mrs Hawley, were released using a writ of habeas corpus, their captors often went unpunished.

It was the very public case of Mrs Mary Leggatt, a citizen of south London, that brought about the first signs of a coherent madhouse reform movement. Like so many others, Mrs Leggatt's case began with a trick that was commonly used to get catch people off their guard so that they could be taken unwittingly to a madhouse. Her husband 'tenderly' suggested to his wife that she might want to accompany him to Kingston, where they could take some air. She agreed but was alarmed to find herself being taken instead to Kennington, where she was delivered into the hands of a private madhouse keeper. Despite showing no sign of insanity, Mrs Leggatt was locked inside a cell and denied any access to the outside world. Such false imprisonment had been meted out to many people, but Mrs Leggatt was to undergo a worse ordeal than most.

On the day of her admission the madhouse Keeper committed a serious sexual assault on Mrs Leggatt, apparently in an attempt to rape her. The terrified woman pleaded with her captor and offered to pay him £20 for her release, but the Keeper refused, saying that he was going to get as much from her husband for her imprisonment. Three days later the Keeper committed another assault on his prisoner, but afterwards she was somehow able to get word of her predicament to friends, who approached the Keeper demanding Mrs Leggatt's release. The Keeper told them that he would 'confine any woman if her husband would put her under his care'. The friends were persistent and shortly afterwards managed to spring Mrs Leggatt from her cell, taking her in their care.

In exacting revenge on her Keeper, Mrs Leggatt chose not to prosecute him through the civil courts for false imprisonment, a charge which would have brought into play all the usual questions about her sanity at the time of her confinement. Instead, she brought a criminal prosecution against him for assault. The case came before the Surrey Quarter Sessions on 26 February 1771 where it was tried before Sir Joseph Mawbey and Sir Timothy Waldo together with 'a crowded bench of magistrates'. The Keeper was charged with assault with an intent to commit a rape and, following a five-hour trial, was found guilty by the jury.

The court expressed its concern at the 'aggravated circumstances that attended the illegal and cruel usage' of Mrs Leggatt and vowed to 'admonish all keepers of such infamous private houses, established under the false pretences of curing lunatics'. The Keeper was given a six-month gaol term, fined 13 shillings and sentenced to stand in the pillory, a most unpleasant, and sometimes dangerous, experience. He also had to pay a security of £200 against his good behaviour for two years. This was considered a harsh sentence and one that would almost certainly see the Keeper lose his business; news of it was greeted with cheers from the public gallery.[89]

Mrs Leggatt's trial was attended by hundreds of people and its details seen by many thousands more through the newspapers. The combination of a sexual assault, a conniving husband and tyrannical madhouse keeper caught the public's imagination. Calls were made for the proper regulation and inspection of private madhouses.

The most vocal protest against the private madhouse system came from a gentleman who published an open, but anonymous, letter to the Lord Mayor. The writer lamented the many instances of false imprisonment whose effect, in some cases, was to lead to genuine expressions of insanity and even suicide.

He cited the case of Mrs Leggatt, commenting that 'no misery on earth is equal, nor so soon destroys the brain, as quick sensibility, wounded by confinement and cruel usage; where no permission is allowed the unhappy [prisoner] to write to anyone, to see anyone he wishes, or by his own behaviour to contradict reports too easily credited, too cruelly spread of him.'

The writer then expressed his wrath at the failure of Parliament to follow through on the recommendations of the 1763 Select Committee. He requested a law that would require the certification of suspected lunatics by physicians and parish authorities, and which could be used in conjunction with a madhouse inspection regime. Perhaps most controversial of all was a plan to persuade madhouse staff to blow the whistle on their employers by offering them a reward of £10 for a successful prosecution.[90]

It was pointed out that these demands would have cost a fortune to implement and were too labour-intensive. They would also have encouraged underpaid staff to make false allegations against their employers in return for the cash reward. The effect would have been to put most madhouses out of business or to have increased their fees so much that only the wealthiest citizens could afford to use them. London could not afford to lose the accommodation provided by its private madhouses (Bethlem and St Luke's were full and had lengthy waiting lists), but neither could it allow the abuses to continue unchecked. A compromise was needed.

Thomas Townshend junior, the Member of Parliament for Whitchurch, had an involvement with the Privy Council (a body that had the power to admit lunatics to Bedlam), which perhaps gave him cause to take an interest in the matter of madness. Townshend was aware of the public's mood and personally undertook to regulate England's errant madhouse system. Aged forty, Townshend was still a relatively young MP, but he was an experienced politician noted for his tenacity and for being a man of principle. The appeal for a madhouse Bill found favour with him and he became determined to see it placed on the statute book.[91]

Rather than initiate another Select Committee investigation into madhouses, which would waste valuable time, Townshend thought it more simple to revive the decade-old recommendations of the 1763 inquiry. Townshend put forward the idea of a new Madhouse Bill on 24 February

1774 and was given parliamentary leave to pursue it. Over the coming weeks the Bill worked its way through the tortuous legislative process of the House of Commons. The first big hurdle came on 25 March when the Committee that had been formed to examine the Bill made its report to the Commons. It proposed some minor amendments to the 1763 recommendations, which, to the relief of Townshend, were accepted by the House and led, a few days later, to it being passed to the Lords for their comment.

The Lords took their time examining the proposed text, engendering a degree of nervousness in Townshend and his colleagues, for it had been at this point that the original 1763 Bill had failed. Several weeks later, on 9 May, the Lords returned the legislation to the House of Commons with some minor amendments that were read to MPs on the following day. The Commons debated the changes and duly ordered 'that Mr Thomas Townshend junior do carry the Bill to the Lords and acquaint them that this House hath agreed to the amendments made by their Lordships'. The Bill had just one hurdle left, and this it cleared on 20 May when the 'Act for Regulating Madhouses' was given Royal Ascent.[92]

For the first time in British history the owners and keepers of private madhouses were to be licensed and inspected in an attempt to stamp out instances of flagrant abuse. The Act was lengthy and was divided into two general sections, one dealing with London madhouses, the other with those in the 'countryside' (ie outside London).

Those madhouses in the London region (about eighteen in total) were to be inspected each September by an officer from the Royal College of Physicians: if the madhouse was up to standard, the following month it would be granted a licence to trade. This was a major breakthrough for, since at least 1754, the College had refused to participate in asylum regulation and had allegedly been uncooperative with the 1763 Committee. When Townshend reported to the Commons that 'the College do agree to the plan,' he had resolved a major problem.

Madhouses outside London, including the county asylums, would be regulated by local clerks who 'have the power to see justice done to those who are unhappy enough to become inmates of those places'. If a premises was found to be breaking the terms of its licence, either the College of

Physicians or the County Clerks could withdraw their licence. Other innovations required that all inmates be certified by a doctor on admission, and a requirement that each madhouse was to have a registry book, open to inspection by all, containing the names of its current and past patients. This was to stop madhouses accepting people who were not insane and thereafter hiding them from both the authorities and their friends and relations.[93]

The Act's emphasis was on preventing people such as Mr Turlington from running madhouses that would take in anyone, regardless of their state of mind, then treat them like prisoners. In this respect it was a step forward, but by not linking the licence with general conditions inside the madhouse there was no compulsion for the College of Physicians or County Clerks to check on the manner in which the inmates were being treated. This would inevitably mean that some of the physical and mental abuse that was being meted out to patients would continue unchecked.

Both Bethlem and St Luke's were purposefully excluded from the Act, possibly through lobbying by some of their Governors. St Luke's was already functioning in a reasonably open manner and was subject to unannounced inspections by outsiders, but the same could not said of Bethlem, which, following the cessation of visitors, was mostly operating behind closed doors. Bedlam's Governors, and especially its Physician, John Monro, disliked outside interference and were consequently happy that the hospital had been entirely exempted from the legislation.

The Act was initially scheduled to last for just five years, after which time Parliament had to vote for its renewal. This clause may have been added to help persuade those MPs who were wavering that the Act could be rescinded if necessary, but in the long term the time limit did not prove to be a problem. In 1779 it was renewed for another seven years and when this expired, in 1786, the Madhouse Law Perpetuation Act was passed, ensuring that the original Act could carry on indefinitely.

Despite some shortcomings, the 1774 Madhouse Act was a landmark in the history of Britain's asylums. It was the first indication that calls for reforms in the mad doctoring business were being taken seriously by the authorities. The reform movement itself was still young and its actions disjointed, but its members were ambitious and on the lookout for newer and bigger targets, including Bethlem Hospital. However, for the time being Bedlam could carry on as usual, and, in truth, it was not the Madhouse Act that was worrying the Governors but the implications of a massive financial crisis that was threatening the hospital's very existence.

In the opinion of some Governors the most important post within the hierarchy of Bridewell and Bethlem officers was not the President but the Treasurer. As controller of both hospitals' purse strings, the Treasurer not only oversaw the finances but had other privileges such as the casting vote during meetings.

The Treasurer was usually associated with the Corporation of London and therefore was often an Alderman or, more rarely, a Lord Mayor. The political prestige that came with being Treasurer to Bridewell and Bethlem meant that on occasion there was great rivalry for the position; this is perhaps surprising given that the financial benefits were few and the workload, which involved keeping the hospitals' accounts, could be heavy and tedious. Naturally, being in charge of so much money brought with it a temptation to embezzle, so the Governors would also appoint an Auditor-General to keep an eye on the Treasurer and his book-keeping. This, in theory, should have protected Bridewell and Bethlem from the sort of disaster that befell St Bartholomew's Hospital in 1760, when its Treasurer, John Tuff, ran off with a chunk of money, but the auditors rarely did their job properly and most were happy to sign off hospital accounts without having studied them in detail. The Governors assumed that they had in place a failsafe system, so took little interest in the Treasurer's affairs. It was a disaster waiting to happen.

In June 1768 the post of Treasurer was offered to William Kinleside, an apothecary who had been a Governor at Bridewell and Bethlem since 1740. Kinleside was an unusual choice, for although he was a successful practitioner, he did not hold any other political office within the Corporation of London. Nevertheless, he lived and worked in a road that adjoined to Bridewell and the Governors must have had some reason for electing him to the post, but after taking up the job Kinleside was by and large left to his own devices and received little attention from his fellow officers.[94]

In December 1774, a month after the Act for Regulating Madhouses came into force, two Governors, Thomas Horne and Deputy Rogers, got wind of some irregularities in the hospitals' finances. As far as can be deduced, the initial warning came from a trader who was owed money by one of the hospitals; this was not an uncommon occurrence, but the allegations made were obviously serious enough for Rogers and Horne to raise the matter at a Governors' meeting on 8 December. In the presence of Kinleside, it was suggested by Rogers and Horne that the hospitals' accounting system ought to be examined to see if any improvements could be made.

The first port of call in this process should have been the Auditor-General, whose job it was to keep an eye on the Treasurer, but as soon as he got word of Rogers and Horne's proposed inquiry, he resigned. The reason for this sudden action was soon revealed: it transpired that the Auditor-General had not looked at the accounts since 1770, leaving the Treasurer to operate unsupervised for four years. This, together with growing rumours of financial impropriety, suddenly seemed very ominous. Rogers and Horne initiated a full examination of the accounts during which it became evident that large sums of money were either missing or were owed to workers, tradesmen and merchants. By February 1775 it was judged that Bridewell and Bethlem had been defrauded of almost £8,000, equivalent to around £725,000 today. Where this money went was never fully realised, although it is possible that Kinleside had used some of it to pay off debts incurred by his father.

The errant Kinleside faced the wrath of the Governors, who made clear their intent at recovering the missing money; he begged and pleaded with them to be permitted to find the funds himself and to be allowed to keep his job as Treasurer. An extraordinary meeting of the Governors was held on 2 March 1775 to decide his fate; the Governors were for once in complete agreement as to what should be done, decision being announced in a newspaper advertisement:

'At a General Court of the Governors of the BRIDEWELL and BETHLEM HOSPITALS, held at Bridewell Hospital, March 2, 1775. It was ordered, nemine contradicente [without objection], that Mr. WILLIAM KINLESIDE should be discharged from the Office of TREASURER, and struck off the List of Governors of those Hospitals. That the House lately built and allotted for the Residence of such Treasurer, should be returned Lady-Day next; and that the Committee of Treasury be desired to treat with any Person who shall offer to rent the said House.

JOHN WOODHOUSE, Clerk.'[95]

Removing Kinleside as Treasurer was a relatively straightforward task; recovering the money was not so simple. The Governors were not in a mood to muck about, so, rather than rely on Kinleside to find the money himself, they took the drastic step of having him declared legally bankrupt. This meant that the ex-Treasurer's assets could be seized and sold, and the proceeds distributed amongst his creditors, chief of which were Bridewell and Bethlem.

The Governors moved with remarkable speed so that, within a month of being removed as Treasurer, Kinleside had been declared bankrupt. Part of this process required advertisements to be placed in the newspapers announcing the bankruptcy and asking any creditors to make themselves known so that they could submit formal claims. It was yet another humiliation for the former Treasurer, whose private affairs were now the topic of coffee-house conversation. The commissioner appointed to oversee the bankruptcy was efficient and managed to recover £3,000 from Kinleside's estate, but this still left a shortfall of £5,000. The Governors decided that they could cover half this using money they were owed from the City authorities, but that the remaining £2,500 would have to be borrowed from commercial lenders; this meant paying an eye-watering interest rate on what was a very large loan. As an end to the process, Kinleside was officially stripped of his Governorship on 22 November 1775; he had no further involvement with either Bridewell or Bethlem, although he did continue to practice as an apothecary in the Paddington area until his death in 1792.[96]

The Kinleside affair left a sizeable hole in Bethlem's annual budget and was to mark a change in fortune for the hospital's finances. While the bankruptcy proceedings were being enacted, Britain started fighting a revolutionary war with its American colonies; this quickly consumed large amounts of men, money and materials as well as having an adverse effect on British trade and therefore also the economy in general. Especially badly affected were aristocrats and the landed gentry, who suffered not just from the general financial decline, but also from a steady devaluation of their land and property, reversing the upward trend of the previous several decades. Bethlem relied heavily on income derived from its property investments and also on the generosity of its rich benefactors; both were now coming up short, while other cash-raising methods, such as the admission of visitors, had ceased altogether. In the wake of Kinleside's misappropriation, the hospital suddenly found itself in desperate need of cash.

A perceived solution to the under-funding came in May 1782 when an Act of Parliament gave Bethlem, Bridewell and the other royal hospitals effective autonomy from the Corporation of London, an organisation that had interfered in their management for more than two centuries. The new rules limited the number of Corporation Governors in each hospital's Court to twelve; prior to this the City had filled the Courts with its own men, which often meant that the hospitals were being run for the benefit of the Corporation of London, rather than its patients. With only twelve out of Bethlem's forty-two Governors being directly elected by the City, the balance of power within the management structure passed to Bethlem; this caused one commentator to remark that the royal hospitals 'have now the satisfaction to be assured that the governance of them is settled in a mode best calculated to promote their prosperity'. As a small hospital, Bethlem had long sought to have more control over its destiny, but the newly independent Court of Governors found itself faced with an immediate lack of long-term funding.[97]

A particular drain on Bethlem's funds were its incurable lunatics who for centuries had been barred from admission until the 1720s and '30s, when specialist wings allowed the hospital to accommodate exactly a hundred incurables (fifty from each sex). By the time of John Monro's Physicianship they formed a third of its total number of 270 patients. Much of this had been funded by a bequest of 3,000 acres of land in Lincolnshire made in 1733 by Sir Edward Barkham, who requested that any income derived from it be spent specifically on incurable lunatics.[98]

Even so, demand for incurable places still far outstripped supply, forcing the Governors to implement a harsh admissions policy. Potentially incurable patients would be assessed in the usual way on a Saturday morning at 11 o'clock by the Physician and several Governors. If their condition was deemed to be hopeless and they were a danger to themselves or the public, the hospital would add them to its 'incurable list'. The patients would then be sent back into the community to await the arrival of a vacant cell. Given the low turnover in incurable inmates (and that the incurable list often contained upwards of 200 names) patients sometimes had to wait several years before being admitted. Many must have died or have been abandoned by their relations in the interim.

Bethlem had originally refused to take incurable patients because it wanted to be able to offer cures for mental illness rather than simply acting as a repository for the hopelessly mad. It was also suspected that caring for incurable patients would demand a disproportionate amount of money, time and other scarce resources; this supposition was proved to be correct. Most incurable patients were also paupers for whom Bethlem could receive only minimal funding (by their parish or friends and relations), yet incurable patients generally required more staff attention and were more expensive to house, feed and care for. As time progressed, the hospital's incurable wings began to take more than their fair share of overall funding; this, combined with the fallout of William Kinleside's embezzlement and a general drop in benefactions and income, was a cause of much concern to the Governors and led to them taking an extraordinary course of action.

The hard times brought by the American war had led some private madhouses to produce pamphlets that highlighted their objectives, facilities and success rates. These were little more than glorified adverts but they did help to drum up business, especially from the wealthy classes. The Governors were aware of this and took the bold step of commissioning their own book, which, they hoped, could be used for promotional purposes. Since closing its doors to the outside world, Bethlem had become notoriously secretive and intolerant of criticism; this made the choice of author a crucial one. The job had to be handed to an insider, and the task fell to the Reverend Thomas Bowen, an Oxford graduate who was also the Chaplain and schoolmaster to Bridewell Hospital.

Bowen spent most of his time in Bridewell and had little practical experience of Bethlem, but he was eloquent and, when approached, happy to undertake the task. His instructions were straightforward: write a short book that would take an uncritical look at Bethlem and, most importantly, would avoid any whiff of controversy. The Chaplain rose admirably to the task and on 30 April 1783 the Bethlem Governors met to peruse his draft manuscript. They were delighted, offered their unanimous thanks and 'ordered that the same be printed and distributed in such a manner, as may tend most effectually to promote the interests of that excellent charity'.[99]

The resultant book, entitled An Historical Account of the Origin, Progress and Present State of Bethlem Hospital, was billed as the first official history of the hospital, but in truth Bowen devoted little time to its background. In fact, the few pages concerning its history are error-prone and in most respects less illuminating than the summary accounts given in many London tourist guides then in print. This is because the pamphlet's true objective was not to look at Bethlem's past, but instead to help secure its financial future. It was the Governors' wish that Bowen display the modern Bethlem in the best possible light so as to encourage new benefactors to their charitable cause.

Bowen was far from subtle in his promotion of the hospital. Almost every one of the sixteen pages contains a reference to Bethlem's charitable status and its need for additional money. The incurable patients receive especial attention and their need for charity is highlighted at every turn; Bowen stresses the length of the incurable waiting list (200 people), the amount of time before admission (up to seven years), and makes the point that more incurables inside Bethlem means that there would be fewer left to roam the streets of London. To stress this last point Bowen comments that there are incurable patients free in London that 'have committed deeds of the most horrid kind'. In appealing for cash, Bowen laid it on thick:

'These manifest evils, that arise from the want of a proper provision for so great a number of incurable patients, have induced many benevolent persons to wish that the hospital might be enlarged. Indeed, many have appropriated their benefactions solely to the incurables; and it is hoped that others will forward and complete their good intentions. True policy must join with humanity in the wish, that, this may no longer be, what at present it is, almost the only branch of charity in this great city that wants a sufficient establishment. Besides, there seems a peculiar degree of generosity in assisting those who must burthen, but can never benefit society, and who, so far from recompensing, cannot even feel the least gratitude to their benefactors.'[100]

Bowen might have played up the cash shortfall, but he chose to play down other inconvenient truths including Bethlem's origins as a Catholic priory, something that would not have gone down well in the aftermath of the anti-papal Gordon Riots of a few years before. Some of Bowen's descriptions concerning the Hospital's general environment and care routines are also exaggerated: the wards are 'spacious and airy', the cells are referred to as 'apartments', and 'every patient is indulged with that degree of liberty which is found consistent with his own and the general safety'. Any notion of physical abuse or restraint is dismissed as 'absolutely erroneous' and Bowen makes the extraordinary claim that visitors and staff are so impressed with what they find that they 'have declared that if God should be pleased to visit them with insanity, Bethlem Hospital is the place into which they would wish to be admitted.'

The remaining couple of pages in Bowen's book spell out some of the costs incurred by the hospital; he even included lists of clothing expenses for men and women, which reveals that a straitjacket for gentlemen costs 13s 6d, while a ladies' gown and petticoat cost exactly 19 shillings. We are left in no doubt that food, clothes, bedding, medicine and other facilities cost a small fortune and that it is the hospital, not the patient or his sponsors, that shoulders the cost.

Bowen's less-than-critical account paints a glowing picture of Bethlem that glosses over some of the more controversial aspects of the hospital, such as John Monro's bleeding and purging regimes, the lack of glazed windows in the cells (Bowen claimed that this made them 'airy') and the cold and damp that permeated the walls and, in winter, numbed the inmates' limbs. Bethlem also had a very serious and long-standing problem with vermin, especially rats and mice, which infested all its buildings. The rodents defied every attempt made to control them, such as the introduction of cats in 1777, and they seem to have become accepted as a natural hazard by many staff. With visitors no longer welcomed, there were few people abroad who were in a position to contradict Bowen's optimistic viewpoint.

The Governors, however, were delighted with An Historical Account and John Woodhouse, the Clerk, ordered that it be 'distributed in such a manner, as may tend most effectually to promise the Interests of that excellent charity'. This meant that every Governor, MP, peer, banker and Alderman received a copy, as did dozens of other people with political connections and/or accumulated wealth. The appeal worked and, according to one source, the book 'benefited the funds greatly' and was especially effective at raising money from some of the City institutions such as its livery companies. Bowen continued to be active within Bridewell and published some further short works about that hospital, but had little further to do with Bethlem, although, as a mark of thanks, he was made a Governor.[101]

In the short term a financial crisis had been averted, but the Hospital remained on a financial knife-edge and it was inevitable that at some point in the future the issue of money would rise again. In the meantime Bedlam had another problem: its Physician, Dr John Monro, was growing old and was suffering from increasing ill health. This raised the question of who should be his replacement.

10

Attempted Regicide

The Madhouse Regulation Act of 1774 had come into existence following concerns that perfectly sane people were being falsely imprisoned inside private madhouses. However, by concentrating their attention on asylum admission procedures, reformers had ignored some of the other controversial practices taking place in both private madhouses and Bethlem. There was, for example, a notable lack of comment about the medical treatments given to lunatics and the general environment in which they were being kept; this was simply not an issue that most reformers saw fit to concern themselves with. Indeed, there had been little comment on this issue since 1758, when William Battie of St Luke's Hospital had made his outspoken opposition to the therapies used by John Monro at Bethlem.

Battie kept up his opposition to John Monro until 1764, when he resigned his post as Physician to St Luke's Hospital. True to his belief that the future of mad doctoring lay with the new up-and-coming generation of medics (some of whom had been apprentices at St Luke's), Battie explained that his old age required him to step down: 'Improvement in medical knowledge being one of the principal objects of Hospital practice for which men growing old in confirmed habits and opinions are not so well qualified, I cannot at present answer your good intentions better than by retiring from this part of the mad business in time, and resigning the care of your patients to some younger physician.'[102]

In fact, there was probably more to his departure than just this; Battie ran a private madhouse of his own as well as a consultancy business, and he had also just been elected President of the Royal College of Physicians. A lack of time must have been a factor in his resignation from his post at St Luke's, which, although prestigious, was not very lucrative. Battie continued to be involved with both St Luke's and Bethlem (where he remained a Governor) and operated his private practice until his death in 1776. Ironically, although he never managed to exert much influence over the mad trade, he did grow rich from it: it is estimated that his personal fortune was between £100,000 and £200,000, a veritable fortune by anyone's standards.[103]

From the moment of Battie's departure, John Monro and the other medical staff at Bethlem were untroubled by any further criticisms from St Luke's Hospital. Indeed, many people outside the medical system were unaware of any rivalry between the two hospitals and, because of their close geographic proximity, often assumed that they were part of the same institution. This so irritated the Bethlem staff that Thomas Bowen was moved to complain that 'the Steward of Bethlem hospital has often received letters from persons of education and credit, who were interested for patients discharged incurable, desiring to know when they would be sent to St Luke's. How such an idea could have been obtained is not easy to say ... but the GOVERNORS, OFFICERS and FUNDS of each charity are totally SEPARATE and DISTINCT.'[104]

William Battie's replacement at St Luke's was Dr Thomas Brooke, who shared his predecessor's medical beliefs but chose not to publicise them. Likewise, Brooke's death in 1781 brought in Dr Samuel Simmons, a gifted and progressive Physician who would be called upon to treat King George III's madness. However, despite rivalry with the Bethlem medics over some high-profile cases (including that of mad King George), Simmons chose not to pick a fight with the Bethlem Physicians. From 1764 onwards, St Luke's and Bethlem continued along separate paths, each barely acknowledging the other's existence.

For St Luke's Hospital this was not a great problem; its policy of openness ensured that it received little or no criticism regarding the admission and treatment of its inmates. For Bethlem it was different matter; with few visitors and no independent inspection regime, the hospital was now operating under a cloak of secrecy and, thanks to John Monro's intransigence, was using medical therapies that were increasingly being seen as out-of-date. Since 1751

St Luke's had kept up with latest ideas and theories. Monro, on the other hand, had adopted his father's treatments, most of which were more than two centuries old, and had altered them not one jot. Hence, as the eighteenth century started to draw to a close, Bethlem was still practising seventeenth-century medicine on its inmates, something that seemed to bother neither Monro nor the majority of the hospital's Governors. There must, however, have been some that wondered exactly when John Monro's reign would end and whether his replacement could bring about some measure of change. John was also giving thought to his successor, but for an entirely different reason.

By the mid-1780s Monro was more than seventy years old, had been working at Bethlem for more than three decades and was, like his father before him, thinking about how best to ensure that the post of Physician could remain within the family. This was an issue that had obsessed him for some time, but he had married late and his first children were not born until after he had been appointed Physician. His hopes had initially been placed upon his eldest son John, born in 1754, whom he trained to be a medic in the hope that he would take on the family's private madhouse business as well as the duties at Bethlem. Those dreams were dashed when, in 1779, the twenty-four-year-old John Monro junior became ill and died while still studying at Oxford University. This loss was severely felt by John senior, who was endeared to his son 'by his many amicable qualities and promising abilities'. Worse was to come when, shortly afterwards, his daughter Charlotte died from tuberculosis, a long and lingering illness that, by all accounts, sapped John's strength. 'He had hitherto enjoyed an uncommon share of good health,' wrote a friend, 'but the constant anxiety he was under during his daughter's illness preyed upon his mind.' John's attention now focused on Charles and Thomas, the elder of his three remaining sons; both were young men barely out of their teens and were in the process of training to be lawyers. Charles showed no signs of wanting to be a doctor, so it was down to Thomas to take on the family business; he switched his training from law to medicine.

It is alleged that the stress of losing his son and daughter brought about the serious stroke that afflicted John Monro in January 1783. At this time Thomas was twenty-three years old and still studying for his Masters at

Oxford; even in the nepotistic traditions of the eighteenth century, he was not in a position to take over from his father. Anxious to safeguard his legacy at Bethlem, the crippled John Monro carried on working as Bethlem's sole Physician, a situation that must surely have led to a decline in levels of care and attention. In 1785 he managed to get both Charles and Thomas elected as Governors to Bethlem (assumedly the former was being held in reserve in case anything happened to the latter) and shortly afterwards Thomas started working alongside his father as an apprenticed medic. Thomas had yet to receive his medical degree, which meant that John could not shoehorn him into Bethlem but, with his father's health declining, the son was forced to take on more of his duties.

On 24 May 1787 Thomas was awarded his MD and thus the final piece of John Monro's plan fell into place. As his father had done before him, John applied to Bethlem's Governors to have Thomas upgraded to the position of Physician's assistant. The matter was just a formality, and on 19 July 1787 another Monro father-and-son team began operating as the joint Physicians to Bedlam Hospital. This move came at a time when, after many years of being out of the limelight, Bethlem was once again coming under the public gaze. This renewed interest came about because, within the space of a few years, the hospital had received a number of high-profile patients. The first of these, Margaret 'Peg' Nicholson, arrived during the time when Thomas and John Monro were working together, and was to put both men in an awkward position. Nicholson's unusual case brought Bedlam back into the public domain but it also drew attention to a serious legal loophole that was to have consequences not only for Bethlem, but eventually for the whole system of charitable mental health provision across England and Wales.

John Monro came into contact with Margaret Nicholson on 2 August 1786 after receiving an urgent request to attend the Royal Palace at St James's where, he was informed, an attempt had been made on the life of King George III. The monarch was unscathed but his would-be assassin, who was female and behaving erratically, was a cause for concern; the King himself had requested that the Bedlam mad doctor be summoned to offer his opinion on the woman's sanity. John Monro went at once to St James's, leaving instructions that his son Thomas should join him there as soon as possible.[105]

The attempted assassination had occurred a few hours earlier outside the palace's garden gate near Marlborough Wall; prior to King George's expected arrival from Windsor there had been a handful of well-wishers waiting to see him, including a woman dressed in a flowered linen gown with a black silk cloak and a cap with blue ribbons. Her complexion was pale and her features undernourished, but there was nothing in particular to set her apart from the crowd except perhaps her 'serious cast of countenance'. The woman engaged two girls in conversation, cryptically asking them not to interrupt her if she should make an approach towards the King.

Just before midday the Royal coach drew up and His Majesty alighted; as his feet touched the ground the woman stepped forward and handed him a piece of paper. The King accepted it but as he did so the woman's left hand, which had remained hidden, came lunging forward; in it was an aged dessert knife whose ivory handle was cracked in several places. The King did not spot the danger and was in the process of making a polite bow to the woman as she attempted to stab him. The blow missed but a second attempt found the breast of his waistcoat; fortunately the blade had been worn so thin through use that it bent and did not penetrate the sovereign's clothing. Before any further damage could be done two of the King's attendants grabbed and disarmed the woman.

The King was immediately concerned that his assailant not be harmed. 'I have received no injury! Don't hurt the woman – the poor creature appears to be insane!'

She was bundled into the palace's guardroom and, a few hours later, was removed to the Queen's Antechamber. Here she was placed before members of the Board of Green Cloth, a committee within the Privy Council made up of members of the royal household and usually in charge of mundane tasks such as auditing or making the King's travel arrangements. However, the Board of Green Cloth also had the power to form a court and to sit in judgement on those who had committed an offence within the boundaries of the royal palaces. The woman's attack on the King was certainly a case in point, and she soon found herself greeted by the sight of several royal and government officials, including the Prime Minister, the Solicitor General and the Master of the Rolls. All had been summoned specifically to interrogate the woman.[106]

Until that point the would-be assassin had remained silent, but when the questioning began she became talkative. She gave her name as Margaret Nicholson and explained that she was thirty-six years old and had been living and working in London since her early teenage years. When asked about her motives that day, Nicholson became highly animated and at times incoherent claiming that she wanted 'nothing but her right', which, to her mind, included taking the crown of England for herself. Further questioning led the men to conclude that Nicholson had probably lost her mind; this view was reinforced by the discovery of a written petition she had submitted to the King a few days earlier, which 'was found to be such stuff and nonsense that no notice was taken of it'. Among its contents was a threat that 'England would be in blood for a thousand generations' if Nicholson herself was not made Queen.

The question of Nicholson's sanity was a matter of great importance both to her and the gentlemen of the Privy Council; it was, as we shall see, quite literally a matter of life or death, so it was at this point that Dr Monro was sent for to cast his judgement on the woman's mental health. It must therefore have been thought fortunate that not one but two Dr Monros were present to offer their professional opinion, but father and son found themselves in a difficult situation.

As a would-be royal assassin, Nicholson had committed treason, a crime that carried a mandatory death sentence by 'drawing the woman to the gallows and burning her alive'. Given her public attack on the King, there could be little doubt of her guilt, but Nicholson's execution was not a foregone conclusion as the law provided just one possible means of escape; if her lawyers could convince a jury that she was 'not guilty through reason of insanity' then the case of treason would have to be dismissed. This was an outcome that could cause alarm and embarrassment to the Privy Council, hence their need for John Monro's judgement on Nicholson's state of mind.

However, John Monro understood that any opinion he offered the Privy Council would later become subject to intense scrutiny in a court of law; he had been subject to legal cross-examination before and had found the experience to be tedious and professionally demeaning. It was something to be avoided at all costs, so he decided to duck the issue.

When asked if Nicholson was mad, Monro refused to offer a diagnosis, even though such snap decisions were routinely made by him at Bethlem's weekly admission sessions and madhouse visits. 'She must be taken under care and inspection for three or four days,' Monro replied, perhaps hoping to buy himself some time. The Board of Green Cloth were not pleased to hear this and refused Monro permission to take Nicholson away, the objection being that such a detention might be illegal. She was instead committed to the custody of a Mr Coates, one of the King's Messengers. It was agreed that a member of Bethlem's staff (probably a nurse or the Matron) would attend to Nicholson, although it was later rumoured that both John and Thomas Monro made regular visitations as well.

Over the next few days a vigorous debate raged among the courtiers and magistrates as how best to deal with Nicholson's crime. All were agreed that the act of imagining a monarch's death was enough to bring a charge of treason, but the King and his magistrates thought execution was too harsh a sentence for someone who might well be insane. Their mood softened further as Nicholson revealed more about her past life to the men from the Board of Green Cloth. The unfortunate woman had been rendered insane by an unhappy love affair during her younger years during which she had been 'debauched' by an army officer with whom she had lived in sin before his premature death. To make ends meet Nicholson became a seamstress, a very low-paid profession that left her 'in want of nourishment with the attendant anxiety attendant on it'. Both her brother and landlord noticed that Nicholson's senses appeared to be slipping away, although they did not suspect her capable of inflicting physical harm on anybody, let alone on the King. They saw the attack as proof that Nicholson had finally lost her sanity, but others disagreed with this, claiming that she was merely delusional or frustrated.

'Mrs Nicholson may possibly be in a state of insanity,' wrote one commentator, 'but it is equally possible, that a woman may, from a real cause, or pretended one, petition his majesty, and repeat it seventeen times, and then attempt to assassinate him, and yet be in her senses. Nor is it less possible, that though she may be disordered in her mind the instant she finds her attempt frustrated, she might, nevertheless, have been, at the moment of making it, entirely free from the least tincture of insanity.'[107]

The King himself erred towards the insane option but this would have seen Nicholson acquitted of treason and released back onto the streets, an unappealing prospect for the monarch and other Londoners. With growing public unrest surrounding the matter, it was up to the Board of Green Cloth to find a way through this legal minefield, and its members did so by invoking their right to admit patients to Bethlem Hospital without the need of a formal assessment by the Monros. This would avoid the need for a trial and, by royal command, Nicholson could languish in Bedlam for as long as was deemed necessary.

It is ironic that the decision to commit Nicholson to Bedlam fell to Thomas Townshend, the man who had guided the 1774 Madhouse Act through its tortuous Parliamentary process. Townshend had since joined the House of Lords as Lord Sydney, the Secretary of State for the Home Department. He had retained an interest in the issue of madness and had taken it upon himself to review Nicholson's case. On 9 August he informed the King that, in his opinion, Nicholson was mad. The monarch had long ago decided this for himself, so, with the prospect of a criminal trial unappealing, he ordered Townsend to confine Nicholson to Bedlam for life but to ensure that she was 'supported and taken care of, in case of sickness; but while in health, to be kept at work, or whatever employment she is capable of, in order to earn her own subsistence.'

Margaret Nicholson had spent the previous week lodging with Mr Coates, the King's Messenger, and his wife, during which time they had become great friends. It was with some sadness that Coates called in on Nicholson and asked her if she would join himself and his wife in a coach on 'a party of pleasure'. As the trio wound their way towards London's East End Nicholson calmly told Coates that she knew where the coach was heading. As the coach passed through Bedlam's ornate gates Nicholson expressed no emotion.

'Do you known where you are?' asked Coates.

'Perfectly well,' she replied.

'I hope you will patiently and quietly submit to the regulations here,' Coates remarked.

'Certainly,' she said. Coates's conscience was much eased by Nicholson's calm behaviour and the apparent acceptance of her fate. Only once did he become alarmed when Nicholson asked him when the King would be coming to visit her.

The meek, undernourished woman was handed over to Bedlam's Steward, who took her to a cell where a chain was put around her leg and fastened to the floor. Nicholson did not resist and, when asked whether the chain was uncomfortable, replied: 'No, not at all.' With that the cell door was closed and locked, leaving Nicholson to contemplate her life in Bethlem.[108]

Nicholson's internment in Bedlam may have got the King out of a tight spot but it did not go down well with Londoners, many of whom were concerned to see the Board of Green Cloth using a legal loophole to deny Nicholson a court trial. If they could do this to Nicholson, what was to stop them putting other innocent people in Bedlam?

'Bedlam was never before understood to be a Government hospital for lunatics,' wrote a *Times* journalist, 'but if it was, it might want some additional wings to contain the madmen who depend on Ministerial promises. Can the decision of the Privy Council be carried into effect without leave being obtained from the Governors?'[109]

The answer was that yes, the Privy Council could ignore the wishes of Bethlem's Governors, but there were more serious implications than this from the case. In using Bedlam to settle Nicholson's fate, the King and his ministers had chosen to ignore the fact that there was no due legal process to deal with those who, like her, were adjudged to have committed crimes while wholly or temporarily insane. The courts had no power to detain criminal lunatics and were forced to release them, no matter what their crime, even treason. This loophole was left open and would in time cause further problem cases that would require the help of Bethlem's Governors to rectify. In the meantime, Margaret Nicholson became one of Bedlam's most famous patients and was in most respects a model patient, rarely creating any problems. However, the King's desire that Nicholson should remain in Bethlem for life was taken literally; the unfortunate woman would never again be allowed her freedom and remained in Bethlem for forty-two years. During her later years she developed an aversion to bread and an addiction to snuff; she became totally deaf and could rarely be persuaded to speak, but was said to be in good health and spirits right up until her death in 1828.[110]

The reluctance displayed by John Monro to involve himself publicly in Nicholson's case may also have been as much to spare his son's reputation as well as his own. At the time of Nicholson's attack Thomas Monro was in his final year of medical training and had been in joint private practice with his father for only a few months. Despite the fact that he was being groomed for the Physician's job at Bethlem, Thomas was a most inexperienced medic.

When John Monro had been appointed Bethlem Physician he had been in general medical practice for over a decade, giving him a wide experience and a genuine love of medicine. Thomas had no such advantage. He was a late and, to judge from his behaviour, reluctant convert to medicine, whose experience came entirely at the hands of his ageing father. John Monro's fixed views on madness and his dogmatic teaching ensured that his increasingly outdated treatments, such as the use of bleedings, evacuative medicines, cold baths, etc, would carry on to the next generation. Thomas became joint Physician in 1787 and from then onwards shouldered an increasing amount of his father's responsibility; the old man, now well into his seventies, was rarely seen in Bethlem or at the family's private madhouses in Hackney and Clerkenwell. Despite Thomas's limited medical experience, his heritage ensured that he was made a candidate of the Royal College of Physicians in March 1790 and, a year later, was made a Fellow. With his son's succession at Bethlem all but guaranteed, in 1791 John Monro retired from the mad doctoring business and moved from central London to the village of Hadley on its outskirts. His retirement was a short one; during the Christmas period he became ill and, on 27 December, passed away.

Dr John Monro was Europe's most famous and respected mad doctor, who had treated patients from nobility (such as Lord Offord, Horace Walpole's nephew) to 'crack-brained' academics as well as Bethlem's pauper lunatics. His bedside manner may have been abrupt and his methods old-fashioned, but Monro's passing was greatly lamented by his colleagues.

One friend wrote that 'Dr Monro was tall and handsome in his person, and of a robust constitution of body. Though naturally of a grave cast of mind, no man enjoyed the pleasures of society with a greater relish. To great warmth of temper he added a nice sense of honour: and though avowedly at the head of that branch of his profession, to which he continued his practice, yet his behaviour was gentle and modest, and his manners refined and elegant in an eminent degree.'[111]

With opinions like this doing the rounds, Thomas must have wondered whether he could live up to his father's reputation, but the old man's will made it clear that he expected his eldest son to keep the family business together as a going concern. Thomas was bequeathed half the profits from the business with the remainder being split between his brothers Charles and James (the latter would eventually become a captain in the East India Company's merchant navy) while their mother was to get £500 a year. Other sizeable cash bequests reveal just how profitable the mad business must have been to John Monro, whose estate was worth several thousand pounds, a very tidy sum.

One month later, on 2 February 1792, the Governors confirmed Thomas's appointment as Bethlem's sole Physician. The lack of any formal election for the coveted post did not produce any objections but, in choosing what must have looked like the safe option, the Governors were opening themselves up for trouble. Thomas may have secured the post of Physician but he did not inherit his father or grandfather's drive, ambition or devotion to duty. Bedlam was entering dangerous times and, by handing the job of Physician to Thomas Monro, it would bring shame onto itself.

PART THREE

The Madhouse Reformers

11

Rules and Regulations

In 1789, at the time when the French Revolution was sending shockwaves across Britain, the prison reformer and philanthropist John Howard (of whom we shall learn more later) completed a detailed and far-reaching survey of all the principal prisons and hospitals in Europe. His report included details of a visit to Bethlem that had taken place on 26 September 1788 when there was a total of 272 patients in residence (133 men, 139 women), of whom 110 were adjudged to be incurable. Howard had mixed feelings about the hospital: he considered the food and beer to be very good but had concerns about the building itself, which he thought unsuitable for housing lunatics.

'On the four floors there are about two hundred and seventy rooms,' he wrote. 'These were quite clean and not offensive, though the house is old and wants white-washing. The galleries have, very properly, rooms only on one side. The patients communicate with one another from the top to the bottom of the house, so that there is no separation of the calm and quiet from the noisy and turbulent, except those that are chained in their cells. To each side of the house there is only one vault: very offensive. There are no cisterns at the top of the house, nor water in the upper floor.'

Howard was impressed that the incurable patients were charged only half a crown a week for their upkeep, but was concerned that on admission ordinary patients had to deposit a bond of £100 ('from two householders') to cover their bedding, clothing and, if necessary, funeral costs. This, he thought, would 'bear hard upon the poor, and absolutely exclude many of those who have the greatest occasion for charitable relief'. However, by the time his report was published, the weekly price for incurables had doubled to

5 shillings, matching the rate being charged at St Luke's Hospital and a sure sign that Bethlem was short of money and drifting toward financial trouble again.

Howard's observations about Bethlem's age and unsuitable design did not apply to St Luke's Hospital, which he visited the next day. In 1786 St Luke's had moved from its original Moorfields site, opposite Bethlem, to nearby Old Street Road. Here the 162 patients (54 men and 108 women, including forty incurables) were properly separated from each other and had full access to water, toilets and large 'airing grounds'. His only real gripe concerned the absence of a chapel, a facility that most mental institutions purposefully omitted for fear of agitating the sensibilities of their more religiously minded inmates. In terms of its maintenance and general environment, Bethlem had fallen a long way behind St Luke's.[112]

Howard's concerns over Bethlem's age, poor layout and lack of whitewash was not news to its Governors; they were perfectly aware that the hospital was structurally unsound and no longer an ideal place to house lunatics. There may have been an awareness of this as far back as 1776, when the architect James Gandon was given £100 as the winner of an open competition held by Bethlem to design an entirely new hospital. The design was never used and the experience left Gandon with mental health issues of his own to deal with.

'The design I made for that hospital very nearly terminated my existence,' recalled Gandon in his memoirs. 'It was necessary that I should visit every apartment in the original structure. In these visits I encountered the most deplorable cases. At last I experienced sleepless nights, and when I did at last procure any rest, I was troubled with horrible dreams of the affecting scenes I had witnessed. I was at last attacked by brain fever, and my medical attendants had no hope of my recovery. But through the affectionate care of my wife, aided by a strong and vigorous constitution, I gradually recovered.'[113]

Details of the circumstances surrounding this competition are non-existent, but it is probable that the Governors commissioned it prior to the financial crisis brought about by William Kinleside, the revelation of which forced the Governors to abandon all thoughts of spending money on the hospital's infrastructure. As the years passed Bedlam became steadily more dilapidated, and in July 1790 the Governors were spurred on by Howard's description to find out just how bad the situation had become. They employed the architect Henry Holland to survey every inch of the Hospital; his report was delivered just under a year later, but it made for some alarming reading.

It appeared that John Howard was being unduly generous when he commented that the hospital was in need of some whitewash and general repairs: the situation was far more serious than this. Henry Holland made it apparent that there been no basic maintenance, decoration or repairs undertaken since the early 1770s, leaving most parts of the hospital in a poor state with some areas actually dangerous. He discovered crumbling plaster, rotten beams and windows, rusted ironwork and endless areas of damp. Furthermore, the entire eastern wall of the hospital was in such a poor condition that it was in danger of collapse. The combined effect of this neglect was to produce an environment that Holland believed would endanger the health of the inmates, but the greatest shock came at the report's end when Holland gave his estimate as to how much would be needed to rectify the situation. The total cost was a staggering £8,660 (about £760,000 today), with the work projected to take at least five years to complete. The Governors knew that they did not have even a fraction of this sum to hand, yet without it the hospital was in danger of becoming uninhabitable; Holland's pronouncement immediately plunged Bethlem into another financial crisis.

With the hospital's infrastructure crumbling and its funding in a state of disarray, the Governors took an unprecedented step: they appointed a Select Committee of Enquiry to look into every aspect of Bethlem's management and finance. With donations declining, the idea was to provide some reassurance to the outside world that Bethlem was still a worthy charitable cause. It would also acquaint the Governors with all the problems and liabilities that they were facing so that they could devise a long-term strategy to handle them. While the Committee conducted its investigations the purse strings remained closed, leaving the hospital to survive as best it could in difficult circumstances.

The Select Committee's work commenced on 10 January 1792, and throughout the winter and spring its members asked for, and were given, access to the hospital's written and financial records; they were also permitted to observe staff practices and to talk to people about their job specifications and routines. It was a thorough audit and the resultant report was placed before the senior officers on 12 June. It was immediately apparent that it was not just Bethlem's buildings that were in bad shape: the hospital's management and staff were also in serious need of attention. This was a moment of crisis for Bethlem: at a time of acute financial shortage, both the physical structure and management were in dire trouble. Unless the Governors could plot a course through the mess, the hospital's very existence was under threat.

The President of Bridewell and Bethlem called for a series of exceptional General Courts so that Governors could discuss the contents of the Special Committee's report. An advert placed in *The Times* on 13 June instructed all Governors to meet at Bridewell Hospital the next day at midday when 'the punctual audience of every governor is exactly requested'. The exceptional meeting was chaired by Bedlam's President, Brass Crosby, an alderman, former Lord Mayor and one-time inmate at the Tower of London. The start of his tenure had coincided with the financial crisis sparked by William Kinleside and it looked set to finish with a management crisis.

After expressing initial shock at the findings, Crosby proposed tackling the findings head-on. It was evident that the entire management system had been operating without close supervision for decades and that this self-regulation had allowed some terrible practices to become established. When faced with mismanagement of this magnitude there was little point in tinkering around the edges – only a radical solution would do. The Governors grasped the nettle with both hands by voting to abandon the Hospital's existing rules, orders and duties so that they could be rewritten from scratch.

'All [existing] rules, orders and duties respecting both hospitals shall be rescinded,' the Governors unanimously decided. In their place would come a new set of regulations, better and more comprehensive than before, but this was no easy task.

The previous rules and regulations had been drawn up in 1677, shortly after the Moorfields building had opened. This short list of ten items placed a heavy emphasis on general routines within the hospital but had little to say on its management or about individual job descriptions. Several of these older rules concerned themselves with trivial matters, such as when individual gates should be shut or when a bell should be rung, but only gave cursory a mention to anti-corruption measures. The only relevant direction was that 'No servant, or other person whatsoever, shall take any money given to the lunaticks, to convert the same to their own use.' Of course, there had been some amendments to, and expansion of, these regulations over the years, but they had been done in an ad hoc fashion, leaving the hospital without a coherent set of rules. That was about to change.[114]

In an unparalleled burst of activity, the Governors convened special meetings on 14, 18, 26 and 28 June 1792, from which emerged many ideas as to how both Bridewell and Bethlem might best be managed in the future. Some were based directly on the findings of the Select Committee, others were based on suggestions from those Governors who ran their own businesses or had been involved with other institutions. The rules were further reshaped and refined so that, by the end of June, a general consensus had been reached. On 6 July a draft document of the new rules was placed before the Governors, every single one of whom voted to accept it. The Clerk then ordered that copies of the new regulations be printed and distributed to all staff, officers, servants, Governors and anybody else connected with the hospitals.

Whereas the original 1677 rules had be accommodated on a single printed sheet of paper, the new booklet of regulations, entitled *Standing Rules of Orders for the Governors of the Royal Hospitals of Bridewell and Bethlem*, stretched to fifty-two pages. From the outset it is clear that the Governors wanted every person associated with the hospitals to know exactly what their duties and responsibilities were, as well as telling them which practices were deemed unacceptable. For example, in future each new Governor would be forced to listen to a statement that would be read out to him by a chaplain in the presence of the President or Treasurer. Its wording was meant to leave an incoming Governor in no doubt that any perks that came with the role were to come to them in the life hereafter and not via the hospitals' cash funds:

'Sir,

You have been elected, and come now to be admitted, a governor of the Royal Hospital of Bridewell and Bedlam; which is a station of great honour, trust, and influence; and will afford you many opportunities of promoting the glory of God, and the welfare of your fellow creatures: for in these hospitals a provision is made for employing idle and vagrant, lewd and disorderly persons, as well as those who desire and want employment in honest and useful labour and also for maintaining and curing needy, deplorable lunaticks.

'The distribution of the revenues designed by royal bounty, and many charitable persons, for those truly noble and excellent purposes, is now about to be committed to your care. And you are hereby solemnly required, and earnestly requested, to discharge your duty in this behalf with a conscientious regard; that you may appear with joy at the judgement seat of Christ, when a particular account will be taken of all the offices of charity in which we have abounded towards our poor brethrens and a peculiar reward conferred on those who have performed them with fidelity and zeal.'[115]

In the pages that followed were printed more than fifty individual rules and orders concerning the good governance of both Bridewell and Bethlem. In light of the Special Committee's discoveries and the ongoing dire financial situation, particular emphasis was placed upon the hospital's bookkeeping and auditing procedures. A standing committee of seven auditors was to be appointed from among the Governors; they were expected to inspect the accounts quarterly, and in addition all the 'cash books, books of accounts and books of legacies and benefactions' were to be brought to each official meeting. This represented an earnest desire by the majority of Governors to move away from the muddled, wasteful, and sometimes corrupt accountancy practice of previous years. However, the depth of the current financial crisis was such this was would not be enough to bring Bethlem back into credit; in the best tradition of cash-strapped organisations, Bridewell and Bethlem needed to make some serious economies as well.

The new rules declared that all commercial land and buildings had to be let to the highest bidder while any contracts for building work, catering, medicines, etc, had to be put out to tender via newspaper advertisements. The stipulation that no Governor would henceforth be allowed to organise contracts or 'be concerned with serving wines, provisions of goods' suggests that there may have been a certain amount of corruption in this area. Further rules made sure that all incoming charity money and donations were properly logged and that, once in the system, the money did not disappear. Probably the harshest economy affected the officers and servants whose entertainment budget was stopped 'except for one dinner on Easter Monday, one of St Matthew's day and one annual dinner at a tavern for the auditors'. Worse still, all staff salaries were to be 'fixed, suited to their service, to be paid quarterly by the Treasurer and all perquisites and emoluments of every kind be avoided and discouraged'.

The economy on salaries proved to be especially disastrous to the joint Clerks of both hospitals, the brothers John and Richard Woodhouse. They saw their joint salary lowered and fixed at £200 per annum. This was the final strain on John Woodhouse's frayed nerves and, shortly before the publication of the new rules, he was forced to retire on grounds of ill health. The Clerk was, in the best tradition of Bethlem nepotism, replaced by his son John, who in the coming decades proved to be feckless and a drunkard. John junior muddled on until 1805 when he was forced to resign. 'I cannot defend my remissness and my irregularity of conduct,' he wrote, 'but my life, though tarnished by folly, has never been stained with dishonour.'[116]

Budget cuts and anti-corruption measures dominated the report, but the object of the hospitals' care, namely its patients and inmates, did get five pages devoted to them. In a total of thirty-four rules, the Governors outlined the admission and discharge procedures, the restrictions on visitors and the inspection regime to be performed by the servants. Only a handful of rules dealt with how the patients themselves should be treated and then only in the most general of terms. For their own safety, patients would not be allowed a 'box with a lock and key, or any razors, knives, scissors, or dangerous instruments of any kinds'; nor were they to be permitted 'tea, sugar, wine or strong beer'. In terms of specific treatment, there were only two rules, both of which concerned the use of chains. These were not to be applied without the approbation of the Apothecary, and afterwards the chained patient must have his or her feet 'carefully examined, well rubbed, and covered with flannel every night and morning during the winter months'. Should any abuses occur, a book was to be placed in the hospital's entrance hall so that the officers, servants or visitors could make them known to the Steward.

The duties of all the officers and servants were also set out in detail across thirty-five pages that covered everyone from the President, which was still very much a ceremonial role, down to the 'basketmen', gallery maids and laundrywomen. All were expected to be at their posts by 6am (7am in the winter), to variously light fires, clean cells, mend clothes and shunt patients about the hospital; all were expressly forbidden from interfering with the patients and accepting gratuities, on pain of losing their job. Even the visiting barber had his role outlined and was warned to have 'a sufficiency of shaving cloths and towels'.

Perhaps the only surprise came with the roles of the medical officers. The Physician and Surgeon were given minimal job descriptions that required both of them to be present on a Saturday morning when patients were admitted and for the Physician to come in on a Monday and Wednesday morning to make a round of patients. The lengthy job description afforded to the Apothecary confirms that the bulk of medical care and decision-making was in his hands. In contrast to the freelance roles of the Physician and Surgeon, the Apothecary was a full-time position that required him to make a daily morning round or 'oftener if necessary'. He had to 'furnish medicines', 'attend the administration of the medicines ordered by the Physician', deliver a weekly list of drugs to the Bethlem Committee, and 'direct the Keepers in their management of the patients during the absence of the Physician'.

Seeing the roles laid out in writing confirms that the Apothecary was the central pillar in the medical triumvirate and vital to the inmates' welfare. He was the only medical officer to have daily contact with the inmates; he was in charge of their routine care and administered the treatments prescribed by the Physician and Surgeon. It was up to the Apothecary to draw the Physician's and Surgeon's attention to any illness, change in mental condition, signs of abuse or any other notable aspect of the patients. Despite taking the lion's share of the work, the Apothecary to Bethlem and Bridewell did not share the same status level as the Physician and, with the long hours, opportunities for work outside the hospital were limited. Although Bethlem's Apothecaries did not die in poverty, none reached the same levels of wealth as even the poorest Physician, but placing so much power in the hands of just one of the medical officers was to have its dangers, as Thomas Monro would in time discover.

The implementation of the 1792 *Standing Rules and Orders* was not just an exercise in staff and financial management: it had also been a chance to prove to the hospitals' benefactors that the charities were well run and that any donations would be spent wisely and not frittered away through corruption or perks for the Governors. There was, however, always the danger that the public expression of intent shown by the new regulations would not be matched by action behind Bethlem's gates, which had been firmly closed to the public for many years. Certainly, the driving force behind the changes, President Brass Crosby, did not live long enough to see them fully implemented; he died a few months later, early in 1793. There is no evidence that the food and building contracts were, as promised, put to tender by advertisement, or that any of the new accountancy practices or revised job descriptions were ever adhered to.[117]

Nor did the publication resolve Bethlem's immediate financial crisis. The £8,000 that Henry Holland had wanted to spend on making Bethlem structurally safe and habitable was simply not available. The Governors agreed to spend just £1,000 in February 1793 on emergency repairs, with a further £1,500 the year afterwards. As the eighteenth century drew to a close Bethlem looked to be in a more precarious situation than ever before.

12

Haslam, Crowther and Matthews

In June 1795, as the Governors continued to debate Bethlem's crumbling infrastructure, the resident Apothecary, John Gonza, died. Like other medical staff, Gonza wanted his job to remain within the family and had been preparing his son Thomas to take over from him. On 11 July Thomas Gonza was made temporary Apothecary but, for reasons unknown, he did not put himself forward as a candidate for the vacant post. When the election was held on 30 July there were only two candidates, Christopher Buck and John Haslam. Such a small field was unusual and favoured Haslam, who had obtained a list of the Governors' names and had been lobbying them for weeks. The tactic worked: Haslam received ninety-two votes against just six for Buck.[118]

In fairness, it was not just lobbying that won Haslam the post – he was also better qualified and more experienced than his rival. John Haslam was thirty-one years old when he entered Bethlem and already had a string of accomplishments behind him. A Londoner by birth, he had taken an early interest in medicine and undertook an apprenticeship before entering St Bartholomew's Hospital as a student surgeon. Many people entered the medical profession because of family tradition or because of the advantages it could bring them in other spheres of life. Haslam was different: he had an academic interest in medicine and in 1785, after serving as House Surgeon at St Bartholomew's Hospital, he enrolled on a medical degree at the esteemed Edinburgh University. Here he became something of a student activist, campaigning for the right of trainee medics to be admitted to the Royal Infirmary as well as fronting the University's Medical, Natural History and

Chemistry societies. Strangely, Haslam left Edinburgh early in order to study first at Uppsala, Sweden, then at Cambridge University, but despite the considerable expense his education must have incurred, he did not receive an MD from any of these institutions. Being unable to practise as a qualified physician probably meant that Haslam was making his living as a surgeon, and it is thought that he may have operated a medical practice in Shoreditch, where he was living prior to entering Bethlem.

Thus, in July 1795, the Governors were able to fill the Apothecary's post with a candidate who had a solid medical background but whose lack of a degree prevented him from competing with either the Physician or the Surgeon. The Apothecary's job was full-time, residential, not especially well paid and gave little opportunity for additional income through private practice; the annual wage was just £100 (now about £7,000), although this was raised to £335 a few years later. This suggests that Haslam may have wanted the position to boost his medical credentials, but he did at least have an interest in mental health issues and came to Bethlem with some predetermined thoughts about their causes and treatments.

All this should have been excellent news for Bethlem and its patients, but Haslam had the misfortune to arrive at a time when the other two medical officers, Thomas Monro and Bryan Crowther, the Surgeon, were becoming more erratic in their attendance at the hospital. This situation left the Apothecary with near-total responsibility for the patients' care, but ironically with very little power to change their medication or treatment. Haslam was overworked and underappreciated: it was not long before a tense situation developed between himself, Monro and Crowther.[119]

Almost from the start of his career at Bethlem, Thomas Monro had exhibited a disregard for his duties, which he considered to be both time-consuming and poorly paid. His job description required him to attend the hospital three times a week, but he would commonly be absent for one or more of these sessions, although he did make an effort to be at the Saturday meeting when new admissions would be examined and, more importantly, one or more of the Governors would be present. When he did attend in his capacity as Physician, Monro refused to enter the hospital's galleries; he would instead occupy a room in the main building and request that any ill patients, as diagnosed by the Apothecary, Steward or Matron, be brought to him for examination. To Monro the title of Bethlem Physician was useful as a means of boosting his prestige and his personal income via his thriving private practice, which consisted mostly of wealthy clients. The funds from this were used to finance his preferred interest, namely art, and especially painting; with much of his time and cash being devoted to this cause, the needs of his charitable patients were very much a secondary concern. In particular, Monro had given little thought to the medical treatments he should offer to his patients and, rather than seek modern solutions, had adopted wholesale the practices of his father and grandfather, which consisted of a regime of purges, vomits and bleedings. Monro refused to entertain the idea of new practices and eschewed the notion of publishing case histories or of allowing students into the hospital to observe the medical staff in action. Monro's conservatism was an instant and ongoing source of irritation to John Haslam, whose extensive medical training and wide reading had led him to adopt a more progressive attitude towards the insane.

Unlike Monro's one-size-fits-all treatment using medicines, Haslam believed that the key to helping and treating lunatics lay in careful individual management rather than brutalising them with lancets and poisons. His later writings recommend that lunatics should never be threatened, punished or coerced, and should only ever be restrained or chained if they become a danger to themselves or others. Haslam believed that asylum superintendents should use reason and force of personality to make sure that the patients knew that they were under the control of the institution. 'I can truly declare', he wrote, 'that by gentleness of manner, and kindness of treatment, I have never failed to obtain the confidence, and conciliate the esteem of insane persons, and have succeeded by these means in procuring from them respect and obedience.'[120]

Haslam also chose not to subscribe to some fashionable cures, and vocally rejected one of the most popularly used suppression techniques of the day, which was known as 'the eye'. William Pargeter offers a description of 'the eye' technique, which was supposed to render obedience from troublesome inmates simply by giving them a certain look. 'The maniac was locked in a room', wrote Pargeter, 'raving and exceedingly turbulent. I took two men with me, and learning he had no offensive weapons, I planted them at the door with directions to be silent and keep out of sight, unless I should want their assistance. I then suddenly unlocked the door – rushed into the room and caught his eye in an instant. The business was then done – he became peaceable in a moment – trembled with fear, and was as governable as it was possible for a future madman to be.'[121]

> 'The eye' had even been used on insane King George III, but Haslam was dismissive of the technique. 'It has, on some occasions, occurred to me to meet with gentlemen who have imagined themselves eminently gifted with this awful imposition of the eye, but the result has never been satisfactory, for, although I have entertained the fullest confidence of any relation, which such gentlemen might afterwards communicate concerning the success of the experiment, I have never been able to persuade them to practise this rare talent tête-à-tête with a furious lunatic… Whenever the doctor visits a violent or mischievous maniac, however controlling his physiognomy, such patient is always secured by the strait waistcoat: and it is, moreover, thought expedient to afford him the society of one or more keepers.'[122]

Aside from displaying his non-reliance on conventional practice, Haslam's comments on 'the eye' show off two other aspects of his personality. The first is his absolute belief that one could only learn about the causes and treatment of madness through practical experience, something that led him to dismiss any ideas that emerged from people outside the asylum system. The second is his arrogance, a trait for which he was notorious and which is immediately apparent in all his writings. Haslam could be dismissive and acerbic and was not averse to ruffling the feathers of his superiors, an action that often served to alienate him within the wider medical community.

Underlying all Haslam's writings is a belief that mental illness originated from within the body, most especially the brain, an organ with which he was fascinated and had been so since his days at Edinburgh. Haslam used his position in Bethlem to gain access to the bodies of those patients who had

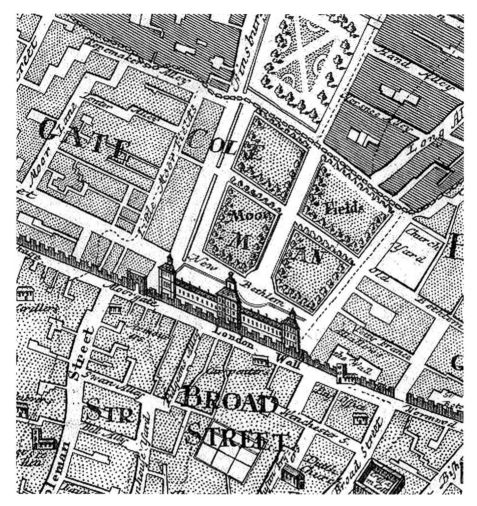

Above: A 1746 map of Moorfields showing the location of 'New Bethlem' Hospital next to the London Wall.

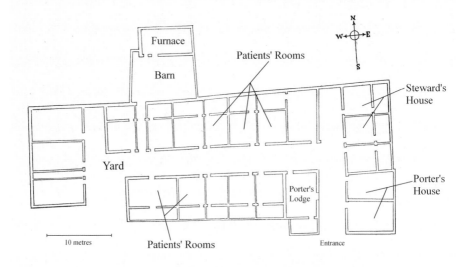

Above: A plan of the original Bethlem Hospital at Bishopsgate based on a 1677 drawing. *(After O'Donoghue, 1914)*

Below: The statues of 'melancholy and raving madness' greeted patients and visitors as they passed through the gateway of the New Bethlem Hospital.

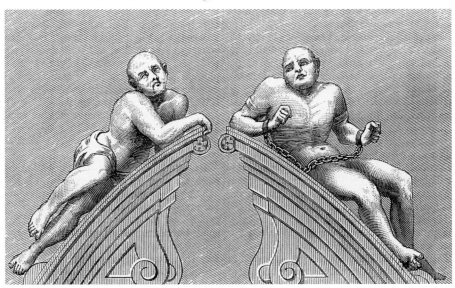

Above and Below: 'The Madhouse': the final scene from William Hogarth's 'A Rake's Progress' series (1735). This is probably the most familiar historical image of Bedlam which depicts both patients and visitors inside the hospital's gallery.

Above: The New Bethlem Hospital at Moorfields as it looked in 1676. For decades it was a major London landmark, a tourist attraction and the focus of pimps, prostitutes and drunkards.

Below: An 1823 plan of the new Bethlem Hospital St George's Fields showing 'Criminals' Buildings' and the strictly partitioned airing grounds.

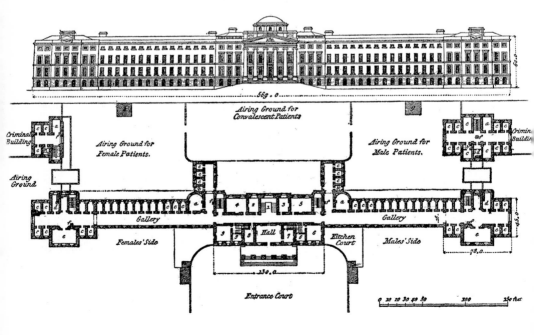

Above: The St George's Field Bethlem Hospital as it looked on its opening in 1815. The building was a great improvement over the appalling conditions of the old Moorfields hospital.

Above: 'A Peep into Bethlehem', a satirical cartoon from the 1790s. The raving woman in the background is said to be Margaret 'Peg' Nicholson, who attempted to murder King George in 1786.

Above: Dr James Monro, physician at Bethlem and Bridewell between 1728 and 1752. He was the first of four Monro 'mad doctors' to work at the hospital. *The Royal College of Physicians*

Above: Dr John Monro, son of James, was Bethlem physician from 1752 to 1791. His methods and understanding of madness were the subject of much controversy. *The Royal College of Physicians*

Above: Dr Thomas Monro, son of John, was a reluctant physician and was sacked from his post in 1816 following a major scandal. *The Royal College of Physicians*

Below: William Battie, physician of the rival St Luke's Hospital, advocated humane treatment of the insane and was a thorn in the side of the Bethlem physicians.

Above: Margaret 'Peg' Nicholson was one of Bethlem's most famous patients but by the time of her incarceration, in 1786, the hospital was no longer admitting visitors.

Above: The allegedly violent patient James Norris was chained to a post for over a decade before he became the subject of a vocal reform campaign in 1814. His case awakened the wider world to poor conditions within the Moorfields Bethlem building.

Above: The York
Retreat, a model
'madhouse' built
by Quakers in 1796.
Its design and methods
would be advocated
as a blueprint for the
treatment of the
mentally ill.

Right: An 1810 picture
and plan of James Tilly
Matthews's mysterious
'Air Loom', a devious
machine which he
believed could control
the thoughts of
politicians and
monarchs.

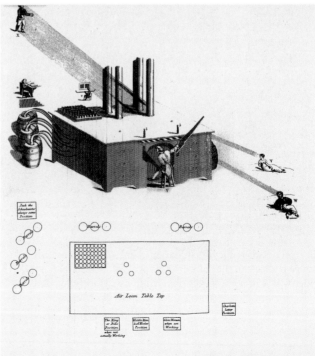

Above: John Haslam was the Bethlem apothecary between 1795 and 1816, when he was sacked following a parliamentary inquiry into the hospital.

Above: 'Cooling his Brains', a satirical cartoon from 1789 depicting a Bethlem inmate having his head shaved, as was often the case with raving patients.

Above: The male ward in the St George's Hospital following a series of reforms ushered in by Dr Charles Hood in the 1850s and 60s.

Above: A set of restraining irons of the sort that were routinely used in Bethlem until the mid-nineteenth century.

Above: Dr Helkiah Crooke (stood on the left) was a notorious figure whose time as Bethlem physician, between 1619 to 1633, was marked both by beneficial reform and serious scandal.

died at the hospital and, in the damp, darkened conditions of the basement, would dissect their skulls, making meticulous notes on the pathology of their brains. Although Haslam believed passionately that it was physical defects in the brain that were producing the mania, melancholia, hallucinations and other symptoms exhibited by his Bedlamites, after twenty-nine autopsies he still had difficulty relating the morphology of his dead patients' brains to their particular mental disorders.

Despite his prickly nature, Haslam's views were quoted extensively by mental health reformers including the pioneering French asylum reformer Philippe Pinel, who described Haslam as being 'in the habit of discharging the important duties of his office with integrity dignity and humanity'. Given the way events were to turn, comments such as these would eventually look ironic indeed.

Despite making strident claims for himself and his theories, Haslam was limited as to what he could achieve at Bethlem. He was entirely subordinate to Thomas Monro and as such was forced to administer the violent 'physicks' that the doctor would prescribe as a cure for madness. He was also subordinate to the Surgeon, Bryan Crowther, whose visiting hours were just as irregular as Monro's and who, like the Physician, had replaced his father at the hospital. Crowther was one of Bethlem's more bizarre characters, about whom little is known. He was certainly a severe alcoholic, was subject to extraordinary mood swings, and was in absolute agreement with Monro about the benefits of vomits, purges, opiates, bleeding and cold baths.

'I never saw or heard of the bad effects of vomits,' wrote Crowther, adding that 'maniacal people, as is frequently observed, require a quadruple dose of opium.' But it was the purgatives that were his favourite method of treatment, a consequence of his belief that maniacs were liable to suffer from constipation and trapped urine. He was not a very conscientious medic and once even confessed that he had 'not been educated in the practice of physic'. Many of his cures were haphazard and quite possibly home-made, including such things as the curing of mortification of the buttocks by covering them in bandages soaked in wine and water. At least one patient died of a ruptured bowel because of his lack of care, all of which would seem to support a remarkably candid confession by Crowther given, of all places, in a textbook he wrote about the nature of insanity: 'I disclaim all pretensions as a theorist on the subject of insanity, and still more any presumption in directing others in the treatment of its unfortunate victims.'[123]

Haslam's dislike of Monro and Crowther and their methods was in tune with the thinking of others. A reviewer of one of Crowther's books (entitled Practical Remarks on Insanity) takes the Surgeon to task for adhering to the use of vomits, cold baths and purges. The reviewer suggests that Crowther should listen to the views of Haslam, who believes that 'such practices don't work and are rarely employed in lunatic hospitals.'[124]

But Haslam's freedom in Bethlem was limited by his subordinate role to such an extent that he could not even alter the conditions inside Bethlem's galleries and cells, which he would tour daily. His powers here were curtailed by those of the Steward, the Matron and even some of the lower servants who were in day-to-day control of the galleries and who took their orders from Monro or the Keeper. In essence, Haslam's role was that of a medical caretaker, carrying out the orders of others, providing basic care for the patients and drawing attention to individuals who required more detailed treatment.

Under this system Bethlem's medical officers tended to operate in isolation from one another with no clear lines of communication or a coherent vision of the hospital's future direction. The Governors should perhaps have picked up on this problem, but they rarely interfered in the medical officers' domain and almost never set foot inside the patients' galleries. There were, however, occasional incidents that should have prompted the Governors to dig a little deeper into some of the practices operating within Bethlem. One of these was a monumental and extraordinary battle that developed between Haslam and one of his patients, James Tilly Matthews. Although this started as a spat, the importance of Matthews's case grew exponentially and eventually caused the downfall of the hospital's entire medical regime.

James Tilly Matthews was born some time around 1760 and for many years worked as a tea dealer in London's Leadenhall Street. Following the French Revolution of 1789 he began to take an interest in radical politics and made friends with the English intellectual David Williams. Both Williams and Matthews were concerned that the British Government might want to declare war on France and, in 1792, the pair embarked on the first of several self-appointed diplomatic missions to Paris, their aim being to prevent the outbreak of hostilities. Even at this early stage Williams had concerns about his friend's mental health, claiming that he had 'suspicions that Matthews was affected in the head'. In 1793 a sudden and brutal change in the French political system led to Matthews's arrest in Paris as a suspected double-agent; he was detained in France for three years, where he was starved, left half-frozen and dragged from prison to prison with the constant threat of the guillotine hanging over him. Perhaps unsurprisingly, he was seriously affected by this experience and started to form a complex series of paranoid delusions that fused together various aspects of his experiences in Paris, his political interests and a long-standing fascination with hypnotism.[125]

When Matthews returned to London in March 1796 he found that his tea business had been declared bankrupt, leaving him short of money and isolated from his former high-society contacts. Increasingly disturbed, he began to write letters to people of influence, outlining his treatment at the hands of the French but also offering some unorthodox opinions about the cause of the uneasy relationship between the French and British Governments. It would appear that Matthews's views were ignored and, on 30 December 1796, he took direct action by attending the public gallery in the House of Commons. At the height of a debate concerning British-French relations, Matthews stood up and shouted out the word 'treason!'. He was arrested and, when examined before the Bow Street Magistrates, told such a bizarre series of stories that he was committed to Bethlem Hospital as a dangerous lunatic. After a brief spell in a workhouse, Matthews entered Bethlem on 28 January 1797, much to the annoyance of his wife, brother and other family members who insisted that he was perfectly sane. A few months later his relations brought Matthews's case before Lord Kenyon but, on interviewing him, the judge immediately declared that Bethlem was by far the best place for a person in his state of mind. A year after being admitted, Matthews was declared to be incurably insane, which effectively gave him an open-ended stay at the Hospital.

During his first year of incarceration, Matthews's wife and brother had much contact with the hospital, a process that seems to have drawn in the

Apothecary, John Haslam, who, in the general absence of Dr Monro, was left to defend the diagnosis of insanity. Haslam became involved with Matthews, and was intrigued by his brand of insanity, taking a special interest in his peculiar ideas and behaviour. From the outset Matthews refused to associate with any other patients, who, he believed, were actually sane but had been paid 'by certain agents to counterfeit the disease [of insanity]'.

A few months later Matthews claimed that there was a man standing upon Bloomsbury Church who held a 'Doomsday Book' underneath his arm but that 'no one could open that book save himself'. Such delusions were the tip of the iceberg, but it was only after he had been declared incurably insane that Matthews began to reveal to Haslam a complex conspiracy theory that surrounded him and his experiences in France. The Apothecary, who was perhaps aware that Matthews's family had the potential to cause the hospital trouble, kept a record of his patient's beliefs, which were, according to him, 'a matter of curiosity'.[126]

At the heart of Matthews's beliefs was his insistence that in London there was a gang of four men and three women who had invented a machine called an 'Air Loom', which they kept in an underground room near Bethlem. The gang, who had names such as Jack the Schoolmaster, Sir Archy, Middle Man and Glove Woman, could use the Air Loom to control the thoughts and actions of people anywhere in Europe, forcing them to say and do things against their will. This was achieved chiefly by feeding the Loom with a clever concoction of ingredients that, according to Matthews, included 'seminal fluid, male and female; effluvia of copper; ditto of sulphur; the vapours of vitriol and aqua fortis; ditto of nightshade and hellebore; effluvia of dogs; stinking human breath; putrid effluvia; ditto of mortification and of the plague; stench of the cesspool; gas from the anus of a horse; human gas; gas of the horse's greasy heels.'

The smell of the Loom must have been extraordinary, but by these means it could influence people in more than two dozen different ways, each of which was given a name by Matthews. Many of these techniques (eg 'kiteing', 'thought-making' and 'apoplexy-working') would either implant or rid the brain of certain thoughts, but the Air Loom could also induce physical pain and even death (so-called 'lobster cracking' and 'bomb bursting'). By these means, the Air Loom's operators had served to control the minds of key figures in the British and French Governments, ensuring that the two countries were kept in a permanent state of war. The Air Loom was also directed at Matthews in particular after the gang had placed a magnet in his brain 'by which a number of event workers and political chemists were enabled to attain his thoughts and persisted that these persons he said he constantly heard. They forced him to utter various noises and had the power of directing his thoughts; they also endeavoured to poison him by admitting into his room various stenches.'[127]

Although Haslam held a fascination with Matthews, their relationship was adversarial with the inmate being convinced that he was at the centre of a vast political conspiracy that pitched not only the Bethlem Apothecary against him, but also most of the political and royal figures of Europe. 'In this situation he continued for many years,' wrote Haslam of his patient, 'sometimes an automaton moved by the agency of persons, at others the Emperor of the whole world, issuing proclamations to his disobedient subjects, and hurling from their thrones the usurpers of his dominions.'

From the moment of Matthews's committal, Haslam had received a continuous series of threats and petitions from the man's family, who continued to protest his innocence. In 1809, following another failed petition for Matthews's release, the family smuggled into Bethlem two physicians, Henry Clutterbuck and George Birkbeck, both of whom declared Matthews to be of sound mind and suitable for release into the community. Thomas Monro and Haslam vehemently disagreed, but the two doctors' diagnosis allowed the family to take out a suit of habeas corpus in the court of King's Bench.

Habeas corpus suits (which give the courts the power to release falsely imprisoned people) were an occupational hazard for the staff and managers of madhouses, including Bethlem, but in this instance Haslam was greatly affronted that two ordinary medics should have had the nerve to contradict his professional opinion. In reply to the charges, Haslam produced a lengthy deposition that outlined Matthews's history in Bethlem and detailed his ideas about the Air Loom and its operators. In addition a number of eminent people turned up in court to testify in favour of Matthews's continued detention. The most powerful of these came from one of Bethlem's Governors who insisted that, if released, Matthews would present a physical danger to the Royal Family and certain other political figures. In the light of recent attempts on the life of King George by lunatics such as Margaret Nicholson, there was no way that a judge would risk releasing into the community a person with potentially regicidal thoughts. After only a brief trial, Matthews was declared insane by the judge and ordered to remain in Bethlem.

The court case was in most respects a routine affair and did not receive much publicity, but the challenge it presented to Haslam's authority riled him to such an extent that he decided he would silence his critics once and for all. Over the coming months he gathered together his notes on Matthews and wove them into a book that sought to demonstrate the extent of his patient's insanity. The resultant work was called Illustrations of Madness and was the world's first full-length examination of a single patient, but Haslam did not produce the book with a view to understanding Matthews's state of mind: he merely wanted to prove that his diagnosis had been correct. To this extent, Illustrations offers no analysis of Matthews's condition, but instead sets out the story behind the Air Loom and its operators, the assumption being that anyone who read the book could quickly work out for themselves that Matthews was mad. Included in the text was an elaborate diagram of the Air Loom as drawn by Matthews, complete with an explanation of its various components and operators. It is an impressive piece of artwork and certainly helps to strengthen Haslam's assertions. However, it was not just against Matthews's relations that Haslam was rallying, but also the two doctors, Clutterbuck and Birkbeck, who had seen fit to diagnose Matthews as being sane.

Haslam let the doctors' actions speak for themselves by printing their diagnosis in full, assuming that the reader would be able to spot their error. 'How they could fail to detect his insanity is inexplicable,' rants Haslam, 'as his disorder was evident to all who saw and conversed with him; even his fellow-students derided the absurdity of his doctrine.' Just in case there are should remain any doubts in the mind of his audience, Haslam finished his book with a stark warning:

'There are already too many maniacs allowed to enjoy a dangerous liberty and the Governors of Bethlem Hospital, confiding in the skill and integrity of their medical officers, were not disposed to liberate a mischievous lunatic to disturb the good order and peace of society. These gentlemen can have no advantage in detaining a person in confinement who has recovered his senses. Their interest consists in the numbers who are restored to the community and their friends; and their only reward the incense which Gratitude projects on the altar of Reason.'[128]

Haslam believed that he had won his argument and continued to treat Matthews as an incurable lunatic, much to the irritation of his family. It was, however, not just Haslam who would torment Matthews during his time in Bethlem; general conditions within the hospital had deteriorated to such a degree that parts of the building were beginning to collapse. It was a situation that the Governors had been ignoring for years but they would soon be forced to take the issue more seriously.

13

Relocation

The year 1798 saw the completion of an extensive renovation at Bridewell Hospital, which included the addition of a new prison section. The building work had been accompanied by the publication of a report that put forward several ideas as to how the prison could be made more efficient; one of these suggested that Bethlem, its sister hospital, was adsorbing too much of Bridewell's cash and that it might be time for the two institutions to go their separate ways. This idea received support among many of Bridewell's Governors, but was publicly rebuffed by Thomas Bowen:

> 'Bethlem, whose exigencies are pressing, would be left without her usual resource. And here, it cannot but appear extraordinary that the Committee, in their allotments of the estates and revenues of Bridewell, should have left the UNITED HOSPITAL wholly out of the account... No part of the Revenue of Bridewell has ever been more usefully employed, or perhaps so unexceptionally, as that which has gone in aid of the poor lunatics at Bethlem'.[129]

Bowen's intervention ensured that the financial link between Bridewell and Bethlem remained intact, but the Governors had had good cause to want to distance themselves from the charitable madhouse at Moorfields. It had been almost a decade since Henry Holland had recommended the application of urgent and extensive repairs at Bethlem, but a lack of cash meant that only essential maintenance had been undertaken. By 1799 Bethlem's ruinous state was such that it could be ignored no longer: 'There was not one floor which was level, and not one wall which was upright: settlements and fissures were visible everywhere,' wrote one author.[130]

The Governors commissioned Bethlem's Surveyor, James Lewis, to undertake an architectural examination of the building with a view to discovering 'the probable annual expense of keeping the same in repair'. A number of Bethlem's architecturally qualified Governors volunteered their services and, together with Lewis, they set about examining 'the whole of the building from end to end, and from the foundations to the roofs [including those places] where the eye could not reach'. Lewis's report appeared early in 1800 and, at fourteen pages long, looked slim; this turned out not to be a reflection of the Hospital's sound infrastructure but was instead the result of Lewis's economical use of the words with which he spelled out a blunt message: Bethlem was in a perilous state and almost beyond repair.

Lewis's inspection had uncovered dozens of serious structural flaws, many of which were directly related to deficiencies in Hooke's design for the building; chief among these were its foundations, which had been laid upon soft sediment infilling a former moat. Instead of using deep piles to underpin the building, the foundations were shallow and had for decades been sinking into the ground beneath. This process had been expedited by the weight of the roof, which was far in excess of anything the foundations could reasonably have been expected to bear, and by the design of the walls, which, by not being properly tied together, had warped and buckled. The Governors were seeing the results of the miraculous speed at which Bethlem had been erected a century earlier (although more recent alterations, particularly to the brick piers in the basement, had also contributed to the subsidence). This diagnosis was far worse than the Governors had expected and was compounded by Lewis's reluctance to place a figure on the cost of annual upkeep. His solution to the problem required more than just a few repairs: it required the demolition of the entire hospital.

'I am clearly of the opinion', wrote Lewis, 'that the present condition of the buildings is not in such a state as to warrant any other repair to be made thereto, than to preserve it, with the common care and attention, by such works as may be requisite... To do more would be unwise and improvident in the highest degree. The parts defective, and to be rendered stout for duration, are so extensive and intermixed with others; that not only great expense, but danger will be derived therefrom, which, of itself must be foreseen and prevented.'

Bethlem was cramped, damp, dark and dreary, which meant that, according to Lewis, it was ultimately 'incurable', having been fatally wounded by its inadequate foundations. Recent attempts at shoring up the walls and roof had been a waste of time, he said, and there was little point in throwing more cash at a structure that was ultimately doomed. Lewis's conclusions were stark and his evidence clear and concisely delivered, but his report was the last thing the Governors wanted to hear, especially given the fuss that Bridewell had been making about its continuing financial responsibility towards Bethlem. Like all good bureaucratic bodies, Bethlem's Governors managed to postpone making a decision by forming a special House Committee, which was tasked with studying Lewis's report and, based on his evidence and recommendations, to make recommendations of their own. This process took several months, but the delay actually worked in Bethlem's favour.[131]

When opened in 1676, the Moorfields Bethlem building had looked out upon a landscape that was only semi-urbanised. To the north lay the open pastures of Moorfields and beyond these the artillery ground and parklands, giving a sense of space in what was an otherwise highly built-up area. The financial boom of the eighteenth century created a need for land on which to build new houses, shops and factories. Moorfields possessed some of the last sizeable tracts of lands within the City of London, so, as the years progressed, Bethlem found itself being increasingly hemmed in by man-made edifices.

The Victorian journalist William Harvey recalled Moorfields at the turn of the nineteenth century:

'It was a large open quadrangular space, shut in by the Pavement to the west, the hospital and its outbuildings to the south, and lines of shops without fronts, occupied chiefly by dealers in old furniture, to the east and north... It was interesting to inspect the articles exposed for sale: here a cracked mirror in a dingy frame, a set of hair-seated chairs, the horse-hair protruding; a tall, stiff, upright easy chair, without a bottom; a cupboard with one shelf left of three, and with half a door; here a black oak chest, groaning to be scraped, so thick with ancient dust that it might have been the den of some unclean animal in Noah's ark... Escaping from this uncomfortable mart to the hospital footway, a strange sense of utter desertion came over you; long, gloomy lines of cells, strongly barred, and obscured with the accumulated dust, silent as the grave, unless fancy brought sounds of woe to your ears, rose before you; and there, on each side of the principal entrance, were the wonderful effigies of raving and moping madness, chiselled by the elder Cibber. How those stone faces and eyes glared! How sternly the razor must have swept over those bare heads! How listless and dead were those limbs, bound with inexorable fetters, while the iron of despair had pierced the hearts of the prisoned maniacs!'

As Harvey makes clear, by 1800 inmates such as James Tilly Matthews and Peg Nicholson did not gaze upon open fields but instead a mass of terraced housing and second-hand shops that formed Finsbury Place and South Street, while beyond this lay Finsbury Square, designed by George Dance so as to appeal to London's 'middling sort' of merchants, traders, actuaries and others. The Square certainly achieved this aim and even became famous for a bookshop known as 'The Temple of the Muses', which was so large that it was rumoured that a coach and six could be driven around its central counter. In 1800 the Corporation of London wanted to see the success of Finsbury Square repeated elsewhere in the City, but it was hampered by a lack of available space. This crisis was well known and, as the House Committee settled down to discuss the grave implications of James Lewis's report, one of its members realised that Bethlem was occupying one of the most expensive pieces of real estate in the world.[132]

In November 1801 the House Committee delivered its opinion on how best to solve the problem of Bethlem's crumbling infrastructure. It concluded that the hospital building was worth far less than the land on which it stood, so, rather than spend a fortune shoring it up, it made sense to sell the Moorfields plot to developers and to use the cash this raised to move Bethlem to a new site elsewhere in London. Lewis's original report had given the

House Committee little room to manoeuvre, but the idea of demolishing Bethlem was one that many of the Governors simply could not entertain. A serious and earnest debate took place between the Governors with impassioned pleas on both sides; eventually a vote was taken to settle the issue, from which emerged a compromise. The Governors voted to adopt the House Committee's report concerning the building's perilous condition with one crucial exception: they would ignore those recommendations 'relating to the expediency of rebuilding Bethlem Hospital'. In other words, they chose to ignore the vast and obvious problem confronting them and instead buried their heads in the sand, perhaps in the hope that another less drastic solution would present itself.[133]

The folly of this policy must have been evident to some of the Governors, for within a year there were rumours that people with connections to Bethlem were actively searching for sizeable tracts of land to the north of London. Official policy remained against relocation, but nonetheless in the semi-rural district of Islington landowners were being approached with a view to finding a new site for the hospital. One of those contacted was the Drapers' Company, a London guild that, like the original Bethlem, had its medieval origins in the Bishopsgate area of the City. The Drapers' Company was of interest to Bethlem because it held seven acres of land at Gossey Field, located on top of a hill in the central part of Islington. The site offered not only enough room to build a new hospital, but also benefited from being away from the noise and dirt of the City. It also had a commanding view over the rest of London and, perhaps by coincidence, was close to John Haslam's recently purchased family home.[134]

With a potential site having been found, the Governors' meetings were dominated by talk of the hospital's crumbling walls and roof, but the financial implications of rebuilding still scared a majority. It was argued that Bethlem could perhaps be patched up for several years to come, but James Lewis put paid to this idea when he was asked to address the Governors on the issue. He dismissed all talk of repair and instead declared the current building to be in a 'decaying and crippled state' and irreparable.

In the spring of 1803, and with their options decreasing, the Governors agreed to ask the Drapers' Company if it would sell Gossey Field but, having done so (and without receiving an answer) they then went quiet on the issue of rebuilding. One year later (and after much prompting from Lewis) it was agreed that possible means of financing a new hospital should be identified and that in the meantime they should prepare a contingency plan for the old hospital, parts of which were unfit for human habitation.

At this time Bethlem was operating at capacity and held at least 260 inmates, with dozens more names on its waiting list. James Lewis had foreseen a situation where parts of Bethlem Hospital would have be made off-limits for reasons of safety, and the Governors reluctantly agreed that, with parts of the building collapsing, alternative arrangements would have to made for some patients. It had been hoped that patients could be housed in other London hospitals, but all were either full or unwilling or unable to house lunatics on their premises. The Governors looked at the problem they were facing and decided to take a proactive decision: it was decreed that the waiting list should be closed to new names, an action that would in time reduce the number of inmates (because those that were released or died would not be replaced) and thus allow certain parts of the hospital to be shut down.

It had been hoped that these measures would be short-term, but Bethlem's Governors were in no hurry and it was yet another year before a newly formed Building Committee instructed James Lewis to start designing a new hospital to fit on the Gossey Field site. With this in motion, the issue of how to finance the project became more critical: it was thought that the high value of the Moorfields site would offset the cost of buying Gossey Field, and the expense of erecting the new hospital building could be met from other as yet unknown sources. An appeal fund was launched using newspaper advertisements, and the Governors' abundant political connections were asked for help, but the British economy was depressed and the money only trickled in. The fund alone would not provide the tens of thousands of pounds needed for the project, which meant that the taxpayer was going to have to stump up some cash as well.

Many of Bethlem's Governors were or had been politicians and knew how best to approach the country's parliamentarians. Rather than go cap in hand looking for money, it was explained to MPs that the current hospital was on the verge of closing its doors to new admissions, a decision that would have been disastrous for the soldiers and sailors ('the mental wreckage of the French Wars') awaiting treatment there. It was suggested that a sizeable donation to the building fund by the Government would ensure that a certain number of spaces was made available in the new hospital for those suffering from combat stress. This ploy gave MPs the impression that, rather than offering a handout to Bethlem, they were investing in the future of their armed forces. A sum of £10,000 (now £580,000) was offered by Parliament and gratefully accepted by the Governors. It was a good start but still just a drop in the ocean; it was thought that several times as much might eventually be needed. It was at this point that Bethlem's careful plans, which had been played out by the Governors over a period of six years, started to fall apart.

The prospect of selling the Moorfields site in order to pay for Gossey Field in Islington had been an integral part of the relocation plan, but the careful strategy started to unravel when it was discovered that Bethlem did not actually own the land on which it stood. This discovery was made in 1806 only after somebody took the trouble to check the original 1674 deeds, which revealed that the Moorfields land had been given to Bethlem by the City of London on the strict condition that it could only ever be used to house a hospital. Should Hooke's celebrated building ever be demolished, ownership of the land immediately reverted back to the Corporation of London. This meant that Bethlem would be unable to utilise the value of its site and thus could not raise enough money to buy the land in Islington.

It was, however, suggested that the wording of the deed would allow the Moorfields land to be swapped for a real estate location elsewhere in London. The Drapers' Company was approached with a view to exchanging Gossey Field for Moorfields, but it declined, explaining that it wanted less, not more, property in its portfolio. Bethlem did not have the cash to buy Gossey Field and after years of prevarication the Drapers' Company's patience had worn thin. The deal collapsed, initiating a frantic search by the Bethlem authorities for other suitable sites.

The new search was again focused on the north of London, but during the years of Bethlem's wrangling over Gossey Field this area had become fashionable and the cost of real estate had soared; few landowners were interested in the possibility of swapping their valuable property for a plot in the less exclusive Moorfields district. It was with some reluctance that the search for a new site moved from the modish north to Southwark, across the River Thames from the City of London.

For centuries land to the south of the river had been considered an undesirable place to live because it was low-lying, swampy, subject to tidal flooding and occasional outbreaks of cholera. However, the dramatic expansion of London during the eighteenth century saw the developers cross the river into Southwark in search of suitable land on which to build houses. One such expanding population centre was St George's Fields, a small area of higher ground that sat about half a mile inland from the Thames at a junction for several major roads. It was this area that caught the eye of the Bethlem Governors.

St George's Fields had been inhabited since Roman times but held a reputation for housing refugees, political insurgents and armies. The parish had been used as an assembly point for the armies of Henry VII and Charles II as well as by the anti-Catholic Gordon rioters and, in 1666, it was where homeless victims of the Great Fire were housed. Although St George's Fields was never considered as to be as desirable as the northern parts of London, it was not subject to flooding, had a clean water supply and was situated on direct roads leading into and out of central London. It was an area ripe for development and, as chance would have it, Bethlem's surveyors discovered a large patch of land owned by the Corporation of London that looked to be a suitable size and shape for the new hospital. The site comprised eleven acres of land in a triangular plot that was bounded by public roads on two sides and on the third by a fashionable residential development called West Square. The land was occupied but the lease only ran until 1810, which gave Bethlem's Governors hope that a deal could be struck that would see the new hospital under way before then. Negotiations started with the Corporation of London and at first the prospect looked to be extremely promising.[135]

The piece of land in question was famous for having once been home to the Dog and Duck, a notorious tavern that had stood there since at least the early seventeenth century. At the time that the first Bethlem Hospital was moving from Bishopsgate to Moorfields, the Dog and Duck began marketing itself as 'St George's Spa', a resort whose natural spring waters were claimed to heal a variety of common diseases including scorbutic pimples, scrofula, leprosy and even breast cancer. Dr John Fothergill recommended it highly and suggested drinking 'one pint to three; it generally purges easily and briskly, and without affecting the strength, unless in very tender constitutions.'[136]

St George's Spa proved popular, so the Dog and Duck expanded to include tea-gardens, bathing pools and sporting facilities that played host to the rich and famous, including the likes of author Dr Samuel Johnson, the actor David Garrick and others. However, in the later part of the eighteenth century the resort fell under the influence of drunkards, prostitutes and criminals. 'I have seen flashy women come out to take leave of the thieves and to wish them success,' complained the moral campaigner G. R. Porter, while actor David Garrick stopped attending because it was populated with 'fawns half drunk' and 'dryads breaking lamps'.

In 1787 local magistrates put an end to this tomfoolery by refusing to license the tavern, but a lengthy courtroom battle by the landlord meant that it did not close down entirely until 1796. After this the building was used variously as a bakery, a soup kitchen and, at the time of Bethlem's initial interest, by the School for the Indigent Blind, which had already made arrangements to move elsewhere on expiry of the lease.[137]

At first the negotiations between Bethlem and the Corporation of London appeared to go well. It was agreed that the hospital could swap its Moorfields site for the larger but less valuable plot in St George's Fields. Such a move would require assent from Parliament, something that was not considered to be much of an obstacle, but as talks progressed so arguments erupted over the relative values of the two estates. It seems that this began after some of the Bethlem Governors suggested that their Moorfields site was worth far more than the St George's Fields one. The Corporation of London disagreed and for nearly two years there was a stalemate during which the existing Moorfields building became further degraded and its inmates less numerous. In the end it was the Corporation that backed down and, in July 1809, it agreed to a direct swap of its St George's Fields site for the Moorfields one, while also allowing Bethlem to retain a financial benefit from the remaining portion of its lease. Parliament ratified the deal on 15 June 1810, backdating the 865-year lease to the previous Christmas so that the hospital could take immediate possession of the new site.

It had been exactly twenty years since Henry Holland had first been employed to examine the hospital's crumbling walls and roof, allowing the situation to progress from bad to desperate. Parts of the hospital were too unstable and damp for human habitation, and thanks to the closed waiting list the total population had shrunk to around 150 patients. With habitable space at a premium, Bethlem's officers decided to merge all the remaining patients into two galleries, one for men and the other for women, but this had the unfortunate side-effect of mixing together the quiet inmates (such as the melancholics) with those who were violent and/or raving mad. The troublesome patients had originally been housed in separate galleries, but placing them in close proximity immediately created additional problems for Bethlem's staff, who were too few in number to keep a close eye on the inmates' behaviour. Following a series of violent assaults, the decision was taken to restrain many of the more unpredictable patients, which in practice meant chaining them either to their beds or to a wall within their cell. This was viewed as a pragmatic solution by all the staff, including Bethlem's three medical officers, and, in the absence of visitors and official inspections, it could be carried out without fear of outside complaint. Even if any complaints had arisen, there was little that the staff could do to rectify the situation; for decades the Governors had been warned about the state of the Moorfields buildings but had chosen to drag their feet over the issue. The need to move had, however, become imperative, placing enormous pressure on the Governors to find enough money to build the new hospital at St George's Fields.[138]

14

Better by Design

A first step towards building the new Bethlem at St George's Fields was taken in July 1810 when the Governors initiated a public competition to find a design for the new hospital. The prizes were to be £200, £100 and £50 for the top three entries as judged by Bethlem's surveyor James Lewis and the architects Charles Dance (designer of the new St Luke's Hospital) and Samuel P. Cockerell. Entrants were given just under seven months to draft and submit their designs.

Bethlem's fame and architectural reputation ensured that the judges had a wide field from which to choose their winners; a total of thirty-six entries was received, and on 30 January 1811 the three winners were announced. William Lochner, an up-and-coming architect, won first place, with second going to the brothers John and George Repton and the third to John Dotchen. It may be of little surprise to learn that the winner Lochner was a pupil of the competition's organiser and chief judge James Lewis. However, none of the designs submitted was thought to be entirely suitable, so it was left to Lewis to draw up a new blueprint that incorporated the best features of the winning entries, all of which depicted an elongated, south-facing two-storey building with a central entrance block and two wings for the patients.

Part of Lewis's problem stemmed from the triangular layout of the St George's Fields site, which was bounded by roads, existing developments and an open sewer, making it an awkward shape to develop. It had also been decided that, of the eleven available acres, three should be kept separate from the hospital so they could be leased out privately to help bolster the annual income. Lewis's final design blended the ideas of Lochner, Dotchen and the

Repton brothers into a practicable, functioning building that could house the mentally afflicted; it cleverly utilised the available space and even managed to incorporate the old St George's Spa into the gardens. It was approved by the Governors and, on 18 April 1812, the foundation stone was laid by Sir Richard Carr Glyn, Bethlem's new President.[139]

The competition to find a new design had been a straightforward process, but it had an unexpected side-effect that opens a small window into the lives of the hospital's inmates. Bethlem's records reveal that of the thirty-six competition entries, only thirty-two were posted back to their owners. Of the remaining four entries, three belonged to the competition winners and were retained by the hospital, but it is the fate of the fourth entry that is of interest. This losing design was not posted out because its owner occupied a cell within Bethlem's incurable gallery: the architect was none other than James Tilly Matthews, promoter of the mysterious 'Air Loom' and long-time tormentor of the Apothecary John Haslam.

Matthews had been inside Bethlem for thirteen years when Lewis announced the competition to design the new hospital at St George's Fields. The previous year had seen the publication of John Haslam's Illustrations of Madness, a book that focused on Matthews's extraordinary case. This publication may actually have flattered Matthews's sense of self-importance, and its inclusion of his illustration of the Air Loom may have awoken within him a passion for technical drawing, an art at which he was proficient. Being stuck inside Bethlem provided few opportunities for a budding designer, so when Lewis's competition was announced, Matthews became determined that he should not only enter a design, but be the winner. Matthews believed that he could achieve this by drawing upon his experiences as a Bedlam inmate to create a design for a new hospital that would not only look impressive but also provide its inmates with the greatest degree of comfort and convenience.

Matthews's plans were submitted in April 1811, three months after the winning designs had been chosen, and they therefore could not have been considered by Lewis, but he was nonetheless awarded a consolation prize of £30. This award, which came at a time of financial prudence, may not simply have been a sop to pacify the temperamental Matthews but may have been a reflection of the high quality of his design. His plans were exact, displaying a breathtaking level of detail and a wonderful level of artwork. His ideas for the general design of the new Bethlem went along the same lines as the other entrants: the building had two wings on either side of a central office/accommodation block. At four storeys it was taller than the other entries, but this was a reflection of Matthews's desire to house 400 patients, rather than the 200 that the Governors wanted. That Matthews should have produced a design of such merit was amazing enough, but together with his drawings came a series of hand-written notes that were more extraordinary still. Matthews used these to justify key features in his design and in doing so he provided a rare and surprisingly lucid insight into what daily life inside Bethlem was really like at a time when the building was close to collapsing.

Given Matthews's opposition to his confinement and his unshakeable sense of self-belief, it is surprising to see that his comments are not a list of moans and whinges about his particular circumstances. Instead they are mostly sensible complaints based on the collective experience of many inmates, to which he tries to offer sensible solutions. Take the problem of damp inside the hospital, an issue that had been ignored by Thomas Monro under the pretext that lunatics could not feel the cold. Matthews notes that the Moorfields building was riddled with damp, that the basement was unusable and the ground floor cells so prone to water penetration that inmates resorted to plugging the gaps in their floorboards to prevent 'wet from penetrating through the joints'. According to Matthews, adding extra storeys to the new building would solve this problem by elevating the patients into cleaner, drier air and by removing the need for a basement.

The design of individual cells also came in for criticism. The ones used in Moorfields were apparently fractionally too small, which, according to Matthews, gave disruptive patients who were chained to their beds the ability to reach their doorway. These inmates would amuse themselves by 'forcing the door to shut with violence sufficient to produce almost cannon report and spring back for them to repeat it, nearly forcing the door case out of the wall; and standing advanced they can hold at bay and obstruct the Keeper, etc, who would enter.'

One can see why this continual din of slamming doors would be disruptive, but rather than shortening the inmates' chains, as was done at St Luke's,

Matthews advocated lengthening the cells. The physical comfort of his fellow inmates was also foremost in Matthews's mind when he advocated that the cells be for sole occupancy only, heated by hot air and, above all else, be given a decent view of the outside world. 'A view of the public passing and re-passing', wrote Matthews, 'is highly gratifying to patients in every stage [of madness]. The great consolation in Bethlem is the busy world moving to and fro in the fine opening of Moorfields.'

His other ideas include placing the infirmary within the main building so that some of the more capable inmates could be used as carers, and the removal of bars on the windows to make the building look more like a hospital than a prison. Matthews pleaded that the incurable galleries be properly segregated so that the raving, door-slamming patients could be kept away from others who, like himself, are 'utmost orderly, clean and extremely well-behaved'. As a final act, Matthews could not resist taking a swipe at his old enemy John Haslam, who, a few years previously, had forsaken his private quarters inside Bethlem for a large house in Islington, leaving the hospital without a residential medical officer. In his design Matthews gives Haslam a large new office situated in a prime position as a 'sure means to force him from home to see how the world goes elsewhere'.

On the whole Matthews's suggestions were a sensible reaction to the increasingly difficult and overcrowded conditions brought about by Bethlem's poor state of repair. It is evident that Bethlem in Matthews's day was cold, damp, smelly, noisy and ill-staffed, his only compensation being a good view of the outside world (the food may also have been adequate, as Matthews has little say about it). The quality of Matthews's design and the measured, incisive nature of his comments do not give the impression of a man who was mentally ill, but instead of an intelligent, rational human being. Based on this, one could perhaps be led to believe that Haslam and Monro had made a mistake and that James Tilly Matthews was, as his relations claimed, merely an eccentric, rather than a madman. As ever, it would be Matthews himself who ensured that this view could not prevail for long.

Having received both money and praise for his drawings, including from Haslam himself, who offered to lodge the plans with the Royal College of Physicians, Matthews went on to draft a further set of recommendations for the new Bethlem building. These, however, were radically different from his previous efforts and were neither succinct nor rational, but formed dozens of pages across which Matthews had splurged his thoughts about those issues that he found irritating.

Chief among these is the fate of the straw that was used to line the patients' cells and, in some case, also formed their beds and even blankets. Once used, the straw was often soaked in 'sufficient excrement and urine to cause an intolerable stench' and it would be disposed of by pushing it down a purpose-built refuse shaft after which it would be burned. According to Matthews the flames from the burning straw often reached back into the galleries, causing staff and inmates to flee for their lives in avoidance of being scorched. This was a valid criticism, but it was one that Matthews was unable to convey without being diverted into a dozen other issues, such as the construction of compost heaps outside the kitchen and the need for a full-time gardener at the hospital.[140]

When talking about soiled straw, the coherent and measured image of Matthews the architect was replaced by the jumbled, paranoid thought-process belonging to the man who saw himself at the centre of the Air Loom plot. As one of Matthews's modern biographers correctly notes, 'In the first plan, Matthews made a revolutionary case for why the architects should be listening to the views of a patient; in this second plan, he is unwittingly reminding them why he's a patient in the first place.' Although Matthews did not stop producing designs during the remainder of his time in Bethlem, he stuck to conventional buildings and did not trouble himself with the architecture of mental asylums.[141]

It is clear from Matthews's comments that conditions inside Bethlem in 1811 were immeasurably worse than they had been in 1788 when the reformer John Howard had made his inspection. With so few visitors touring the galleries, the degradation had occurred largely unobserved by outsiders, although some did gain access and were shocked at what they saw. The Naval Surgeon John Weir complained that, while in the process of visiting some distressed sailors, he had been appalled at the sight of 'patients lying perfectly naked and covered up in straw; from their mixing the mild and the frantic patients together, and others being unnecessarily loaded with chains; I am of the opinion both that the medical treatment is injudicious, and that uncalled for severity is practised toward them.' Weir put his observations into a report, but it did not prompt anybody to take any further action, least of all the Governors, but the outside world would not stay ignorant of the plight of the Bedlamites for ever.

15

The Criminal Department

Despite the Madhouse Act of 1774, the late eighteenth century had not seen the formation of a mass campaign calling for the reform of Britain's mental asylums. This was partly because the issue of lunatic asylums had been pushed into the background by the publication of John Howard's The State of the Prisons in England and Wales, which, in 1777, started a comprehensive and effective prison reform movement. Thanks to Howard and his supporters, several changes in the law were enacted to improve conditions within Britain's prisons and county gaols, including the segregation of female and male prisoners and the payment of regular salaries to prison staff. At first the prison reform movement seemed to have little in common with earlier attempts to legislate against the madhouses, but the boundary between the two issues began to blur following another attempt on the life of King George III.

On 15 May 1800 King George had been witnessing the Grenadier Guards exercising in Hyde Park when somebody fired a shot in his direction. It missed the King but injured a Navy clerk who was standing nearby; the origin of the shot was never discovered and it was adjudged to have been unintentional. That evening the King attended a theatre in Drury Lane; as he entered the Royal box, the orchestra struck up the national anthem, which prompted the audience to rise to its feet. In the pit a man stood on a chair and raised his arm upwards – in his hand was a horse pistol. A shot rang out and in the Royal box the startled King felt a bullet pass a few inches above his head: had he not been bowing politely towards the audience, it would have undoubtedly found its mark.

There was a stunned silence followed by loud cries of 'Seize the villain!'

The would-be assassin was grabbed and bundled away to a secure room. In the Royal Box the King appeared unconcerned; on seeing that their monarch was unhurt, the orchestra struck up a rousing chorus of 'God Save the King', much to the delight of the audience.

In the back room the assassin was interrogated. He gave his name as James Hadfield and it was evident from his clothing and the scars across his face and head that he had at one time been a soldier. This was confirmed when the Duke of York entered the room: he recognised Hadfield as having served with him in the French wars a few years previously. When asked about his actions, Hadfield replied, 'It is not over yet; there is a great deal more and worse to be done.'

In time a magistrate arrived and questioned Hadfield, who admitted firing towards the King in the theatre but denied that he was trying to assassinate him. 'I am as good a shot as any in England,' explained Hadfield, implying that he had deliberately aimed above the King. Asked why he would do such a thing, Hadfield said that it was an act of suicide, his hope being that the enraged audience would beat him to death. This presented the magistrate with a problem. If Hadfield had attempted to assassinate the King, this was a clear-cut case of treason. If, however, his mental state was in doubt, this may not be a criminal offence at all. Hadfield also denied being the person who had fired towards the King in Hyde Park that morning. The matter could not be resolved that night, so Hadfield was taken to Newgate Prison while the matter was given further thought.

The next morning light was thrown on the matter when a special convention of the Privy Council interviewed witnesses to the shooting as well as several other people who knew Hadfield personally. Slowly a picture emerged of the man's life and habits.

James Hadfield was a Londoner who in 1792, when aged 21, had signed up to be a soldier in the Fifteenth Light Dragoons. Only a few months later France declared war on Britain and the Army was mobilised; in August 1793 Hadfield was present at the Battle of Lincelles when the British forces found themselves outnumbered by the French. He was involved in hand-to-hand combat and showed much bravery, but he received eight sabre wounds to his head and had his wrist shattered by a bullet. After lying in a ditch for three hours the severely wounded Hadfield was taken prisoner by the French and remained captive until 1795, when he was returned to England.

Hadfield had suffered greatly and his injuries meant that his army career, most of which had been spent as a prisoner of war, was over. As compensation he received a disability pension from the Chelsea Hospital and was offered an apprenticeship as a spoon-maker with a silversmith named Hoffman. It was Mr Hoffman who was to give the Privy Council their first insight into Hadfield's temperament on the day of the attempted assassination.[142]

Hoffman testified that four days beforehand he and Hadfield had gone to watch two soldiers being publicly flogged at White Conduit Fields. While there Hadfield had talked with a strange character named Bannister Truelock who had told him that 'it was a shame there should be any soldiers and that Jesus Christ was coming and that we should have neither King nor Soldiers'. Bannister Truelock, who was said to be a cobbler from Islington, sounded like Hadfield's accomplice, so soldiers were despatched to arrest him.

Truelock turned out to be a man of some passion and, having answered several questions rationally, he started to expound his religious views, which were, to say the least, somewhat unconventional. Truelock believed himself to be a revolutionary prophet named Saturn who knew that the Virgin Mary was a 'bloody whore', that Jesus Christ was 'a thief' and that God himself was 'a blackguard'. Truelock was quickly bundled off to prison, but before leaving he admitted to knowing Hadfield who, he prophesied, would become a very great man.

If this admission didn't seal Hadfield's fate, other witnesses certainly would. A member of the orchestra in the theatre testified that he had seen Hadfield aim purposefully and carefully at the King, while some of Hadfield's workmates said that he had left them that afternoon because he had to attend to 'business of great importance'. One had even lent him the money to buy a theatre ticket. 'You shall hear something of me,' said Hadfield before departing. Finally, Sarah Lock, Truelock's landlady, testified that her lodger had talked of killing the King several months previously and that he was a fervent radical and 'a believer in the French Revolution'. This was all the evidence the Privy Council needed to convict Hadfield of treason, a crime that carried a mandatory death penalty. The unfortunate Hadfield, whose mind may not have been right after his battlefield injuries, had become a pawn in the revolutionary politics of the day.[143]

In the years following the 1789 French Revolution, Britain had entered a period of political and economic instability that led to the setting up of several radical societies, some of which promoted the idea of an English Revolution, others of which took a more religious view of the situation. In a climate of paranoia, the Government frowned upon all such political societies and even tried some of their leaders for treason. In 1799 Parliament outlawed all revolutionary parties, clubs and societies of all kinds, driving them underground, but this did not lessen their passion for a British version of the 'justice and reform' that France had meted out to its populace a few years previously.

The aims of these would-be revolutionaries (who were collectively nicknamed 'the English Jacobins') were disparate, but among the usual cries for equality and suffrage was a small group of religious fanatics who had interpreted the upheaval in Europe as a portent to the Second Coming. One such visionary was Bannister Truelock, whose charismatic personality gave him a small but devoted band of like-minded followers, including Hadfield.

When Peg Nicholson had attempted to murder the King in 1786, the Privy Council had bundled her off to Bethlem rather than risk a trial for treason. Nicholson was, however, a relatively harmless individual in comparison to James Hadfield, who had all the appearances of being both mad and a revolutionary. Unlike Nicholson, whose case never went to trial, the Privy Council brought a charge of treason against Hadfield, but in doing so they presented the courts with several problems. Treason was a serious charge that was usually levied upon members of the political elite or the aristocracy; it was also a charge that had been much ill-used historically and it was deemed necessary that those accused of treason should have special privileges. This included being given access to the prosecution's papers and the names and addresses of their witnesses and jurors; the accused also had the right to select a defence counsel of his choice (provided free of charge) and the right to consult with two further counsellors appointed by the court.

At his arraignment Hadfield was made aware of these privileges and he asked that his two court counsellors be Thomas Erskine and Sergeant Best, and his solicitor be Charles Humphries. All three men were top-flight lawyers and a plea of poverty ensured that their considerable fee would be met by the State. In making this choice Hadfield must have had outside help, for he had been especially astute; Thomas Erskine had already successfully defended several high-profile people, the most notable of whom was Lord George Gordon, whom Erskine had acquitted of treason in 1780 after he inspired the famous anti-Catholic riots that bear his name. Under the privileges afforded to alleged treasonous persons, Hadfield and his counsel had to be given time to prepare their case, so it was several weeks before the proceedings opened.

On 26 June 1800 Hadfield stood in the dock at the King's Bench with Erskine as his representative. Facing him was the judge, Lord Kenyon, and Sir John Mitford, who was acting on behalf of the Crown. Erskine began proceedings by objecting to the presence of half the potential jurors, another privilege that came with treason trials; several were subsequently ruled ineligible. Sir John Mitford then gave his opening remarks, sketching out his belief that in buying a pistol and travelling to the theatre Hadfield had acted in a premeditated fashion. However, it quickly became clear that ideas such as premeditation were irrelevant; as some in the press had predicted, Hadfield's case was going to come down to whether or not he was a sane man at the moment he pulled the trigger. If so, then he would be acquitted of the crime and be eligible for release; if not then he would be executed for treason.

Despite instances such as that presented by Margaret Nicholson, for years Britain's legal system had purposefully ignored the issue of criminal insanity, but the Hadfield trial brought it sharply into focus. Mitford began his prosecution by offering a lengthy legal definition of madness, as he saw it. A man cannot be guilty of a crime, said Mitford, if he 'is completely deranged, so that he knows not what he does, if a man is so lost to all sense, in consequence of the infirmity of disease, that he is incapable of distinguishing between good and evil; that he is incapable of forming a judgement upon the consequences of the act which he is about to do, that then the mercy of our laws says, he cannot be guilty of a crime.' He then quoted from two cases where a plea for insanity had been dismissed. One of these was a shooting that occurred in 1723, the other the trial of Lord Ferrers, who had shot and killed a servant in 1760. In neither case was the defendant proved to have been suffering from 'absolute madness' or a 'total deprivation of memory'.

With this view established, Mitford went on to talk about Hadfield's actions in relation to the shooting. He proved that Hadfield had earlier bought the pistol and that he was using real bullets; he also noted that Hadfield had chosen to sit in the most advantageous place for firing directly at the King. The Duke of York was then called as a witness. He confirmed that during questioning Hadfield had acknowledged that by firing at the King he understood that he was in effect forfeiting his life. Erskine cross-examined the Duke and attempted to get him to state that Hadfield was in an agitated state during the interrogation; the Duke refused, claiming that Hadfield was 'perfectly collected'. All this, said Mitford when summing up, amounted to the actions of a man who knew what he was doing and what the likely consequences would be. Satisfied that his point had been well made, Mitford rested his case and handed the court over to Erskine.

Like his learned colleague, Erskine knew that Hadfield's only hope of obtaining an acquittal came from convincing the jury that he was insane. He began by demonstrating that the legal definition of madness just offered by Mitford was incompatible with the medical knowledge of madness. How could a man, argued Erskine, be absolutely mad or totally deprived of memory, as the legal definition required? Even the most insane persons would have some aspect of their memory and reason preserved; indeed, some madmen had proved themselves to be highly cunning not only when committing crimes but also at concealing their mental disorder from those around them. Erskine reminded the jury that in order for a man to be acquitted by reason of insanity they only need believe that his crime was the 'unqualified offspring' of his mental disease. Thus he set about proving that his client did indeed suffer from bouts of insanity.

Erskine's case rested on the testimony of many of Hadfield's former acquaintances, but before calling these witnesses the lawyer outlined the influence held by Bannister Truelock over his client. Truelock was, claimed Erskine, a man whose revolutionary instincts had become blended with the apocalyptic religious thoughts that were then in fashion and as a consequence he had become insane. Truelock had 'overpowered and overwhelmed'

Hadfield's mind, causing him to believe that his own death would help trigger the Second Coming. It was for this reason that Hadfield had fired a pistol in the direction of, but not directly at, King George, in the hopes that he would be lynched by the angry audience. Erskine then reminded the jury that all the King's would-be assassins, by which he chiefly meant Margaret Nicholson but also John Frith, who assaulted the King in 1790, had thus far been found to be insane and not political revolutionaries. To ensure the safety of the King, argued Erskine, did not require Hadfield's conviction for treason but instead relied upon British people being content with their political masters, something that was best achieved by the 'impartial administration of justice'. Erskine then began to call his witnesses.

First were people who had known Hadfield during his days as a soldier. They confirmed that he had been brave and dutiful and that it was only after his terrible experiences on the battlefield that signs of insanity emerged. John Lane, a fellow prisoner of war in France, testified that Hadfield had been temporarily hospitalised after believing himself to be King George. A surgeon, Henry Cline, told the court that Hadfield's head wounds were sufficient to have caused brain damage, while another physician confirmed that Hadfield was rational on all subjects other than those relating to politics and religion. Apparently Hadfield held a belief that 'he was ordained to die, and to die as Jesus Christ did'. Hadfield was undoubtedly insane, the physician said.

Hadfield's friends and relations gave instances of his bizarre behaviour and of his strange relationship with Bannister Truelock. The ex-soldier had apparently attempted to kill his eight-year-old son, whom he loved dearly, because 'God had told him to kill the child'. Truelock and Hadfield had, according to the latter's sister-in-law, planned to set up house together in which Hadfield would be God and Truelock would be Satan. As Erskine summoned one witness after another and the trial entered its sixth hour, Judge Kenyon started to get agitated.

'Are you nearly finished?' he asked.

'I have twenty more witnesses to examine,' replied Erskine. This produced a look of despair from Kenyon, who turned to Mitford and asked whether he had any further witnesses. Mitford had not, but evaded the question by telling the judge that what mattered was whether Hadfield was insane 'at the very time when the act was committed'.

Judge Kenyon was not impressed, adding that Hadfield was obviously in a 'very deranged state'. If I let the trial continue, mused the judge, then I shall have to acquit him, an act that would set free a man who was 'a most dangerous member of society' and who 'for his own sake, for the sake of society at large, must not be discharged'.

On this point everyone was agreed; if Hadfield were released then it would only be a matter of time before he committed another grave criminal act, but how could they detain him once he had been acquitted? It was Mr Garrow, one of the prosecution attorneys, who found an answer. He ventured that if the jury were to explain the exact reason why they were acquitting the prisoner, then this would provide Judge Kenyon with 'legal and sufficient reason for future confinement' of Hadfield.

Only moments later, and without even leaving their seats, the jury declared: 'We find the prisoner is not guilty; he being under the influence of insanity at the time the act was committed.' This was all the information Kenyon needed and he ordered that Hadfield be confined to Newgate as a suspected lunatic to await further arrangements. It was hoped that this would buy enough time to get Hadfield formally declared insane and taken to a mental asylum, but the nature of this case presented the Court with yet another problem.[144]

Getting Hadfield declared insane was not difficult; under the Vagrancy Act of 1744 two magistrates could pronounce him to be a lunatic and order his confinement until his senses returned. This last point was, however, a cause for concern to Kenyon because Hadfield's bouts of madness were known to be followed by periods of lucidity. What if Hadfield were to be released during one of his sane moments only to lapse again later? The public (and perhaps the King) would surely be at risk. For this reason it was decided that declaring him insane was too risky a strategy, but, having been acquitted of treason, Hadfield could not remain in Newgate gaol for any length of time either. Another solution was needed, and it was needed quickly.[145]

Behind the scenes there was a scramble by the Government and its legal advisers to find a means of permanently confining Hadfield to an asylum.

Within four days of the trial ending the Attorney General had prepared a draft Bill for Parliament to consider. It was entitled 'Regulating trials for high treason in certain cases (murder, or attempted murder of the King), and for the safe custody of insane persons charged with offences'. Its aims were simply to downgrade the assassination (or attempted assassination) of the monarch from treason to an ordinary criminal offence while at the same time providing a legal means of confining a criminal lunatic to an asylum until such time as they were considered not to be a threat to the public (if ever). This meant that any future assassins would be denied the special privileges associated with treason trials and, moreover, that anyone found to have committed a criminal act while insane could be locked up and only released at the Court's say-so.

Although the Bill passed its first two readings in Parliament without trouble, not everyone was happy with the proposed changes. The press worried that being able to lock up criminal lunatics for an open-ended length of time would erode an individual's civil liberties. Conversely, some MPs thought that the Bill was offering murderers a means of escaping the gallows by pleading insanity. Others asked whether the Bill removed the deterrent of execution to murderers.

On 11 July 1800 Parliament was presented with two separate Bills. One, the Treason Bill, dealt with the legal reclassification of the act of murdering a monarch, while the second, 'An Act for the safe custody of insane persons charged with offences', sought to give the courts the power to confine those whose mental health made them a danger to the public. Despite some minor objections, both passed into law. Of the two statutes, it was the second, known as the 'Criminal Lunatics Act', that was to have a profound effect on the British legal system. Within the act were four sections that gave the courts sweeping powers to deal with those that were thought to be insane, and its effects are still to be seen today.

The first part of the Act was tailored to Hadfield's situation; it gave judges the power to detain anyone who had been acquitted of a serious felony because of insanity. The person could then be held until 'His Majesty's pleasure be known', which, in most cases, meant a life sentence.

The second section gave the courts permission to detain those who were thought to be unfit to plead or incompetent to stand owing to insanity. This part of the Bill applied to Bannister Truelock who, although guilty of inciting Hadfield to murder the King, could not be tried because the only witness to the event was Hadfield himself. The third section denied bail to arrested persons who were thought to be insane, while the fourth section allowed the detention of insane people trying to break into the royal palaces.

Once on the statute books, the Criminal Lunatics Act immediately allowed James Hadfield to be removed from his gaol cell and, on 10 October 1800, he was admitted to Bethlem. Two months afterwards he was joined by Bannister Truelock, who had been sent there by the Privy Council with instructions that, if there was no sign of any improvement in his sanity within a year, he was to be detained indefinitely as an incurable. Once inside Bethlem neither man stood any realistic chance of release, especially as they did not prove themselves to be model patients.

Hadfield was particularly disruptive and in 1802 was reported to have murdered a fellow patient with a blow to the head, although this was later denied by Dr Crowther, who blamed the death on a seizure. A few months later Hadfield and another patient, John Dunlop, made a daring escape from Bethlem, after which they travelled as far as the port of Dover before being recaptured. By this time the Governors no longer felt that they could hold Hadfield and had him taken to Newgate Prison where he remained until 1816 when, as we shall see later, he was returned to Bethlem as a 'criminal lunatic'. In later life Hadfield is alleged to have regained his senses and he made several petitions to Parliament to be freed and, on one occasion, to be allowed to 'hold communications with a female through the railings'. All such requests were denied and in 1841 Hadfield died of tuberculosis within the hospital.

Truelock was better behaved but never lost his religious mania and was, as a consequence, often kept in solitary confinement so as not to disturb other inmates with his preaching. He did once escape to London, where he spent the night with a 'vulgar, Billingsgate and apparently abandoned woman' before returning to the hospital the next day. He too died in Bethlem, in 1830, and was noted for always signing his letters as 'Bannister Truelock, madman'.[146]

The 1800 Criminal Lunatics Act may have solved the problem presented by the attempted regicides, but its hasty passage through Parliament was to have some unforeseen consequences. Just prior to his death in 1790, the prison reformer John Howard had noticed that 'in some few gaols are confined idiots and lunatics. These serve for sport to idle visitants at assizes, and other times of general resort. Many of the bridewells are crowded and offensive, because the rooms which were designed for prisoners are occupied by the insane. Where these are not kept separate they disturb and terrify other prisoners. No care is taken of them, although it is probable that by medicines, and proper regimen, some of them might be restored to their senses, and to usefulness in life'.[147]

The 1800 Act made this overcrowding much worse. It had plugged a hole in the law but, with nowhere else to put them, county gaols and other prisons began to receive an increasing number of people who were deemed by the courts to be criminal lunatics. Little thought had been given to the special circumstances associated with the confinement of lunatics, especially ones that might be violent, abusive or otherwise dangerous, and it was soon clear that housing lunatics with ordinary prisoners was creating a dangerous situation.

It was a young MP by the name of Charles Watkin William Wynn who, in 1805, was the first to raise the issue in the House of Commons. Wynn highlighted the problems associated with housing lunatics in ordinary gaols, but his words were ignored by Parliament. It was only after Wynn's uncle, Lord Grenville, had been made Prime Minister in February 1806 that the young reformer was able to make himself heard.

With the help of his uncle's patronage, Wynn was made non-permanent under-secretary to the Home Secretary, Lord George Spencer. The 'Ministry of All Talents', as Lord Grenville's Government was known, marked a shift in the British political landscape by pursing a reformist agenda that included proposals to outlaw the slave trade and to emancipate Catholics. Wynn utilised his position by attempting to interest the Home Secretary in the issue of criminal lunacy; the ploy worked and in the spring of 1806 Lord Spencer asked all local authorities to provide him with figures detailing the number of criminal lunatics in their prisons. He then wrote to Sir George

Onesiphorus Paul, whose vocal campaigning in the field of prison reform had touched on the issue of criminal lunacy, asking him to look at the effects of the 1800 law with a view to adjusting it, if necessary. In October Paul delivered a lengthy letter that spelled out some of the problems he had encountered and how best they could be rectified.

A major issue uncovered by Paul was the great expense incurred by local authorities when maintaining lunatics. Gloucester Gaol, for example, held only two criminal lunatics, both of whom were maintained entirely at the gaol's expense with no contribution from the Government or the prisoner's home parish. However, their special needs meant that the annual cost was about £25 per person (now £1,500). Paul related instances where parish authorities had encouraged troublesome lunatics to commit crimes so that they could be placed on trial and sent to gaol under the Criminal Lunatics Act. This removed the financial responsibility of caring for the lunatic from the local parish (which was liable under the Vagrancy Act) to the gaol (which was responsible under the 1800 Act). 'Local officials,' wrote Paul, 'would rather encourage than prevent an outrage that may bring a man to trial and thus effect this important saving to the funds of his parish.'

Paul's solution was relatively simple: rather than house lunatics in prisons, workhouses, etc, it would be better to build a network of county mental asylums within which these unfortunate people could be housed and cared for properly. The building of these institutions should, he argued, be funded by the Government and the county authorities but, once completed, the upkeep of individual patients would be the responsibility of either their relations or, in the case of paupers, their parishes (ie much like Bethlem). Paul complained that the various wars fought by Britain during the previous fifteen years had led to successive Home Secretaries taking their eye away from the plight of the counties and parishes in favour of the armed services. Lord Spencer, wrote Paul hopefully, was a man who was 'distinguished for his attention to provincial evils'.[148]

Paul's letter had its desired effect and in January 1807 Charles Wynn went before the House of Commons to explain the plight of England's criminal lunatics. He did so by giving an account of the number of lunatics held in county gaols, workhouses and other places of correction. Wynn observed that this figure almost certainly underestimated the scale of the problem. He suggested that a Select Committee be formed to look at the issue and evidently made a good case because he had little trouble in getting Parliamentary assent. Wynn formed a Committee that comprised seventeen people, including such luminaries as William Wilberforce (who later helped to abolish slavery) and the MPs George Rose and Samuel Whitbread, who would go on to become key players in a madhouse reform movement. Wynn's Committee based its evidence largely on the statistics provided by several county authorities and the letter written by Sir George Paul: its report was delivered on 15 July 1807.

The Committee's conclusions were almost identical to Paul's recommendations, and even though Lord Grenville's 'Ministry of All Talents', which included Wynn and Spencer, had collapsed in March, the Bill went forward and was given Royal Assent in June 1808. The 1808 County Asylums Act gave county authorities the power, and a means to finance, the building of mental asylums that would be solely used to house criminal, pauper and other types of lunatic. The first asylum was started in Bedford, John Howard's former home town, in 1809 and opened three years later, but the creation of such institutions was voluntary and there was not exactly a rush to erect them.[149]

Together with the establishment of a county network of asylums, the 1807 Select Committee recommended that England should have a separate purpose-built asylum specifically for criminal lunatics. When it came to looking for a place that could accommodate such a facility there was really only ever one serious contender, Bethlem Hospital, which was at that time in the process of trying to move itself from Moorfields to St George's Field.

In June 1810 the House of Commons ratified the hospital's relocation plans, allowing the Home Secretary, Lord Sidmouth, to approach the Governors about the idea of the new site housing a specialist criminal lunatic wing. Given Bethlem's fame and that it was already housing several criminal lunatics, including Peg Nicholson and James Hadfield, the request was not an unnatural one. Indeed, until a few years previously the hospital had been home to some twenty murderers and, in 1808, still had thirty-two inmates who were considered to be criminally insane. It was the only asylum in

England that offered purposeful care for violent inmates, so building a criminal lunatic facility at Bedlam seemed perfectly sensible, but the Governors had their reservations.[150]

Under the 1808 rules, any new county asylums were bound by the conditions given in the 1774 Madhouse Act, which meant that they were subject to an annual inspection and to patient certification. Bethlem had fought hard to be exempted from these requirements and, since the cessation of general visiting rights in 1770, its staff and Governors had done everything in their power to avoid coming under independent scrutiny. They feared that, by accepting to manage a specialist criminal lunatic facility, they would be opening themselves up to official inspection and would, as a consequence, lose some of their autonomy. The Home Secretary offered reassurances that this would not be the case, but the Governors remained doubtful; then one of their number pointed out that the situation could be used to get further Government funding for the St George's Fields project.

Negotiations started and quickly led to the Bethlem Governors being assured that the proposed 'criminal department' would be entirely funded by the Government, both during its building phase and afterwards, when the maintenance and medical care of each patient would be paid for by the Exchequer. The Parliamentary Law Officers had to provide written statements before the Governors could be convinced that the criminal lunatic wing would be exempt from inspection and that they alone would have authority over its management. As a final point, the Governors insisted that only the most serious cases of criminal lunacy should be housed in Bethlem, with all others being taken in by the new county asylum network. This was undoubtedly a good deal for Bethlem, especially as they had been promised £19,800 for the new building (although the eventual bill would actually be £25,144), but the negotiations and assurances had taken so long that it was not until 1814 that the building work began on the criminal department.

The Government had estimated that it would need around fifty cells to house England's entire population of criminally insane persons but, to be on the safe side, it ordered that space be made for sixty people. To ensure that there was strict segregation, there were to be two criminal buildings, a male one capable of holding forty-five people, and a female one with just fifteen places; both were to be erected behind the main hospital and were to have their own walled airing grounds. When these amendments were added to the plans it could be seen that the new units would remove a sizeable chunk of the hospital's gardens, but the benefits they bought in terms of additional finance from, and influence with, the Government more than compensated for this.[151]

With both the main hospital building and criminal units being erected at speed and with the Government having agreed to underwrite sixty per cent of the entire project's cost (which would eventually amount to £122,572 8s), many at Bethlem must have believed that they were standing on the threshold of a new and glorious age in their hospital's history. And indeed they were, but before the dawning of this new age Bethlem was to undergo a long and terrible period of darkness that would see its charitable image dragged through the mud and its staff publicly humiliated: after years of disorganisation, the madhouse reformers had become a force to be reckoned with. [152]

16

The York Retreat

The seeds of a coherent madhouse reform movement were not to be sown in London, which was home to a majority of Britain's private madhouses and charitable asylums, but 200 miles north in the industrial city of York. Prior to the County Asylums Act of 1808 York had a sizeable number of curable and incurable lunatics but no purpose-built facility in which to house them. Those afflicted by madness were being sent either to the workhouse or to 'places of correction' (ie prison), but awareness of this problem led to the formation of a committee of inquiry that, in August 1772, determined how many lunatics there were within the county that needed proper housing. The returns were so numerous and individual cases so alarming that the committee acted immediately; within a year land had been purchased near York and work had begun on an asylum that would be capable of holding sixty-four inmates. It was another three years before the first patients were admitted into York Asylum, a charitable institution aimed primarily at pauper lunatics but which, according to its Governors, would accept all-comers regardless of their age, sex or mental condition.[153]

Within two years of its foundation York Asylum had already received criticism for being overcrowded and for operating entirely behind closed doors. In 1788 the poet William Mason directly accused the Governors at York of corruption and mismanagement, claiming, among other things, that they were purposefully taking in private patients, who could pay as much as a pound a week, in preference to pauper lunatics on parish welfare of just 6 shillings. The Governors denied this and mounted a vocal defence against Mason's allegations, reassuring the public that any money donated to the

Asylum was not being squandered, but in addition to allegations of corruption some terrible stories were beginning to emerge about the manner in which the patients were being treated by the staff.[154]

On 15 March 1790 the Physician at York Asylum admitted a melancholic widow from Leeds by the name of Hannah Mills. She was not in the best of health and had been a cause of concern to her friends and relations, many of whom were, like her, followers of the Quaker faith. In the weeks following her admittance, the Asylum authorities consistently refused to allow anyone to visit Mrs Mills, including some Quaker ministers who wished to pray for her good health. Whether this action was malicious is open to question (many asylums banned preachers for fear of upsetting their inmates), but the Quakers concerned certainly believed that a member of their congregation was being abused. This view appeared to be vindicated when, on 29 April 1790, Hannah Mills died. There was uproar. Rumours of neglect and ill-treatment began to circulate, as did talk of prejudice by the Asylum against the Quaker movement.

One of those who bore Mrs Mills's death particularly heavily was William Tuke, a wealthy tea merchant and leading member of the York Quaker community. Tuke was a man much troubled at the sight of injustice and he spent much time fretting over what had occurred at York Asylum. In the end, it was Tuke's younger daughter Ann who jolted him into action after she innocently asked, 'Father, why cannot we have an establishment for such persons [ie lunatics] in our own Society?'[155]

The thought of creating an asylum specifically for distressed Quakers appealed greatly to Tuke, but his wife Esther thought that the idea was in itself mad. 'Thee has had many wonderful children of thy brain dear William,' she said to her husband, 'but this one is surely like to be an idiot.'

William Tuke was a notably strong-willed individual who, once afflicted with a thought, could not be easily deflected away from taking action. Using Mrs Mills as a case in point, Tuke campaigned for the establishment of a Quaker Asylum, but his plans were resisted, with few people showing any concern about the plight of York's lunatics. The stubborn Tuke refused to drop the issue and bit by bit he started to win the argument so that, at a

Meeting of the Society of Friends in March 1792, he was in a position to propose the erection of a 'Quaker Retreat for the insane' in York. Tuke was allowed to bring an outline of his plans to the next meeting, at which he suggested that his Retreat be built to hold thirty patients 'in an airy situation', that it be located a short distance from the city and that it be surrounded by gardens and fields so that the patients and relatives could take exercise and some cows be kept on site.

The scheme was seen as idealistic and continued to meet with resistance, but a charitable fund was set up and, in time, enough money was found to buy several acres of land and start the building work. In January 1795 the money ran out and, with the Retreat only half completed, the Governors were forced to borrow in order to build a west wing. In June 1796 the York Retreat 'for persons afflicted with disorders of the mind' admitted its first patients, who were placed under the care of Dr Thomas Fowler, a non-residential physician.

From the outset the Retreat provided a regime that was different from that of every other madhouse in Britain, including Bethlem and St Luke's. William Tuke and his son Samuel eschewed the ideas of the Monro family and even those of William Battie and his successors. They instead investigated the more liberal ideas of Philippe Pinel, a post-revolutionary French physician who is considered by many to be the father of modern psychiatry. Pinel had been appalled at the state of the Parisian asylums and in 1793 had famously liberated the insane from their chains and in their place established a much more 'moral' approach to treating the insane, which was based upon 'kind compassionate firmness'. Like Pinel, the Retreat chose not to restrain its patients using chains, nor did it leave them languishing about their cells all day, preferring to get them outside into fresh air or keeping them busy by allocating jobs. No violent medicines were used and the doctors encouraged the staff to keep a close eye on the patients and to interact with them.

The York Retreat offered a profoundly different type of regime and went far beyond the 'liberal' practices of St Luke's Hospital, which were themselves considered to be humane in comparison to other madhouses. Indeed, when designing the Retreat, William Tuke visited St Luke's to get some idea as to how the insane should be housed, but was appalled at what he saw and immediately made a number of recommendations to the Retreat's builder, John Bevans. Although financial constraints limited some of these ambitions, between them Tuke and Bevans conceived a design that had the patients' comfort foremost in mind. For example, rather than add additional storeys to the building, as Bethlem and St Luke's had done, the Retreat's galleries were lengthened so that the inmates would be forced to take more exercise. Individual cells were insulated from the weather while also being airy, with the entrances and staircases being positioned so as to give the staff good visibility of the patients. Most important of all, the Retreat had extra-thick walls that could amply accommodate the weight of the roof and upper floors. On this point Tuke had been adamant: he had seen the problems caused by inadequate design at the London Foundling Hospital and may also have been aware of the state of Bethlem's crumbling, damp-infested walls.

In most respects the Retreat was a new type of asylum, designed not just to house the insane but also to care for them. According to a visitor who saw the Retreat some years after its opening, the hospital was 'surrounded by beautiful gardens [and] its internal arrangements are everywhere characterised by the most admirable order and refinement. The whole system of treatment pursued, is one of invariable mildness and benevolence, founded on the principle of kindness, as the only rational mode of influencing the insane.'[156]

Part of this 'rational mode' included making the Retreat look less like a madhouse and more like a normal home. Instead of sawdust and straw on the floor, and windows without panes, the Retreat was filled with normal-looking furniture, including wooden chairs and tables, which sat next to glazed windows. Needless to say, chains were nowhere to be seen while any obvious security features, such as iron grills and heavy locks, were hidden behind curtains and leather flaps. If patients should become violent or threatening, they would be placed in a straitjacket but only for as long as it took them to calm down.

Perhaps the most extraordinary decision taken by those at the Retreat was to shun the use of medication as part of a curative regime. Instead its two floors were structured in such a way that all its patients could be kept busy either by exercising or, more usually, by being put to work on simple but rewarding tasks such as gardening, sewing, cooking and cleaning. Those who were considered better behaved were allocated space on the upper floors and given extra privileges, while the less cooperative inmates were placed on the lower floors. All patients were encouraged to see themselves as part of the 'Retreat family', a situation that some visitors viewed with disdain. 'It appears,' wrote the Swiss-French medic Auguste Delarive in 1798, 'that they consider [their patients] rather as children, who have too much strength, and who make a dangerous use of it. Their punishment and rewards must be immediate, since that which is distant has no effect upon them. A new system of education must be adopted to give a fresh course to their ideas. Subject them at first; encourage them afterwards, employ them, and render their employment agreeable by attractive means.'[157]

The founding of the Retreat was undoubtedly a major initiative, but its remote location and limited intake (only Quakers were admitted as patients) meant that there was no public or private pressure on other asylums to emulate its practices. This was not just a matter of intransigence; the 'moral therapy' advocated by the Retreat required additional space and staff that most madhouses, whether private or public, simply could not afford. Besides, William Tuke and his fellow Governors were not at that time interested in starting an asylum reform movement, so did not promote themselves as an alternative to the status quo; yet, in time, the Retreat would prove to be a great nuisance indeed for the rest of Britain's madhouses, including Bethlem.

The post of Bethlem Physician was famous for having been occupied for eighty years by three generations of the Monro family, but the York Retreat was able to match this when, in the space of just fifteen years, it was managed by three generations of the Tuke family.

William Tuke had founded the Retreat but soon afterwards passed the baton to his son Henry who, unlike his father, became concerned that the good work being performed at the Retreat was being ignored by the outside world. Henry Tuke was especially troubled by the nearby York Asylum, which was still subject to accusations of physical abuse and financial corruption. Henry decided that the time had come for the Retreat to promote its humanitarian message to the outside world, which included mounting a vocal opposition to the practices seen in most madhouses. To facilitate this, in the New Year of 1811 Henry drafted in help from his son Samuel who, although only twenty-six years old, had already been involved with the Retreat for several years.

By the age of twenty Samuel was deep in correspondence with various specialists around the country. 'I shall', he declared, 'collect all the knowledge I can on the theory of insanity, the treatment of the insane, and the construction of lunatic asylums.' Within a short period of time Samuel had written articles with titles such as 'On the State of the Insane Poor' and 'On the Treatment of those labouring under Insanity'. Henry was keen to utilise his son's writing talent and asked him to put together a written account of the Retreat and its practices that could be used to publicise the asylum's aims. Samuel set about the task with youthful exuberance, interviewing staff and patients and going back through the Retreat's archives.[158]

Samuel was true to his word but the task was not an easy one: it was to be another two years before his manuscript was published, but his father considered that the wait was worth it. The aim of Tuke's book had been to promote the Retreat but, at over 200 pages long, the finished product turned out to be a sizeable tome on the treatment and care of lunatics. Description of the Retreat, as the book was entitled, was the first published manual describing how a madhouse could be managed and organised using humanitarian 'moral therapy' methods. It was not just a promotion of the Retreat's methods, but also criticised the regimes operating in other madhouses, suggesting that they were inferior. This irritated many madhouse Keepers, but none more so than Dr Charles Best, Physician to the York Asylum; it was this bumptious individual who was unwittingly to kick-start a nationwide reform movement.

Dr Best was furious at Tuke for writing what was, in his opinion, a sanctimonious and erroneous book that misrepresented the general state of Britain's madhouses. Shortly after the book's publication Best learned that the recently appointed Retreat Physician, Dr Henry Belcombe, was founding his own private madhouse in York, which was to be modelled on Tuke's ideas and which, according to its advertisements, would offer a superior form of treatment to that of other local madhouses, including Best's York Asylum.

This not only implied that Best's methods were inferior, something he denied, but the notion that Belcombe's new institution would accept non-Quaker patients threatened the York Asylum's core business. Infuriated, Dr Best wrote a vociferous letter to the York Chronicle, denouncing both Tuke's book and an advertisement placed by Belcombe in the papers.

It was published on 22 September 1813 under the name of 'Evigilator' but few were fooled by the pseudonym. The letter insisted that Tuke's remarks had set out to discredit Best and were 'thrown out against other establishments for the same purpose, the intended application of which no one could misunderstand and which were as strikingly illiberal as they were unfounded'. As for Dr Belcombe's claims for his new asylum, these was intended 'to impose a belief that methods of treatment of an opposite direction were being employed at other Establishments for insane persons at York'.[159]

A week later Samuel Tuke published his reply to Best's letter. He affected a perplexed tone and questioned why Best had adopted so defensive a manner when his book had been generally critical of all asylums, not just those in York. The inference was that Best's asylum was trying to hide something; this proved to be an open invitation for other letter-writers to flood the newspapers with their opinion of the York Asylum. 'The Asylum has been wrested from its original design,' wrote one correspondent, 'the poor are in great measure excluded; and the institution, it is understood, is committed to the care of a Physician and Apothecary; without the interference of any committee or visitors in the internal management. Thus instead of being a public charity, it has become a source of private emolument.'[160]

Best realised that Tuke's letter had skilfully shifted people's attention toward the York Asylum, an institution whose local reputation was appalling. Best started to play down his disagreement with Tuke in the hope that the matter would be dropped by the newspapers, but he was not to be so lucky. Other letter-writers joined in the fray, expressing their discontent at the York Asylum and its policy of refusing admission to all but the most carefully selected visitors. It was argued that, with all access to patients barred, people could only guess as to what horrors were taking place inside. Complaints against York Asylum had arisen before and had died down again, but this time

Best and his Governors suddenly found themselves confronted with stark evidence of their wrong-doing.

At the height of this spat, the York Asylum chose to discharge a pauper inmate named William Vickers who had been placed there several months earlier by the magistrate Godfrey Higgins. Despite a relatively short stay in the Asylum, Vickers emerged physically wounded, emotionally broken and quite incapable of work. Vickers's wife approached Higgins with an application for poor relief, claiming that her husband had been brutalised while in the Asylum. Higgins insisted on seeing William and was shocked to find him infested with lice and with a leg that was in a 'state of mortification'. On 27 November Higgins entered the asylum debate by publishing a letter in the York Herald that gave a full description of Vickers's case and a medical statement detailing his injuries.[161]

Higgins's allegations unleashed a tidal wave of public anger that uncovered further instances of alleged abuse. Some of these were truly shocking: the Reverend Mr Schorey reported being kicked and thrown down a set of stairs at the Asylum, while the relations of one Martha Kidd complained that she had received a dislocated hip and serious head wounds, the provenance of which were unknown. All this negative publicity came in the week before the Asylum was due to hold a quarterly Governors' Meeting. With a crisis looming, Best was forced to declare publicly that the Governors would initiate an inquiry into these allegations, but, as some predicted, no action was taken on this. Instead the Governors simply declared that Vickers and others had been treated with 'all possible care, attention and humanity' and refused the idea that outsiders should be allowed in to see conditions for themselves. Best decided that it would be better to try and ride the storm than risk opening up his Asylum to inspection by his 'enemies'. He perhaps did this in the belief that in the short term there was little his enemies could do to interfere with the running of his institution; after all, the 1774 Madhouse Act concerned itself with admission procedures, not general conditions. Again Best's arrogance led him to underestimate the dogged determination of the ageing Godfrey Higgins and the energetic drive of young Samuel Tuke.

The closed nature of York Asylum had hitherto presented a problem to those wishing to inspect the facility or who wished to have influence over its affairs, but by making a study of the Asylum's standing orders Tuke and Higgins were able to find a weak point in its defence. Many charitable madhouses, including the Retreat and Bethlem, made special provision for generous benefactors so as to encourage large donations. In the Retreat, for example, a person donating £50 (now £2,225) annually was allowed to admit a patient (provided they were a Quaker and judged to be insane) on 'the lowest terms of admission', while generous donors to Bethlem would invariably be admitted to its Court of Governors. York Asylum followed a similar policy, but in a bid to entice donors it had set a low financial threshold so that any person donating £20 (now £900) would automatically be admitted as a Governor.[162]

Because of its humanitarian aims and association with the Quaker movement, the Retreat was supported by people who were socially motivated, educated and, most importantly, wealthy. Tuke and Higgins appealed to this network for help; they planned to load the York Asylum's Committee of Governors with their own supporters until they had enough people to take control of the institution. Tuke requested that his friends each donate £20 to the Asylum so that they might be admitted as Governors and thereafter use this privilege to make their own assessment of the situation. Nearly forty people took up the challenge, including many members of Tuke's own family, so that in mid-December 1813 fifteen of the Asylum's new Governors were able to join together to form an impromptu Committee of Investigation with Godfrey Higgins at its head.

On seeing so many of his tormentors become Governors, Dr Best must have realised that the York Asylum was no longer his personal fiefdom. It is therefore probably no coincidence that the day after Higgins's investigative committee started its work, a serious blaze broke out at the Asylum, destroying a separate wing of the building and killing four patients. Best insisted that the fire was accidental, having been caused by stray sparks coming down a chimney, but Higgins viewed it as a blatant attempt at destroying damning evidence. The newspapers and many local commentators also questioned the fire's origins but some were more cautious, suggesting that it might have had a natural cause. The same reserve could not be applied when, only a few days later, the Asylum's Steward was caught placing dozens of written records into a roaring fire. When confronted he expressed a fear that Higgins and his men would discover evidence of institutionalised abuse: this they certainly did.

The alarming manner in which Dr Best and his immediate staff had run the Asylum became evident from its archives. It was discovered that instances of financial and physical abuse dated back years (probably to the time of Hannah Mills) and that no Governor had made an inspection of the facilities for at least two decades. In fact, few of them even bothered to turn up to the Committee meetings and those that did were lulled into a false sense of security by a sumptuous reception feast prepared for them by Best and his staff. One of Higgins's new Governors described what he found on first entering the Asylum in December 1813:

> 'It was the habit of the Governors to think that all was right – and in fact they had seen nothing that was wrong – the passage to the committee-room was well swept – a cheerful fire blazed in the chimney – the table was covered with a decent baize cloth – the apothecary bowed – the matron curtseyed – the head keeper obsequiously held the door in his hand.'[163]

As the inspections progressed (sometimes in the company of the Archbishop of York) it became further evident that York Asylum was home to some of the worst abuses seen in any madhouse anywhere in Europe. The staff had made some attempt at cleaning up ahead of the inspections, but the general environment was still considered to be filthy, badly ventilated and damp. The cells were too small and overcrowded and the patients poorly clothed or naked. Many displayed evidence of under-nourishment, hypothermia and physical abuse that included scars derived from multiple beatings and whippings and from lengthy periods spent in chains. It was also discovered that piles of rotting straw had been strategically placed over metal rings, chains and handcuffs that were riveted to the floor. No attempt had been made to prevent access to the female patients by male staff and patients, a consequence of which were allegations of rape and sexual abuse. The investigators discovered two women who, prior to being locked up, 'bore good characters' but who had been pregnant when discharged from the Asylum. One had been assaulted by the principal keeper, the other by a patient. There were even rumours concerning female patients that had disappeared after being admitted, the suggestion being that their deaths had been hushed up by the staff. Possible evidence of this came from an examination of the death and burial registers, which showed every sign of having been falsified, as were many of the financial accounts.

Higgins summarised his findings, claiming that his investigations 'provided evidence of wrongdoing on a massive scale: maltreatment of the patients extending to rape and murder; forging of records to hide deaths among the inmates; an extraordinarily widespread use of chains and other forms of mechanical restraint; massive embezzlement of funds; and conditions of utter filth and neglect.'[164]

Although Higgins was shocked at what he had seen up until that point, the greatest instance of abuse managed to escape him until March 1814 when, by chance, he stumbled across a door that had hitherto been kept locked and hidden from him. Higgins insisted on being given access but the keeper said that he did not know where the key was. The magistrate replied that 'he would fetch it presently from the side of the kitchen fire,' and pretended to set off down the corridor, but as he walked past the keeper he snatched the bunch of keys from his hand and without further ado unlocked the door. It opened into a cell that measured just seven by twelve feet. Huddled inside were thirteen semi-naked old women who were covered in their own excrement from head to toe. Higgins was appalled. 'I became very sick,' he recalled, 'and could not longer remain in the room. I vomited.'

The room was one of four similar cells, described by the guards as 'low grates', each of which was inches deep in human mess, so much so that the ventilation holes 'were nearly filled with filth that the unfortunate women had no other way of getting rid of'. The women had been forced to spend their nights in these cells, sleeping in conditions that were unimaginably revolting; by day they were removed to cells that were not measurably better. Higgins made sure that the scene was properly witnessed, then made a written report that was passed on to the other Governors.

Best attempted to play down the 'low grates', describing them as being 'of a very sufficient size [and] furnished with ventilators, straw beds, blankets,' but even he must have known that this was to understate the horror of Higgins's discovery. When news of it reached Tuke he realised that the problems at the York Asylum could not be dealt with gradually and that drastic action would have to be taken.[165]

The scale of abuse was such that the incoming Quaker Governors immediately set about effecting a root and branch reform of the Asylum. Under Tuke's advice a new set of rules and regulations was drawn up that remodelled the failing institution into a version of his own Retreat. In August 1814 the new plans were brought before the Annual Court, but so few of the original Governors bothered to attend that the reformers were able to get their own way without a fight. In subsequent weeks the majority of the Asylum's staff were replaced and a weekly inspection regime initiated. George Jepson, the Superintendent at the Retreat, oversaw the change in regime, and in little more than a year Samuel Tuke was able to declare that the York Asylum and the Retreat were both benefiting from the same brand of moral therapy. 'I believe the system of one is as mild as the other,' he commented in December 1815.

What had started out as a minor spat between Tuke and Best soon expanded to become a nationwide scandal. Tuke's Description of the Retreat had been locally well-received but the horrific revelations at York Asylum ensured that it gathered national publicity. The madhouse reform movement, which had hitherto been small and relatively disparate, suddenly found itself both with an issue around which to rally (York Asylum) and a cause that it could promote (Tuke's Description). Many private madhouse owners must have felt uneasy at the increasing public outrage that was being expressed against abusive asylum regimes. However, one suspects that Monro, Haslam and others working at Bethlem would have perceived little threat from the revelations in Yorkshire; after all, they had thus far been exempted from all national legislation and there seemed little reason for them to become dragged into an argument about private madhouses and county asylums. If this was the way they were thinking, they were to be proved greatly wrong.

17

Wakefield Investigates

Samuel Tuke's success at taking on, then taking over, the York Asylum was an inspiration to social reformers in other parts of the country. A particular admirer was Edward Wakefield, a wealthy London-based Quaker with a long-standing interest in madhouses. For some time Wakefield had been vocally advocating the building of a new London asylum that would be run along Tuke's guidelines as laid out in his Description of the Retreat. When he learned of the investigation made by Higgins in York, Wakefield took it upon himself to make his own inspection of London's charitable mental institutions, including St Luke's Hospital and Bethlem.

Wakefield had little difficulty in gaining access to St Luke's Hospital and to Guy's Hospital, which held a small number of insane patients, but Bethlem proved to be obstructive and would not allow him to enter unless accompanied by a Governor. On 25 April 1814 Wakefield persuaded an Alderman Governor by the name of Cox to accompanying him to Bethlem. They were greeted by the Steward, Peter Alavoine, who was less than happy to see Wakefield inside the hospital, having been warned in advance of his reformist sympathies. However, because Wakefield was accompanied by Alderman Cox, Alavoine could not refuse him entry but the visit was rather abbreviated. Shortly after entering the men's gallery, Alderman Cox was overcome by the Hospital's atmosphere (which suggests that he was one of those Governors who did not often visit Bethlem) and was forced to retire back to the Steward's office. Wakefield assumed that he would be able to carry on his tour alone, but Alavoine was having none of it; he despatched a member of staff to escort Wakefield off the gallery and back to his office.

Here Wakefield was told that, without an accompanying Governor, he could not continue his inspection.

The Quaker was furious and protested that he had a signed letter from Cox and that the Governor was willing to remain in the Steward's office for the duration of the visit. Alavoine was unmoved: no accompanying Governor, no hospital tour. Alderman Cox declared that he had a weak constitution and told Wakefield that he would probably never be able to accompany him around the galleries. The frustrated Wakefield asked for a printed list of Bethlem's others Governors, but Alavoine refused him, claiming that he would first need written permission from the Clerk, John Poynder. The Clerk was approached but he too was wary of Wakefield's motives and refused to hand over the list of names. Aware that he was not going to be permitted to carry out an inspection that day, Wakefield left the building. 'We were compelled to close our visit for that day,' Wakefield recalled later, but he was nothing if not persistent and immediately set about finding a Governor whose stomach was strong enough to cope with the sights, sounds and smells of Bethlem.[166]

Exactly one week later Wakefield was again requesting to be allowed to tour Bethlem's galleries, this time in the company of Governor Robert Calvert and five other gentlemen, including an MP from Essex. The Steward was unhappy about the presence of such a large party of potential troublemakers but the rules compelled him to unlock the gates to the galleries and let the gentlemen make their inspection. As a precaution, the Steward accompanied them at all times, as did a female keeper; the sights that awaited Wakefield were much as he had feared.

'We first proceeded to visit the women's gallery,' explained Wakefield. 'One of the side rooms contained about ten patients, each chained by one arm or leg to the wall; the chain allowing them merely to stand up by the bench or form fixed to the wall, or to sit down on it. The nakedness of each patient was covered by a blanket gown only ... with nothing to fasten it down the front. One female in this side room, thus chained, was an object remarkably striking. She had been a teacher of languages [but one] can hardly imagine a human being in a more degraded and brutalising condition than that in which I found this female, who held a coherent conversation with us, and was of course fully sensible of the mental and bodily conditions of those wretched beings, who, equally without clothing, were closely chained to the wall with herself.'[167]

The party was visibly shocked but the Steward permitted them to question some of the patients; some gave lucid answers while others appeared to be 'inanimate and unconscious of existence'. Wakefield was especially alarmed to see the lucid inmates chained together with raving or moribund patients, a practice that he described as 'disgusting idiocy'.

More horrors were discovered in the male gallery. The first room contained several men handcuffed to a wall, one of whom was literally raving mad but had nonetheless been chained next to a quiet, apparently rational gentleman. None had shoes on. 'One complained much of the coldness of his feet,' said Wakefield. 'One of us felt them. They were very cold. Their nakedness and their mode of confinement gave this room the appearance of a dog-kennel.'

By now the party was beginning to ask questions not just of the patients, but also of their keepers. On witnessing one patient brutally assault a 'quiet civil man', Wakefield asked how this could be allowed to happen. 'There is no means of separating them,' replied the Steward. Indeed, the lack of any segregation was all too evident; the raving were not kept apart from the meek and melancholic, and the violent patients not prevented from committing acts of violence. The excessive use of restraint was also clear; about a fifth of patients were 'lying stark naked upon straw on their bedsteads, each in a separate cell, with a single basket or rug, in which the patient usually lay huddled up, as if impatient of cold and generally chained to the bed in the shape of a trough'. Wakefield implies that this level of restraint might have been due to the ratio of around seventy patients to just three staff.

Wakefield was in search of a cause célèbre to match Tuke's York Asylum campaign, and within a short while of starting his tour he believed that he had found it. To him Bethlem revealed itself to be a brutal, inhuman place that treated its inmates as though they had no understanding of their predicament: it was the complete opposite to the Retreat's moral therapy. However, Wakefield's visit had one more surprise up its sleeve in the form of James Norris, a patient who was shown to him right at the end of his visit. Norris was to provide Wakefield with exactly the sort of ammunition he needed to take on the Bethlem authorities.

James Norris was aged fifty-five and had been serving as an American Marine when his erratic behaviour saw him referred to Bethlem in February 1800, some fourteen years before Wakefield's visit. His mental condition worsened and a year later he was declared to be an incurable lunatic. Normally he would have been released into the community and his name added to the incurable lunatic waiting list, but Norris's propensity to commit sudden acts of violence made him a risk to the public, so he remained at Bethlem, where he was restrained for the protection of staff and patients. Even Wakefield recognised that violent inmates sometimes needed restraining, but the lengths taken to subdue Norris confirmed to him that the staff at Bethlem were incapable of treating any of their patients humanely:

'He was fastened by a long chain which, passing through a partition, enabled the keeper by going into the next cell, to draw him close to the wall at pleasure; that to prevent this, Norris muffled the chain with straw, so as to hinder its passing through the wall; that he afterwards was confined in the manner we saw him, namely a stout iron ring was riveted round his neck, from which a short chain passed to a ring made to slide upwards and downwards on an upright massive iron bar, more than six feet high, inserted into the wall. Round his body a strong iron bar about two inches was riveted; on each side of the bar was a circular projection, which being fashioned to and enclosing each of his arms, pinioned them close to his sides. This waist bar was secured by two similar bars which, passing over his shoulders, were riveted to the waist bar both before and behind. The iron ring round his neck was connected to the bars on his shoulders, by a double link. From each of these bars another short chain passed to the ring on the upright iron bar. We were informed he was enabled to raise himself so as to stand against the wall on the pillow of his bed in the trough bed which he lay; but it is impossible for him to advance from the wall in which the iron bar is soldered, on account of the shortness of his chains.'[168]

Wakefield was aghast at the extraordinary measures taken by the Bethlem staff to restrict Norris's movement, yet the man himself seemed quite rational. Wakefield conversed with Norris for several minutes during which time he spoke lucidly and clearly; he explained that he had been confined in a lying down position for ten years and that, as a consequence, sitting upright would become painful after a short while. Of all the things Wakefield had witnessed, it was the image of the emaciated and tethered James Norris, his muscles atrophied through lack of use, that stuck with him and his fellow inspectors.

Whatever relief Alavoine must have felt at seeing Wakefield leave the hospital premises was short-lived when, somewhat predictably, a month later he returned in the company of another Governor and several eminent gentlemen, some of them MPs. Despite Wakefield's obvious intent to make regular inspections of Bethlem, there had been little improvement since their previous visitation. The prisoners remained semi-naked and restrained, although he did discover that 'the male patients who were then naked and chained to their beds in their cells, were in that situation by way of punishment for misbehaviour and not from disease.'

But Wakefield's real interest in returning to Bethlem was to show James Norris to his friends; at least this message had got through to the staff, and Wakefield was surprised (and perhaps disappointed) to discover that the former Marine had been freed from the majority of his body irons and that the length of his neck chain had been doubled to two feet. Even so, an artist within Wakefield's party was asked to make a sketch of Norris as he had been by adding in the various iron rings that had once been about his neck and body. This being done, the party departed from Bethlem.

A short while afterwards Wakefield formally started his campaign against Bethlem by writing a series of letters to influential figures, then the newspapers, outlining the deplorable conditions he had observed. Naturally, James Norris was given pride of place and was described as being an innocent victim of Bethlem's brutal policy of restraint. As in York, the letters caught the public's attention and led to an outcry, especially amongst Britain's parliamentarians, some of whom were themselves Bridewell and Bethlem Governors and who, in the light of Wakefield's revelation, used this privilege to make their own impromptu visits. Questions were asked in the House of Commons and, sensing that trouble was brewing, several Governors took it on themselves to organise a midweek Committee meeting on Thursday 23 June 1814. Wakefield's opinions, as expressed in his newspaper letters, were read out and in consequence it was agreed that the allegations of abuse made against the hospital would have to be investigated.

The ultimate fate of York Asylum may have inspired Bethlem's President, Sir Richard Glyn, to assemble an in-house investigative subcommittee of twenty-four Governors that included figures such as the Earl of Shaftsbury and Lord Willoughby de Brooke. A robust response was needed to Wakefield's allegations, so on 25 June the committee interviewed John Haslam, Thomas Monro, Peter Alavoine and John Poynder, together with several other key members of staff. They then made their own inspection of the hospital and retired to write up their findings, which were delivered at a Governors' Court held on 28 June.

The issue that was of most concern to the investigators was James Norris, whose name and circumstances (thanks to Wakefield) had become widely known about London. Haslam was particularly closely questioned about this patient and provided a very different story from the one being peddled about town by Wakefield and his fellow reformers. Yes, agreed Haslam, the American could indeed be quiet and intellectually responsive but he was also capable of breathtaking savagery. Haslam cited an attack on a keeper, William Hawkins, whom Norris had attempted to slash with a knife, and described an occasion when he bit off a fellow patient's finger. Norris was also accused of making several murderous attempts on staff and inmates. 'He is the most mischievous patient that perhaps I ever saw,' said Haslam, who complained that ordinary chains could not hold Norris because 'the bones of his hands are smaller than his wrists'. This allowed him to slip his manacles and convert them into offensive weapons.

With both staff and patients thoroughly frightened of Norris, it had been left to Haslam to devise a solution to the problem. He initially proposed giving him a double cell with a connecting door so that when he was in one half, the door could be locked and the other part cleaned and maintained. It was a good idea but the crumbling Bethlem building was suffering from an acute lack of space and Haslam was overruled by a Governors' Committee. Only then was it proposed that a complicated restraining harness system should be used, but this suggestion did not come from Haslam; it came from a Governor who may have got the idea from a similar device that had been used on a violent prisoner in Newgate Prison. (Indeed, Norris's harness may actually have been bought second-hand from Newgate.) Haslam foresaw trouble over this decision and insisted that the Governors' proposal to restrain Norris be recorded in the minutes so that should there be any complaints others 'might know who was present' at the meeting.[169]

Haslam's explanation of how Norris came to be confined satisfied the Governors and, following an inspection, they also declared themselves generally happy with the conditions and treatment they had observed inside the hospital.

'This Committee are of the opinion that it cannot be satisfactorily established, either that any cruelties have ever been practised in Bethlem Hospital, as has recently been stated, or that the case of James Norris in particular, which has been selected as an instance in support of such statement, affords any proof to that effect.' They furthermore declared that the restraint applied to James Norris had 'in all probability saved the lives of others' and that 'no better mode could have been devised for securing a patient of so dangerous a description'.[170]

The officers and keepers at Bethlem had been given a clean bill of health by its own management, but this system of self-certification was unlikely ever to please Wakefield, who quickly accused the Governors of devising a cover-up. With the scandal of Norris coming so quickly behind those from York, it gave the public the impression that there was something rotten at the heart of Britain's madhouses. In response, a sizeable and coherent madhouse reform movement was taking shape and at its centre was the MP George Rose, who was determined to bring his considerable political influence to bear on the oldest and most famous madhouse of them all.

George Rose was born in 1744 to religious but relatively humble parents and had initially pursued a career in the Navy, which he abandoned after discovering that 'he had no chance of promotion'. The civil service beckoned and, following a successful career at the Treasury, he entered Parliament in

1784 and soon after attached himself to Prime Minister William Pitt. Rose was not, however, a popular figure and was a continual source of irritation to other MPs, one of whom described him as: 'A very low man, and very ignorant in all the higher departments of business, and yet at the same time very presumptuous, and he is the very last man under whose management I should be inclined to act.'

The Earl of Dudley was even less complimentary when he said of Rose that:

> 'It was quite absurd that in a country which has produced such a work as the Wealth of Nations, a man of such limited views should have so great an influence upon almost every branch of its economy: yet ... I had grown accustomed to him in the House of Commons, just as one grows accustomed to an old, clumsy, ill-contrived piece of furniture in an apartment, which one is loath to part with, though it only holds the place of something neater and more convenient.'[171]

This controversial, pompous and sometimes self-serving MP was introduced to the issue of England's madhouses through his association with the MP Charles Wynn, the main promoter behind the 1808 County Asylums Bill. The issue of madhouses conformed with Rose's long-standing interest in the plight of the poor and the issue of reform within workhouses and prisons. This, it seems, led him, in 1813, to propose repealing the entire 1774 Madhouse Act in favour of new and further-reaching legislation. The attempt failed, but shortly afterwards the revelations from the York Asylum caused the tide of public opinion to flow in Rose's direction. It was the discovery of the 'low grates' at York, in April 1814, that prompted Rose once more to seek leave for a new and more effectual Bill that would tighten the regulation of all madhouses, including Bethlem, opening them up to proper inspections and tighter certification and licensing.

Given the strengthening mood against asylums, Rose's vocal denouncements of the 1774 Act received due attention from his fellow MPs. His Madhouse Bill passed its first reading without difficulty, much to the alarm of Bethlem's Governors, who wished to remain independent of state-sponsored certification and inspection regimes. At a meeting in late April it was agreed by the Governors that they should use their collective political weight to pressurise MPs into watering down Rose's proposals. Representations were initially made to Rose but to no effect, so several senior Governors began to lobby other MPs, including Lord Sidmouth, the Home Secretary. In June a number of MPs raised the possibility of deferring the legislation but they were voted down and, to the concern of all at Bethlem, the Bill passed its second reading. If the hospital wished to avoid its inclusion in the legislation, time was running out, but it was just at this moment that Wakefield revealed details of his visit with James Norris.

Bethlem's Governors suddenly found themselves engaged in a fight on two fronts: there was the public battle against Wakefield's revelations and a private one against Rose's legislation. For a while the Governors believed themselves to be winning both battles but then, in July, their opponents joined forces and, armed with eyewitness testimonies to the abuses at York and Bethlem, started to push for the appointment of a Select Committee to investigate the state of all England's madhouses. Given heightened public anxiety over the matter, the case against undertaking such an investigation was hard to argue, and as the weeks passed by Bethlem's Governors watched in despair as the course of events moved beyond their control.

A key moment occurred on 11 July when Rose's Bill received its third and final reading in Parliament. The next day it was passed across to the House of Lords where, on the 12th, it received its first reading. The following week the Physician Charles Best, who was at that point still clinging to power at the York Asylum, submitted his own petition against the Bill to the Lords, but only a few days later this was rebuffed by a strong petition in favour submitted by Godfrey Higgins. All this prevarication meant that the Parliamentary summer break began before the Bill could be passed, forcing it to be carried over into the next year's session.

The lack of serious opposition to Rose's Bill and the ineffectual nature of the Governors' lobbying caused the officers and staff at Bethlem to acknowledge that at some point in the near future they should expect to be scrutinised by a Select Committee of MPs. In addition, many MPs and other dignitaries would doubtless want to make their own personal tours of

Bethlem during the coming months, but they would not be seeing the hospital in prime condition.

The old Moorfields building was in a terrible state and had been deliberately run down in expectation of the move to St George's Fields during the summer of 1815. Most parts of the hospital were being minimally maintained while others had decayed into a state of total ruin. Even with the threat of inspections ahead, there was neither the cash nor the time to make significant changes to the Moorfields infrastructure, but there was still an opportunity to shake up the hospital's management structure as well as to make cosmetic changes to the way in which the inmates were being treated.

At the start of 1815 Bethlem began a damage-limitation exercise whose purpose was to imply that Wakefield's reported abuses were the actions of individual staff members. The obstructive Steward, Peter Alavoine, was sacked and replaced by George Wallett, formerly the manager of a well-regarded private madhouse, while the aged, somewhat ineffectual Matron was retired in favour of a young outsider named Elizabeth Forbes.[172]

Wallett and Forbes were receptive to Tukes's ideas about treating inmates as sentient individuals and had reservations about Thomas Monro's use of violent medication. With Haslam's approval, they began to make changes on the galleries designed to bring Bethlem more in line with public expectations. When later asked what changes he had implemented after his arrival, Wallett replied: 'I observed a good many patients were kept in bed. I desired that they might be taken up and dressed and taken to the fire. I mentioned it to the apothecary, he thought it proper to be done. I believe that the women were kept in bed very much. I do not think I had it in my power to do more than that, and having them washed.'[173]

Across the way, the Matron Forbes, who confessed to never having seen an insane patient before her appointment, was also having an effect on the women's gallery. On arriving she discovered fourteen 'blanket patients' (ie wearing nothing but a blanket) chained to the wall in a day room, some of whom had been there for six years or more. She immediately freed all but five of these and, like Wallett, requested that changes be made in the general routine. When asked about her innovations, Forbes replied: 'In having them washed, and having them cleaned, and their hair cut, and making them as decent as their situations would admit of… Having them brought into the side room and letting them walk about; if they have not been able to walk about without handcuffs, they have been put on, and taken off afterwards.'

Proof of Forbes's effectiveness may be found in her treatment of Ann Stone, a person whom Wakefield had seen chained naked to a wall. Forbes was warned that Stone was 'very troublesome' and apt to tear into pieces any clothes that she was offered. 'I said I would have [her in] handcuffs but I found she was very quiet and took them off. I gave her a couple of caps, and she did not tear them. She looks better and very comfortable and tidy; and every time I go into the gallery, she says, "accept my real thanks for allowing me my liberty".'[174]

There were some things about which Wallett and Forbes could do nothing, either because it was not within their power to do so or because the design of the building did not permit it. For example, Monro's medical regime of vomits, purges and bleedings could not be altered (the Physician would not permit it), nor could the raving mad be separated from the quieter inmates, owing to a lack of habitable space. Even so, the changes that were made had a noticeable effect on Wakefield when he made a return visit to Bethlem on 23 April 1815, in preparation for the resumption of George Rose's Bill through Parliament the following week. Accompanied by a Governor, Wakefield made a repeat tour of the male and female galleries and was mildly impressed at what he found:

> 'Although the number of patients was nearly the same as during the last year, I found but one single one chained to his bed, and not a single patient in any one of the side rooms chained to the wall. Mrs Fenwick, the teacher of languages, was walking about the gallery [and] was an entirely different creature since she had been treated like a human being. She immediately came up to me and asked me how Mr William Fry, with whom she had lived as a governess, was, and his family.'

Not all the news was happy though: Wakefield's central object of interest, James Norris, had died on 28 February, apparently of tuberculosis. Naturally, the death of Norris just prior to a likely Parliamentary inquiry aroused Wakefield's suspicions, but he was informed that the cause of death had been confirmed by an autopsy: it was another issue that would have to be dealt with by the Select Committee.[175]

Wakefield's chaperone Governor tried to persuade his guest that Bethlem had undergone a great reformation and that many of the remaining problems, such as a lack of heating and the non-segregation of patients, would be resolved in the new building at St George's Fields. If this was an attempt to get Wakefield to cease his campaign, it was too little, too late. Five days later Parliament gave George Rose permission to form a Select Committee to investigate the state of madhouses in England and to suggest means by which they could be better regulated.

For more than half a century Bethlem had been struggling to maintain its independence from any form of state certification and inspection, but it increasingly looked like it might be fighting a lost cause. Perhaps as a last act of defiance, a Grand Court of Bethlem's Governors voted to re-elect Thomas Monro and John Haslam to their posts in the near certain knowledge that they would have to face some close questioning from George Rose and a panel of hostile MPs.

18

The Select Committee

Any hope that Bethlem was going to get an easy ride from the Select Committee disappeared when, in April 1815, the names of its members became publicly known. It was, of course, to be headed by George Rose, but the remainder of the Committee was dominated by other known reformers including Charles Wynn (Rose's co-sponsor), Robert Seymour (who had moved Parliament with an anti-madhouse speech the previous year) and Samuel Whitbread (who was concerned with the 1807 Committee), together with Henry Grey Bennet, William Smith and Charles Western (all of whom had inspected Bethlem with Rose).[176]

As might be expected, the Select Committee opened its proceedings with a description of the events that had led to Tuke's seizure of York Asylum and its subsequent rapid turnaround by the Quakers. It was with this recent success in mind that, on 1 May, the Committee began hearing evidence that related to conditions and practices at Bethlem. The first witness to be called was Edward Wakefield, who lost no time in painting a damning picture of the hospital and its staff.

Much of what Wakefield had to say had already been placed in print. He described in detail the state of the prisoners during his first visit ('injudicious and improper'), offered his opinion concerning the practices undertaken there ('disgusting idiocy') and, of course, talked at length about James Norris. Wakefield spoke in a series of lengthy monologues with the MPs rarely finding the need to interject. None argued with Wakefield about what he had seen, nor questioned the motives behind his initial interest in Bethlem. The Committee was shown a sketch of Norris tightly chained inside his harness and told of how, in subsequent visits, conditions were seen to have improved for most patients, including Norris. As the Governors had hoped, Wakefield implied that these changes had in part been due to the removal of the former Steward and Matron. However, the last three questions put to Wakefield revealed that Norris was not the only Bethlem inmate that interested the MPs.

'Were you acquainted with a person of the name of Matthews who was confined for many years as a lunatic in Bethlem?' asked the Committee.

Wakefield confirmed that he had met James Tilly Matthews but only after he had been removed from Bedlam to a nearby private madhouse. 'I have heard that he was frequently chained to his bed,' said Wakefield before confirming that Matthews had died the previous autumn. This last exchange indicated that any witnesses called from Bethlem were going to be asked to defend not just the physical treatment of Norris, who was an undoubted lunatic, but also to justify the confinement of James Tilly Matthews, a man whose diagnosis of insanity had been contested vigorously by his friends and relations. Some of Bethlem's ghosts were coming back to haunt it.

Rather than a general fact-finding mission, as perhaps could have been the case, George Rose and his colleagues had carefully planned their inquiry around a small number of issues that were liable to cause maximum damage to Bethlem's reputation. Prime amongst these were the individual cases of Norris and Matthews, both of whom were known to the public and both of whose treatment could be viewed as controversial. The specific way in which Bethlem staff treated these two men was used to suggest that the hospital as a whole was rotten, but a number of other carefully selected cases were also mentioned, including a man named Hurst, who had died of constipation, and Ann Stone, whose restraint and lack of clothing had shocked Wakefield on his first visit. In addition, a number of other general matters were of concern to the Select Committee including Bethlem's cold environment, the use of purgative medicines and the behaviour of individual members of staff. On this last matter, it was evident from the repeated pattern of questioning that Rose's Committee was intent not just in destroying Bethlem's reputation, but also claiming the scalps of several of its senior officers.

The second witness to come before the panel was Richard Staveley, a man who had spent years campaigning for the release of his uncle, James Tilly Matthews, and who, as a consequence, had come into conflict with the hospital's staff. Naturally, Staveley expounded at length his belief that his uncle had been perfectly sane, a position that received no criticism from the MPs. With a little prompting Staveley was able to tell Rose that John Haslam had held a 'violent animosity' towards Matthews and that, when challenged over his authority to confine his uncle, the Apothecary swore and said, 'Sir, we will soon let you know what our authority is!' Drs Monro and Crowther were portrayed as being subservient to Haslam and of offering Matthews substandard medical treatment. Staveley ended with a long and harrowing description of his uncle's death, the cause of which he blamed on the poor environment of his cell.

'He had very bad abscesses on his back,' said Staveley, 'all of which he attributed to the cell that he had been originally placed in and the damp of the house which, he said, affected most of the patients in the same way, beginning with a numbness about the thighs, and the lower part of the back, and frequently terminating in death.' This terminal prognosis was certainly the case with Matthews, who was ultimately removed from Bethlem to a private madhouse where his ulcers could be better cared for.

Perhaps the last bit of evidence was the most interesting. Staveley accused Haslam of having said to an entire tavern full of people that 'Matthews is as well as I am!' The clear implication was that Bethlem staff were knowingly locking up sane people in their cells, a charge that was more usually levelled at private madhouses and which, from past experience, was guaranteed to excite public anger.[177]

The next witness was William Lawrence, the surgeon who had been asked to perform an autopsy on Norris a few months earlier and who had visited Matthews on a number of occasions. Lawrence was another promoter of madhouse reform but he seemed unprepared to talk ill of the staff at Bethlem, much to the MPs' frustration; he instead confirmed that Norris had died of consumption and that Matthews had not been under restraint during the times that he had seen him. Lawrence's reticence may have been because he was at this time eyeing up the job of Bethlem Surgeon, which, as we shall shortly see, had just become vacant. He perhaps did not want to upset either his prospective employers or the powerful Select Committee, whose judgements would doubtless affect Bethlem's future direction. Lawrence answered the questions put to him succinctly and would not be drawn to criticise the Bethlem medical staff. This did not serve the Select Committee's aims, so the Surgeon was quickly released.

The job of Bethlem Surgeon had fallen vacant following the somewhat timely demise of Bryan Crowther, who dropped dead on 17 April, only a matter of weeks before the Select Committee began its work. Crowther's unpredictability and drunkenness must have led the Governors to dread any prospect of his being interviewed by the MPs; his death was seen as fortuitous as it not only stopped him from being questioned but also meant that he could be made to take the rap for any criticisms of medical malpractice, including the allegation of ill-treatment against James Norris. Crowther thus joined the ex-Steward and ex-Matron as Bethlem's official scapegoats.[178]

Shifting blame onto ex-members of staff should have served Bethlem's remaining staff quite well but this strategy required those being interviewed by the Select Committee to toe the party line. However, inside Bethlem there was a growing sense of panic that, when combined with the hospital's poor staff communications, led most senior officers to reject any idea of teamwork in favour of self-preservation.

Whether by design or luck, the first members of staff to be interviewed by the Select Committee were George Wallett and Elizabeth Forbes, the new Steward and Matron, both of whom had only been in place since February. Although some pressure must have been put on them not to say anything disparaging about their colleagues, both were intelligent enough to understand the seriousness of the situation into which they had been placed. They surmised that the best means of keeping their jobs was to place clear water between themselves and people such as Haslam, Monro and the late Dr Crowther.

George Wallett was interviewed first and was subjected to a determined questioning session during which he tried hard to provide answers that, like Lawrence's, did not pander to the Committee's prejudices. He defended John Haslam's attendance record, claiming that the Apothecary toured the galleries every day and was always on call should any of the patients be taken ill at night. In reply, the Committee tried to make a deal of Haslam living some distance away in Islington but, while attempting to make light of this, Wallett inadvertently revealed that the Apothecary was often in attendance for only an hour a day and that during this time he did not visit every patient. The Committee picked up on this.

'So it might happen that months and months might elapse without his seeing the different patients in the hospital?'

'It probably might happen,' answered Wallett with some uncertainty, 'but as I do not go around with him, I do not know.'

The Committee sensed Wallett's nervousness and put further speculative questions to him, asking for his opinion on the behaviour of others. The flustered Wallett tried his hardest to dodge these but often ended up telling the Committee second-hand stories or gossip that should have been dismissed as hearsay but were instead taken down as evidence. This tactic was further used when the Committee began to ask Wallett about Bethlem's patients, some of whom had died before the Steward had taken up his post. As ever, the topic of James Norris raised its head; Wallett had known the man for just ten days before his death, but the Committee pushed him to repeat any gossip he might have heard. It was as a consequence of this that a piece of damning evidence came to the Committee's attention. Wallett was asked to speculate about Dr Crowther's attitude towards the unusual manner in which Norris had been chained up. As part of his reply Wallett inadvertently told the Committee the real story behind Norris's restraint.

'He said it was not necessary. I heard Mr Crowther say that the keeper went into the cell to restrain Norris from some act of violence, or making a noise, and that he struck Norris, that Norris retaliated, and the consequence was, Norris being a very powerful man, he got him down, and would have murdered him perhaps with a shovel, but one of the patients went to the assistance of the keeper, and that Norris stabbed him with a knife. I believe he stabbed both the keeper and the patient, and that was the reason of Norris being solitarily confined. The keeper was in a state of intoxication.'[179]

This version of events differed greatly from the story given to Bethlem's Governors by Haslam the previous year. Rather than being unprovoked, as Haslam had claimed, Norris's notorious attack had, according to Crowther, been promoted by a blow from a drunken keeper. Whether it was true or not, this played into the Committee's hands. In the minutes following, Wallett also confirmed that the hospital was freezing cold, that there was no warm bath and that the Governors' inspections were infrequent and disorganised. Wallett tried to recover the situation by explaining that the old practices were changing (thanks, in part, to his arrival) and that the new hospital at St George's Fields would rectify the cold, the damp and a lack of segregation – but the damage had been done.

The next witness was John Weir, the Inspector of Naval Hospitals, and an adherent to Tuke's 'moral therapy'. He had visited Bethlem some three years earlier to see some naval patients and, based on this visit, he was asked about Bethlem's medical practices:

> 'I am of the opinion that the present medical establishment is insufficient … From the indiscriminate system of bleeding and purging in the spring months; from having observed patients lying perfectly naked and covered up in straw; from their mixing the mild and frantic patients together and others being unnecessarily being loaded with chains; I am of the opinion both that the medical treatment is injudicious and that uncalled-for severity is practiced toward them.'[180]

When Elizabeth Forbes, the new Matron, went before the Committee she was subject to a similar line of questioning as Wallett but her answers were less guarded, and painted Monro and Haslam in a very bad light.

> Committee: 'How long since Monro has personally inspected the female patients?'
> Forbes: 'He was through the female gallery last Saturday.'
> Committee: 'Prior to last Saturday, how long is it since he has been there?'

Forbes: 'I cannot say.'

Committee: 'How long do you think: a month, two months or three months?'

Forbes: 'I think it may have been a month.'

Committee: 'Have you heard that Doctor Monro was in the habit of personally inspecting the situation of each patient at any given period?'

Forbes: 'I have never heard it.'

Committee: 'And have you ever seen it?'

Forbes: 'No. There are patients who have been in some time and that have not had anything done for them.'[181]

Forbes also revealed a communication problem between Monro and Haslam. This was most apparent when she recounted the story of a woman inmate whom she believed to be dangerously ill.

'I reported her to Mr Haslam and begged him to see her, and said, I thought she could not live long. She died of decline, I believe. Mr Haslam gave her powders, and that was nil that was done. I believe Mr Haslam did not report her case to Doctor Monro. She was confined to her bed for a fortnight.'

Forbes later confirmed that powders were the only medicine she had seen administered, regardless of a patient's symptoms and that the general hospital environment was poor. 'We have a patient now', said Forbes, 'whose limbs are so contracted that she can only crawl, from sitting constantly.'

By the end of May the Select Committee had gathered more than enough anecdotal evidence to imply that Bethlem Hospital was a brutal, unfulfilling place where the needs of the patients were secondary to those of the staff. Furthermore, it was evident to them that this ill-treatment was, for some reason, prevalent only in Bethlem and not in Bridewell, its sister institution, even though they shared many of the same senior staff such as the Surgeon and Physician. It was the medical staff that were the Committee's real target, and this was probably why the two surviving senior officers, John Haslam and Thomas Monro, were interviewed last of all, so that some of the evidence gathered from the previous witnesses could be placed before them.

John Haslam was the first of the medical staff before the Committee and he was not in a mood to be pushed around. He was able to fend off early criticisms of Bethlem's staffing levels with ease and was happy to justify the restraints used on patients, telling them that iron manacles were 'a thousand times' more preferable to straitjackets. He even argued back, something that no previous witness had attempted to do. When the Committee accused Bethlem of restraining more of its patients than most private madhouses, he replied curtly, 'As far as I have seen of the private madhouses, there is more restraint than in our hospital, a great deal.' His inquisitors scoffed at this and asked him which ones.

'All the private establishments I've seen,' he replied, 'and I have seen most of them!'

Only then did it become clear as to which madhouse the Committee had been referring. 'Have you seen the Retreat at York?' they asked.

'No,' replied Haslam.

Haslam must have been aware of the direction in which the conversation was being steered because it was he that chose to raise the issue of James Norris, a man whom he described as having shown 'unabated ferocity for more than twelve years with unabated malevolence and where the necessity for coercion existed the whole of the time.'

This wrong-footed the Committee and although they subsequently tried to use Norris as an example of maltreatment, Haslam fought back by portraying him as a dangerous madman and dismissed out of hand the idea that he had been a victim of institutionalised violence. When asked to provide a precise length of time for Norris's confinement, Haslam told the Committee to work it out for themselves using Bethlem archives.

'You will be able to collect the precise time from the date of the resolution of the Committee that he should be so secured, connected with the order for the release from it, that will give you the time, but that time I do not recollect.'[182]

The Select Committee persisted but Haslam acquitted himself admirably. He denied being the architect of Norris's infamous restraining device, recounting that his less restrictive idea had been rejected by the Governors and that, when Norris had been placed in a straitjacket, he had 'burst it to pieces'. As the questions continued to flow, so Haslam became less cooperative and frequently resorted to telling his inquisitors that he 'did not know', 'did not recollect' or 'could not answer' a particular question. Haslam had proved himself to be very slippery, so George Rose asked him to return on another day for further interrogation. He did so, but was even less cooperative, often answering a lengthy question with just one or two words. He did, however, offer a full version of various attacks that Norris had made during his early days at Bethlem. Haslam explained that Norris had been fully restrained after several violent attacks and not just the one where he stabbed his keeper. He described Norris as an irrational and psychotic man who used his intelligence to try and disarm and trap individuals in his cell with the intention of killing them.

> 'I was coming in on one occasion to give him medicine,' recounted Haslam, 'and he had contrived to preserve all the fat from his broth for several days, with which he smeared the bottom of the floor. I came in the usual way and from the grease was thrown backwards immediately and a shower of bowls came at me. I cannot particularise the consistent and repeated acts of violence of this man but he was, stating it generally, the most malignant and the most mischievous lunatic I ever saw in my life.'[183]

The issue of Norris's restraint did not faze Haslam, but this did not stop the questions from coming: there were nearly 300 in total, a majority of which were batted away with ease by the Apothecary. It was an impressive performance and when, inevitably, the line of inquiry moved from Norris to James Tilly Matthews, the Committee was met with an equal degree of resistance. Haslam repeatedly stated his belief that Matthews was both delusional and a potential danger to the public; when the Apothecary started effectively to discredit the evidence provided by Matthews's relations, the Committee decided to release him as a witness.

Rose and his colleagues had witnessed a magnificent performance by the Apothecary. Haslam was masterful and able to deal with his questioners in an assertive and professional manner. Unlike the Steward and Matron, who had chosen to repeat gossip and blame others, Haslam had stuck to what he knew, refused to speculate and, most importantly, refused to apologise for the treatment and conditions at Bethlem. He instead defended the Hospital, robustly, and he must surely have left the Select Committee convinced that his job was safe.

The same could not be said of the next witness, Dr Thomas Monro, who came before the Select Committee in an aloof and dismissive mood. From the outset Monro saw no real need to justify his medical practices or decisions, especially to a Committee of MPs. This led him to give answers that not only placed himself in a bad light, but also many others inside the hospital. In choosing to interview Monro the Select Committee had found a weak point in Bethlem's defence.

Just two questions into the interview and Monro was already in trouble after casually revealing that his hospital visits were not exactly regular. 'Sometimes I may go twice or three times in the week, sometimes not above so many times in a month. It depends upon circumstances.' He then explained that even when there he almost never entered the galleries: 'I have a room where I have the patients generally; the patients I visit I send for into that room.'

When asked about what cures he prescribed, Monro said: 'We apply generally bleeding, purging and vomit; those are the general remedies we apply.' When pressed further about how he decided individual medicinal doses, Monro passed the buck onto his Apothecary. 'It is generally left to the discretion of Mr Haslam to give the proper dose.'

The Committee moved on to the matter of restraint, but Monro refused to take responsibility for this either, saying that, if Bethlem had more staff, the need for handcuffs, chains and the like would be greatly diminished. It was during this discourse that Monro made a series of comments that were to haunt him and Bedlam for some years to come. It began with a simple enough question, which Monro chose to interpret as a threat.

'Do you know the number of persons now under restraint in Bethlem, in irons?' he was asked.

'No,' answered Monro, 'I have nothing in the world to do with the irons. I never gave an order for a patient to be put into irons in the course of my life.'

'What are your objections to irons and fetters?'

'They are fit only for pauper lunatics. If a gentleman was put into irons, he would not like it.'

Monro had admitted to the Committee that Bethlem's pauper patients were treated in a harsher manner than the patients in his own private madhouse. This bore out George Rose's belief that Bethlem was offering its inmates a second-class service. Monro must have seen the stern look on his inquisitors' faces for he quickly tried to backtrack. 'I mean that pauper lunatics of course cannot pay for the regular attendance to prevent their doing mischief and there are so few servants kept for the purpose, that it is the only mode of restraining them.' The Committee did not have to wait long before receiving further evidence of Monro's distain for the poor.

'What idea do you affix to the words that a gentleman would not like irons?' asked George Rose.

'In the first place, I am not at all accustomed to gentlemen in irons – I never saw anything of the kind. It is a thing so totally abhorrent to my feelings that I never considered it necessary to put a gentleman into irons.'

'Do you think that a man in a superior rank of life is more likely, in a state of insanity, to be irritated by such a mode of confinement, than a pauper lunatic?'

'Most assuredly,' said Monro. For good measure he then contradicted Haslam's testimony by declaring that straitjackets were more humane than chains, but it was Monro's parting statement that showed his true colours. When pressed further on the issue of restraint he summarily managed to blame everyone else in the hospital other than himself:

'I have seldom or never been consulted on the matter. I should rather think, myself, it might be owing to the opinion of the Matron in respect to the women, and very likely the Steward, in respect to the men, exercising their authority, under the direction of the Apothecary, I presume. I believe that no patient is permitted to be liberated without the approbation of the Apothecary.'[184]

These were the last words spoken by Monro to the Select Committee. Despite the Physician's importance to Bethlem, Monro's examination had been short and had ended before the subjects of Norris, Matthews and other topics could be raised. Why this should have been so is perplexing. Monro may simply have walked out or the MPs could perhaps have gone easy on him in recognition of his status and wealth. Either way, during his short interview Monro had reapportioned all blame, especially toward his rival Haslam, whom he portrayed as being central to Bethlem's decision-making process, a situation that was not strictly true. The Committee decided that they needed to recall Haslam.

The Apothecary may have learned something of Monro's behaviour, for on his return to the Committee much of his former bravado had gone and from the outset he gave the impression of being rattled.

The proceedings started with questions being asked about a keeper who had been accused of 'being too familiar with a female patient of great beauty'. Haslam replied that the matter had been unproven but admitted that he had asked the member of staff concerned to leave Bethlem for a job in Liverpool. Then, instead of being tight-mouthed and defensive as he had been previously, Haslam began to divert blame away from himself. When asked who had first employed the errant keeper, he gave a Monro-style answer:

'I have nothing to do with the hiring of keepers. I never recommended him. The servants of the house were always hired by the Treasurer. The male Keeper is hired by the Steward with the approbation of the Treasurer and the Committee. The females are chosen with the approbation of the Treasurer and the Committee.'

George Rose then moved on to the case of a patient who had allegedly died from a blocked bowel. Haslam at first denied any detailed knowledge of the matter but then admitted that the late Dr Crowther had mentioned it to him.

When pressed to reveal what Crowther had to say on the matter, Haslam's patience snapped.

'Knowing the situation of Dr Crowther at that time, I paid no attention to it. Dr Crowther was generally insane and mostly drunk. He was so insane as to have a strait waistcoat.'

This unexpected revelation much excited the MPs, who sensed that they at last had Haslam on the run. 'Then for ten years Mr Crowther was Surgeon to the hospital!' gasped Rose. 'During those ten years he was generally insane; he had had a strait waistcoat, and was mostly drunk?'

'He was.'

'And during that period he was continued as Surgeon to the hospital?'

'He was.'

'Did he attend the patients?'

'Yes, he did.'

'Were the Governors of the Hospital acquainted with the fact of his incapacity?'

'I should think not. His insanity was confined principally to the abuse of his best friends. He was so insane that his hand was not obedient to his will.'

Wishing to continue the momentum, the questioning switched back to Haslam's duties, which, he confirmed, included general responsibility for restraining patients. He made one last attempt at placing himself in a better light by declaring that at all times he enforced 'the humane treatment of the patients and endeavouring, as much in my power lies, to diffuse as much good order and decency of manners among those unhappy people as possible.'

It was a brave last attempt, but Haslam's spirit had been broken and, when questioned about the previous Keeper, he wearily declared that 'for the last five years I think he has been incompetent.' After this Haslam was released.[185]

Only three further witnesses were called, and all of them questioned only briefly. A Dr Latham offered an opinion that Bethlem was as much a place 'of confinement as a place of cure'. Bethlem's Treasurer, Richard Clarke, was able to outline some basic facts, statistics and procedures at Bethlem without undue controversy, while the final witness, the MP Henry Grey Bennet, was actually a member of the Select Committee itself. He gave another gruesome description of Bethlem as he and Wakefield had found it during their visit the previous spring. This ensured that the MPs' parting image of the hospital would be an unpleasant one.

With the subject of Bethlem having been exhausted, the MPs moved on to other issues such as the conditions within private madhouses and charitable asylums. Further witnesses were called, most of whose evidence only served to reinforce the MPs' belief that there was something very rotten with England's mental health institutions. Following this the Committee began a lengthy deliberation on its findings and afterwards formulated its recommendations. This process took months, but in the meantime the staff and inmates of Bedlam had a more important matter to attend to. For the first time in seven centuries Bethlem Hospital was moving to a location outside of the City of London.

19

St George's Fields

On the morning of 24 August 1815 the residents of Moorfields awoke to the sight of dozens of hackney carriages forming an orderly queue outside Bethlem Hospital. For days the keepers, nurses, basketmen and other staff and officers had been preparing themselves and their inmates for the long-awaited move to the new building at St George's Fields. One by one the 122 remaining inmates were released from their cells, escorted out through the main entrance and loaded into the carriages. We must presume that the patients did not travel alone but were given chaperones and that those considered violent, manic or raving were securely restrained by straitjackets, handcuffs or chains.

Each departing carriage headed south across Blackfriars Bridge following the Great Surrey Road through the borough of Lambeth to St George's Fields, where the new Bethlem Hospital lay waiting for its inmates. This building had been long talked about in London, especially in light of the complaints made by Wakefield and Rose. The Apothecary, Steward and Matron had all promised Rose that the new Bethlem would rectify many of the current problems, especially the lack of heating and segregation and, on first sight, the new asylum certainly appeared to offer the prospect of a new and better phase in the hospital's history.

Like its City predecessor, the St George's Fields building was designed to be awe-inspiring and imposing. This new Bethlem Hospital retained the familiar layout of two wings (which housed the patients' galleries) separated by a central entrance block in which were located the administrative rooms and offices. At 570 feet long and with four floors reaching more than 60 feet in height, the new Bethlem towered above the flat ground that surrounded it, dominating the landscape. Even so, it was purposefully less ornate than Moorfields; only the entrance hall showed any element of ostentation, with its dome and six-columned portico. Even the gardens, which had been such an important part of Moorfields, were much scaled back: instead of acres of manicured private grounds visible to the outside world, the new hospital was surrounded by a high brick wall above which a few tree tops could be seen. In place of flower beds and lawns was a simple entrance court and, behind the main building, extensive 'airing grounds', which were separated by large walls so that the male, female and convalescing patients could not come into contact with one another.

The new building was capable of holding 200 inmates (together with another sixty in the separate criminal department being built behind the hospital), although it was hoped that future expansions would double this number. It was a marked improvement on the crumbling edifice at Moorfields, but there were teething troubles, some of which were noted by George Rose's Select Committee, which took a tour of the hospital just prior to its official opening. The Committee's chief complaint concerned a lack of glazing on the upper-storey windows and the limited extent of the much advertised steam heating system. Both problems would be rectified, but in the meantime Bedlam's inmates would have to face one last winter in cells that were exposed to the effects of wind, rain and snow.[186]

The first intake of patients also had to endure a deal of noise and dust from the high-security criminal lunatic buildings, both of which were under construction. The criminal department eventually opened in 1816 and among the first wave of 'criminal lunatics' transferred to Bethlem from Newgate Prison was the former patient James Hadfield, whose court case had alerted people to the inadequacies of the law with regard to the criminally insane.

Even without glazing and heating the new Bethlem was a welcome change from the damp, dilapidated conditions of the old hospital. Furthermore, the new Bethlem had managed to conform to Samuel Tuke's basic principles of good asylum design, even though it had been planned before the publication of his Description of the Retreat. In his treatise Tuke had written that:

'The defects in the construction of asylums which I have had opportunity to observe, have defeated one or other of the following objects, which appear to be of primary importance to the welfare and comfort of lunatics. Firstly, the complete separation of male and female patients. Second, the separation of patients in proper number and distinct apartments, according to the state of their minds. Third, a system of easy and constant superintendence over the patients, by their attendants, and over both by their superior officers. Fourth, that the accommodation for the patients should be cheerful, and afford as much opportunity for voluntary change of place and variety of scene, as is compatible with security.'[187]

The St George's Fields Bethlem met with all these criteria but, although the environment might have changed, its staff and officers had not, and this remained an issue to those campaigning for reforms to the madhouse trade. Despite a generally positive reception for the move, George Rose was determined to keep the memories of the old Bethlem alive and it cannot be coincidental that the day after the first patients settled themselves into the new hospital, The Times began to serialise the transcripts of the Select Committee's interviews with Haslam, Monro and others. This unwelcome newspaper publicity began on 25 August and continued intermittently until October. The articles were lengthy, sometimes taking up a third of a broadsheet page, and printed every word uttered in reply to the MPs' questions. At the same time, the Select Committee published its findings as a booklet available for anyone to buy, although a high cover price of 13 shillings may have dampened the appeal of many casual readers.[188]

If this adverse publicity had any effect on the senior staff at Bethlem, they did not let it show. An air of invulnerability remained within Bethlem, and on the traditional St Matthew's Day feast in September 1815 the Governors affirmed their support by drinking a toast to Haslam's health. Both he and Dr Monro must have believed that the move to St George's Fields and the collective political power of Bethlem's Governors had got them off the hook, and they probably thought that their jobs were safe. They had, however, greatly underestimated the determination of Edward Wakefield.[189]

Despite the activities of the Select Committee, Wakefield continued to operate a personal campaign against Bethlem, but by the New Year of 1816 he was focusing his efforts on just two targets – John Haslam and Thomas Monro – on whose shoulders he heaped the blame for the failings of the old hospital.

The New Year also saw an end to the Governors' complacency after they learned that George Rose's proposed Madhouse Bill might actually get the approval of Parliament. On 10 February 1816 it was suggested to the Governors that they should attempt to stem the tide of criticism by undertaking an internal review of their administration. The main promoter of this idea, Alderman John Atkins, was asked to form an investigative Committee that, under his chairmanship, immediately set about its task.

Atkins was able to report back quickly and informed the Governors that there were a number of areas where the hospital could be improved. These mostly concerned its financial practices and stocktaking, which, despite the malpractice of previous years, were still considered to be lax. Atkins also told the Governors that many of Bethlem's current problems stemmed from its obsession with secrecy and a refusal to acknowledge that the hospital had any duty to the wider world that helped to fund it. To overcome this Atkins suggested that the Governors publish an annual report that would display some basic statistics and reports from all the senior officers, including the medical staff.

Most of Atkins's suggestions met with approval except for his idea of an annual report, which was the subject of much debate among the Governors, something that in itself highlighted the ingrained nature of Bethlem's secrecy culture. However, Atkins's logic was inescapable and the Governors begrudgingly agreed to the idea of a public report, which would be published in January each year. The first one was scheduled for 1817 but, perhaps unsurprisingly, it never appeared and it would be another quarter of a century before one was published. This aside, the Atkins Inquiry found very few major problems with the way in which Bethlem was being run, and allowed the Governors to conclude that:

'The Standing Rules and Orders of the Hospital, together with the regulations adopted this day, will with the assistance of the Treasurer and weekly Subcommittee be found sufficient for the good government of the Hospital and the creation of any new Officer will be unnecessary.'[190]

This self-congratulatory behaviour did nothing to placate Edward Wakefield, although his mood towards some aspects of Bethlem's regime had softened. Wakefield declared himself happy with the new arrangements at St George's Fields and also believed that the recently appointed Steward and Matron could be trusted to treat the patients with dignity and respect. However, one aspect of the old Bedlam regime still bothered him greatly: its medical staff. He did not trust Haslam or Monro and thought them quite capable of repeating mistakes from the past; he correctly sensed that the Atkins Inquiry was a prelude to the reappointment of Haslam and Monro at the annual Governors' General Court, due to be held in early April. The third medical post, that of Surgeon, had just been offered to William Lawrence, an assistant surgeon at St Bartholomew's Hospital, who had on occasion acted as a locum to the mad and drunk Dr Crowther. Lawrence was familiar with Bethlem and his testimony to the Select Committee portrays him as being a straightforward, direct type of man who was medically capable and trustworthy. Despite Lawrence's association with Crowther and the fact that he had autopsied the body of James Norris, Wakefield believed him to be firmly on the side of the reformers, so did not object to his being made Bethlem Surgeon; but he did still have the existing Physician and Apothecary within his sights.

On 31 March Wakefield opened up a new front in his battle against Bethlem by writing to several London newspapers complaining that 'the fact is sufficiently obvious; the Governors and the Public have been deceived by their medical officers'. He then implicitly linked all of Bethlem's past troubles with Haslam and Monro and, in doing so, offered the Governors an easy way out of the tricky situation in which they found themselves. Sack Haslam and Monro, said Wakefield, and he and the other reformers would draw a line under the abuses of the past. This was certainly a tempting offer and one that would leave the Governors and other senior officers free of any blame, even though their haphazard inspections and hands-off management style had contributed to the hospital's neglect.

Wakefield reinforced this by privately approaching George Wallett, the new Steward, telling him that 'so long as your Physician and Apothecary are permitted to hold their situations, I will continue my attacks against Bethlem and its medical officers, through the medium of the daily newspapers and other periodical publications.' Within a couple of days of this, every single Governor had received a copy of the Select Committee's printed report, prominent within which were the disastrous testimonies given by Haslam and Monro as well as accusations of abuse provided by Wakefield, Bennet and others. This, and the public anger being directed at Bethlem, had the desired effect.

When the Governors' General Court met on 5 April 1816 their mood was solemn. As in the past, Haslam and Monro had expected their reselection as Apothecary and Physician to be a mere formality, but Wakefield had created such a difference of opinion among the Governors that it was decided to postpone the vote so that they might have 'an opportunity of investigating the subject'. Haslam and Monro were aghast, especially when they were told that before reapplying for their posts they had to supply a letter that could explain their previous conduct in relation to the Select Committee's evidence.

In the meanwhile the reformers kept pressurising Bethlem by placing an advertisement in the papers suggesting that one James Bevan was 'particularly suited to fill the situation of Architect and Surveyor to Bridewell and Bethlem Hospitals'. The names of the twenty-nine supporters given in this advert revealed the true extent of the reform movement and included twelve members from the Parliamentary Select Committee, fourteen members from Wakefield's self-appointed Committee of Inquiry, plus Samuel Tuke, Godfrey Higgins and Dr John Weir.[191]

Seeing this long list of dignitaries must have made the Governors feel even more uncomfortable about the approaching Parliamentary Bill, the first reading of which had successfully passed earlier that month. Aware that events were slipping out of their control, several of Bethlem's more influential Governors started to lobby MPs to keep the hospital excluded from any resulting legislation. Word of this got back to the Select Committee and, on 10 May, Henry Grey Bennet stood up in the House of Commons and pointedly asked whether there were plans to 'give any allowance' to Bethlem. If so, he argued, the Government 'should resist the payment of one single shilling to that hospital, so long as the management of it should continue in the hands in which it now was.' This was answered with cheers of 'Hear! Hear!' from MPs. Buoyed by this reception, Bennet went on to vent his spleen about the management of Haslam and Monro:

'All those concerned in the hospital were most shamefully neglected by them. There was a physician who walked the hospital once a month – an apothecary who abounded in theoretical views, but who was above attending to anything else – a steward, a matron, and a porter, all too important in their own eyes to attend to the wants and necessities of the patients and a surgeon often mad himself, and almost continually drunk'.

This met with further cheers of support and led Bennet to offer a threat. 'Unless the Governors should dismiss the present officers from their situation, I will move for leave to bring a bill for the purpose of taking away the charter of the hospital.' There were some objections to this last suggestion, and it was pointed out that Bethlem was due to house the country's criminal lunatics, something that would require public funds, but Bennet remained unmoved, stating that 'not one shilling of the public money should remain in the hands in which it would be so scandalously abused'.[192]

A few days prior to this outburst Haslam and Monro had delivered their explanatory letters to the Governors. Both men were still seething at their treatment and pointed out that they were being asked to defend themselves against unknown charges. The tone of the two men's letters was reminiscent of their performance in front of the Select Committee: Haslam admitted that there had been problems but said that these had been resolved, while Monro acknowledged no culpability whatsoever and instead launched a broadside attack on the reformers, especially Wakefield, whom he considered to be ill-informed outsiders. Both men expressed disbelief at the Governors' actions and were at pains to point out that in previous years they had approved of their conduct and had even congratulated them for it.[193]

The letters had been written for the Governors' eyes only, but news of their content leaked out and a booklet containing their full text was published. On reading it, Wakefield was horrified at the attack on his character and those of his colleagues; he chose to reply to the Governors in the form of an open letter published on 13 May by several newspapers. In it, Wakefield rehashed much of his evidence concerning Norris, Matthews and Anna Stone while liberally quoting from Monro's own testimony. It finished with a stern warning to the Governors:

'To conclude: The resolution of the Committee of the House of Commons, signed by the Right Hon George Rose, is before you, warning you of the conduct of your medical officers. Those medical officers, the Physician and Apothecary, have had their re-selection suspended... The Physician defends every circumstance which has taken place. The Apothecary admits most of the charges but says that an alteration for the better has occurred which I know to be the fact, and which I rejoice at – but attribute it to anyone but him... My Lords and Gentlemen – I have none to serve in this business; I throw myself before you, the advocate for the exercise of humanity towards the most wretched of our species; I am opposed by those who are deeply interested that no inspection should take place, that no inquiry should be made, and that the election should go on as formerly. That election comes on Wednesday the 15th of May, at Bridewell Hospital: I pray you to attend and judge rightly.'[194]

It was not, however, just strong words like this that sealed the fate of Haslam and Monro, but also a ghost from the Apothecary's past. Unbeknown to Haslam, a month earlier George Rose's Committee had decided to dig a little more deeply into the case of James Tilly Matthews and as a result took evidence from James Simmonds, a former head keeper at Bethlem. Simmonds had been treated with disdain by Haslam but had formed a friendship with Matthews and, when asked by Rose how he felt Matthews had been treated by Haslam, he replied: 'I cannot think Mr Matthews was treated properly. He was a gentleman; he had a genteel education, and I did not think he ought to have had the treatment he had, for he would never offend anybody that did not offend him.'

Simmonds admitted that Matthews was eccentric but denied that he was a dangerous lunatic, as Haslam had frequently claimed. He then went on to describe how Matthews had been chained by the leg and handcuffed for a period of a couple of years 'because he would not submit to the apothecary … the irons were put on him to punish him for the use of his tongue.'

When asked to comment on this testimony Haslam denied everything and complained that Simmonds hadn't a clue what he was talking about, but the damage had been done. A report detailing Simmonds's allegations was circulated to the Governors together with an old manuscript that had been written by Matthews and made several clear allegations of malpractice against Haslam. The Apothecary was already aware of this manuscript's existence and professed to be unconcerned about its contents.

'As this manuscript was only the record of delusions which constituted his disorder', he wrote, 'and formed the staples of his discourse – as its burthen was a series of imaginary grievances and pretended abuses, thoroughly impregnated with a rancorous hostility against those who were the authors of his seclusion … I conceived that its circulation ought not to be prevented.'[195]

Haslam could not (or perhaps would not) see that he had lost the Governors' support, many of whom found Matthews's posthumous comments deeply disturbing. After nearly two decades spent incarcerated in Bethlem, and more than a year after his funeral, Matthews was exacting revenge against his nemesis Haslam.

The meeting on 15 May was a drawn-out and bad-tempered affair with impassioned speeches coming from Governors on both sides of the divide. At times the proceedings, which, with more than eighty Governors present, were abnormally well attended, became animated as the significance of the Select Committee's evidence was hotly debated. Eleven Governors gave speeches, the central theme of which was broadly the same: should the Governors re-elect Dr Monro and Mr Haslam to the posts of Physician and Apothecary?

The answer was mostly in the negative. Only four people voted in favour of Haslam's selection against seventy-six who did not; it was a resounding defeat for the Apothecary, whose life was centred on the hospital. The vote for Monro was closer, being thirty-five in his favour with forty-five against. Given that Monro had treated the Select Committee's report with disdain and hostility (whereas Haslam had attempted to make amends), the imbalance in this vote could be viewed as unjust. It is easy to suspect that Monro's position as 'a gentleman' may have garnered him more votes than the humble-born Haslam.[196]

This 'de-selection' (ie sacking) had a markedly different effect on the two men. Thomas Monro was a gentleman doctor in his late fifties who possessed inherited wealth, social connections, a string of large houses and a thriving private madhouse business. Although humiliating, the loss of his Bethlem post was not a life-changing disaster, so he accepted the Governors' decision without causing too much fuss. A few months later Monro found himself the subject of a lawsuit concerning his Brook House asylum; the case against him failed but it served to persuade him out of the medical profession altogether. For many years his heart had not been in the madhouse trade, something that was reflected in his frequent absences from Bethlem and his dismissive attitude towards his patients. His real interest lay in the world of art, especially watercolours, and he had acted as a patron to dozens of up-and-coming artists. After bowing out of medicine Monro adopted a less stressful and more fulfilling life that involved inviting his protégé artists up to his country estate at Bushey, Hertfordshire. It was here that he died in 1833, leaving behind him a small fortune and a phenomenal art collection that included works by Turner, Peter DeWint and others.[197]

For Haslam the reverse was true. When he left Bethlem he was in his early fifties and, despite accusations made by Crowther that he held outside interests, he had had neither the time nor the opportunity to build up a substantial private practice. Unlike Monro, Haslam was not wealthy and, thanks to the Select Committee, his name had been associated with abusive and archaic practices limiting his chances of starting up in private practice. He also felt a great sense of injustice at his de-selection and, with nothing else to fall back on, became determined to go down fighting. Thus, when the post of Bethlem Apothecary was advertised as being vacant in early June 1816, Haslam put himself forward as a candidate.

Haslam found himself up against four other candidates of mixed quality. The first two, Thomas Parker and Rees Price, were relative unknowns and not serious candidates. The third, Dr John Propert, was an experienced naval surgeon and noted reformer who liked to call himself 'the poor Welsh Apothecary'. Born near Cardigan, he had arrived in London penniless a few years earlier but had managed to set up a successful practice in Portland Place. However, he was still in his early twenties and was perhaps a little too young and idealistic for the Governors. The fourth candidate was George Wallett, the Bethlem Steward; he had been in the post for just over a year but he had already proved his mettle both in his reforms and in the way in which conducted himself during the Select Committee's interviews. As the internal candidate, he would always be the person for Haslam to beat, and so it turned out to be.[198]

On 19 June the Governors met at Bridewell Hospital to choose a new Apothecary. The resulting vote underlined their determination to make Haslam a scapegoat for the problems at Moorfields. He received just one vote and came in last place behind Parker (three votes) and Price (five votes); Dr Propert acquitted himself well with twenty-six votes, but the winner was never really in doubt: George Wallett received seventy-six votes, even though during his testimony of the previous year he had declared himself ignorant of the medical practices used at Bethlem.[199]

Haslam was furious at the Governors and accused them of having been 'panic-struck at the shadow of your enemy'. Despite writing a vociferous and lengthy letter that sought to justify his treatment of Norris and Matthews, Haslam did accept that he would never again be employed at the hospital. He pleaded with the Governors to give him a pension, as they had done the previous year when they dismissed the Steward and Matron. To reinforce his position he listed the misdemeanours of previous staff members who had received pensions, which included allowing two daughters of a laundry woman to become pregnant via the same lunatic and 'the late Porter, a shattered victim of gin and paralysis, [who] basks in the sunshine of a pension'.[200]

The plea for an annuity fell on deaf ears and a proposal from the Treasurer that Haslam should be offered £200 a year was heavily defeated. When the perilous state of Haslam's finances was revealed, the Governors relented a little and agreed 'to enter into an immediate subscription' for the relief of 'the distressed state of Mr Haslam and his family'. It must only have had a limited effect, for one month later Haslam was forced to auction off his entire library of rare medical books, some of which dated to medieval times. This at least allowed him to purchase an MD from Marischal College, Aberdeen, after which he began to build a career as a medical expert in insanity. To bolster this in 1817 he published Considerations on the Moral Management of Insane Persons, which defended his views on the origins and treatment of insanity but also criticised Wakefield, Tuke and other reformers who, in Haslam's eyes, were interferers in a subject area about which they knew next to nothing.[201]

Madness, wrote Haslam, was 'the peculiar and exclusive province of the medical practitioner', while Wakefield and others were 'zealots of reformation, [whose] powerful and adventurous spirits have the magnanimity to depreciate experience; flushed with hope, and confident of untried speculation, they nobly press forward to surmount the obstacles of nature', but the end result will be 'a dreary waste – a desolate monument of folly and expense'.

The embittered Haslam managed to carve out a new career for himself and regained some respect as a member of London's medical community. He continued to criticise the authorities for their interference with the treatment of the insane and managed to gain something of an academic reputation for his understanding of the human mind. However, and despite becoming a noted comic writer, his new-found life did not provide him with much of an income (or if it did, he did not hang on to it for long). When Haslam died in 1844 his entire estate was worth just £100, but he was fondly remembered by friends as being 'entertaining and full of anecdote'.[202]

The removal of Haslam and Monro did little to divert Wakefield, Rose and other reformers from their goal of revising the 1774 Madhouse Act. On 28 May 1816 George Rose was given leave to present his Bill, which was based on the findings of the Select Committee. On this occasion, and during subsequent debates, Rose and his colleagues highlighted the many deficiencies of the 1774 Madhouse Act, which included the inability of commissioners to get patients liberated, to force improvements onto asylums and to exclude permanently rogue owners from managing madhouses. This, they stated, was contributing to continued abuse at many private and public madhouses, including Bethlem.[203]

Rose argued that in future all madhouses, including Bethlem, 'should be twice a year examined by eight commissioners appointed by the secretary of state for the home department, throughout the kingdom. The commissioners to be assisted by two of the local magistrates in each district, armed with equal powers, and the members for counties to share this privilege. There was also provision in the bill relative to the erection of lunatic asylums in counties, and ordering the reception therein of pauper lunatics, who were allowed at present to range abroad, to their own and the public injury.'[204]

This was exactly the sort of outcome that the Bethlem Governors had spent years trying to avoid as it challenged both their authority and that of their senior officers. Rose was confident that his new Madhouse Bill would be passed, but the attempt to introduce it into law in 1816 failed after the House of Lords stalled its progress. A further attempt was made in early 1817 but this too was halted by the Lords; in neither case did the Peers give a reason for their rejection, leaving the reformers mystified and angry but still determined to carry on.

The death of George Rose in January 1818 led to his friend and fellow MP Charles Wynn taking up the cause in his place, declaring that, despite the Lords' intransigence, 'it is the duty of the House to persist in its purpose'. In March 1819 the Bill again came before the Commons and, in June, was passed over to the Lords, where it was vigorously opposed by the Earl of Eldon, the Lord Chancellor, who argued that it sought too much power and would cause problems with the care and cure of lunatics. He was especially concerned at the idea of offering whistle-blowers immunity from prosecution:

'It is important that the superintendence of physicians should not be interfered with. The Bill gave a number of penalties, half of which were to go to the informer, and it was evident that the informer would be found amongst the attendants and servants who would thus be made the judges of the physicians, and it would be impossible for the latter, under such circumstances, to resort to many of those means which their experience taught them were most effectual for the cure of their unhappy patients: for there could not be a more false humanity than over humanity with regard to persons afflicted with insanity.'

Eldon admitted that the 1774 Act was problematic and offered to make provision for pauper lunatics, but he was fundamentally opposed to Rose's Bill as it stood. His opinion carried the weight of his colleagues and it was yet again rejected by thirty-five votes to fourteen. Eldon had been known to oppose other reform bills, but his arguments against the transfer of power away from medics bear a similarity to the views of John Haslam and other professional mad doctors. This suggests that the Lords could have been influenced by the medical establishment or perhaps even Bethlem's Governors themselves who, after all, were not above lobbying Parliament. Eldon suggested that the Bill be totally revised before being brought before the House again, but Wynn did not have the heart to continue the fight, so the matter of reforming the 1774 Madhouse Act was dropped.[205]

The madhouse reform movement had achieved much over the previous few years, not least the transformation of conditions at several asylums, including York and Bethlem, but its ultimate goal of forcing England's madhouses to adopt the practices recommended by Samuel Tuke had ended in failure. Private madhouses were still subject to the 1774 Act and Bethlem remained a self-regulating institution that was beyond the reach of the inspectors and reformers. However, the campaign orchestrated by Tuke, Rose, Wakefield and others had led to a public awareness about mental health and the treatment of the insane. This, surely, would prevent some of the alleged instances of abuse from happening again, wouldn't it?

Bedlam

PART FOUR

The Last Battle

20

Sketches in Bedlam

The dismissal of John Haslam and Thomas Monro had been demanded by Wakefield and other reformers in a belief that their replacements would be more familiar with Samuel Tuke's moral therapy. What they did not reckon on was the degree of irritation felt by Bethlem's Governors, many of whom were seething at the outside interference in their affairs. The election of a new Apothecary had been a relatively uncontroversial procedure that resulted in the appointment of George Wallett, but the election for the all-important post of Physician was not so straightforward; it was a far more politically charged affair.

The first hint of controversy came in May 1816 when Edward Wakefield wrote to Bethlem's Governors expressing, among other things, his concern about a rumour that a Dr Edward Monro had put his name forward for the post of Physician. 'Is the gentleman, or not, the son of Dr [Thomas Monro] to whom I alluded in my last letter? If he is not then it is an extraordinary coincidence.'

In the week before the election those who wished to be considered as candidates for the post announced their interest by placing advertisements in The Times. Many eminent names came forward including the reformers Henry Clutterbuck (who had examined James Tilly Matthews in 1809 and declared him sane), George Man Burrows (a retired general practitioner) and Robert Williams (who had once put himself forward as a madhouse inspector for the College of Physicians). The other candidates were, as Wakefield had feared, Edward Monro (the son of Thomas) and George Leman Tuthill, the Physician to Westminster Hospital.[206]

It is said that there was a mood of defiance amongst the Governors when they met at midday sharp on 13 June to select their new Physician. They had suffered much at the hands of Wakefield and cannot have been best pleased to find that the majority of the candidates for the job were sympathetic to the ideas of Samuel Tuke. The last thing the Governors needed was a Physician who would make their lives yet more awkward, so a message of non-cooperation was sent to the outside: the Governors selected the one person who was guaranteed to get people's hackles up, Dr Edward Monro. This act did not go entirely without remark; some of the Governors were active in the reform movement and questioned Edward Monro's suitability for the post. The debate became heated and was only diffused after it was suggested that Bridewell and Bethlem should have not one but two Physicians. (It was even suggested that a third Physician should be added to the staff, but this idea was rejected.) Having more than one Physician was a commitment that had first been made in 1728 but, at the insistence of the previous three Dr Monros, had not been acted upon. However, in the current circumstance this solved not only the questionable decision to place yet another Dr Monro in sole charge of the patients, but also allowed the attendance rota to be split so that the Physicians could visit on alternate days, thus increasing the medical staff's overall hours of attendance. This having been agreed, the new created post of joint Physician was given to George Leman Tuthill, the only other non-reformist candidate on the list.

The announcement that the Monros had managed to get a fourth gen-eration of their family shoehorned into Bethlem was greeted with incredulity by Wakefield and his colleagues. A few days later Sir Robert Seymour was drawn to criticise Bethlem's medical regime in Parliament: 'The patients are periodically physicked, bled and vomited, and this too, without much reference to any difference of circumstances which may exist between case and case.'

There was little that could be done and, much as Wakefield and his colleagues would have liked to have had a Tuke-style reformer as Physician, their influence over the Governors was limited. They would have to hope that Edward Monro was capable of escaping from his family's reputation for conservatism and arrogance and that Tuthill was a forward-thinking and considerate practitioner.[207]

At the time of becoming Bethlem Physician, Edward Monro was still a very inexperienced medic and had only received his MD from Oxford University just over a year earlier. There was little on his CV to recommend him for the post other than his genetic relationship to the previous incumbent. At nearly forty-four years of age, George Tuthill was seventeen years older than Monro and had led a rich life that included a lengthy spell as a prisoner inside a Parisian gaol at the hands of Napoleon. He did not receive his MD until after his appointment to Bethlem, but by this stage he already had several years of experience as the Physician to Westminster Hospital where he was renowned for being a good chemist. Although not directly connected with the madhouse reformers, Tuthill was a progressive thinker and, in the years to come, would become known for the changes he made within the Royal College of Physicians.[208]

To many people's surprise, the partnership between the inexperienced Edward Monro and the ambitious George Tuthill proved to be successful. From the outset Dr Monro did not display the stubbornness and egotism attributed to his ancestors and appears to have been happy sharing power with Tuthill. As far as can be gathered, it was left to Tuthill to devise changes to the medical regime at the new Bethlem Hospital. Tuthill was by far the more experienced medic and, while not a follower of Samuel Tuke, he seems to have recognised the value of some of the practices operating at the York Retreat and other institutions such as St Luke's Hospital.

Within months of his appointment Tuthill had initiated a series of reforms within Bethlem that saw a reduction in the use of chains and fetters to restrain patients (although the practice was not abandoned entirely, as some reformers had requested) and a reduction in the use of purgative medicines and venous bleeding. In their place came some ideas that were taken directly from Samuel Tuke, most notably the encouragement of inmates to take exercise in the airing grounds and, more importantly, by dividing them into separate groups.

The crumbling infrastructure in the Moorfields Bethlem had forced Haslam to collectivise all his patients into the same space, a practice that James Tilly Matthews and the 1815 Select Committee had found especially repugnant. Tuthill rectified this by suggesting that the St George's Fields building should have a hierarchy of male and female galleries based on the nature of the patients' behaviour and their degree of recovery. The worst sort of patient, those who were violent or raving, were confined to the basement, while the ground floor housed those who showed signs of recovery and the first floor those who were on their way to being cured. In addition, patients with specialist needs, such as those who were ill, aged or incurable, would be placed in other parts of the hospital.

This was a great improvement on the old system, but Bethlem's limited resources sometimes led to problems with a lack of cells in one gallery necessitating some patients to spend the night elsewhere in the hospital. 'It sometimes happens', wrote Francis Martin in 1836, 'that patients belonging to the upper galleries are compelled by their infirmities to pass the night in the basement while, on the other hand, some who sleep in the upper galleries are placed in the basements in the day.'[209]

From the moment of his arrival George Tuthill was very careful to keep a record of his actions and of any problems he perceived with the hospital. Each year he would gather these notes together and turn them into a report from the medical staff, which would be submitted to the Governors for their assessment. This ensured that, unlike the days of Thomas Monro and John Haslam, the Governors could not use ignorance as an excuse should any complaints be levied against the medical staff.

Such complaints appear to have been few in number and there was a general consensus that, following the revelations made by the Select Committee in 1815, the new Bethlem Hospital was operating under a humane regime. The degree to which the Governors had become aware of their public image was demonstrated in 1818 when an ex-patient named Urbane Metcalf self-published a pamphlet that purported to give a description of everyday life for some of Bedlamites.

Metcalf was a controversial character who had at one time hawked garters, laces and other sundries in and around London and who would occasionally suffer from the delusion that he was heir to the throne of Denmark. In October 1817 Metcalf caused a disruption during a Royal performance at the Weymouth Theatre, which, in common with other potential assailants on Royalty such as Margaret Nicholson and James Hadfield, ended with a trip to Bedlam. In fact, Metcalf had been a regular private madhouse patient for more than twenty years before his admission to Bethlem and although deluded he was generally considered to have been a co-operative patient by the hospital's staff. He had, for example, never been known to refuse medicine or to become objectionable and violent. In the autumn of 1818, and after responding well to treatment, Metcalf was released, although one of the medical staff noted that: 'There is something peculiar in his manner... I cannot help thinking that there is some latent disorder existing.'

A few months later saw the publication of Metcalf's *The Interior of Bethlehem Hospital*, a thruppenny leaflet that gives a curiously detached description of everyday life within the hospital. Metcalf was not very complimentary about his stay but, rather than providing lurid descriptions of physical abuse, as might have been the case in the old building, he instead chose to highlight perceived shortcomings among several members of staff, most notably George Wallett the Apothecary, Alfred Humby the new Steward, and Dr Edward Monro.

The seriousness of Metcalf's charges have been subject to much debate over the years, some believing him to have been nothing more than a troublemaker and a peddler of half-truths. Certainly many of the abuses he describes are in the eye of the beholder and can be interpreted in different ways. Take, for example, his description of Bethlem's basement, which he accurately describes as being 'for those patients who are not cleanly in their persons, and who on that account have no beds, but lie on straw with blankets and a rug.' However, he makes it sound more sinister by adding, without further evidence, that 'it is too often made a place of punishment to gratify the unbounded cruelties of the keepers.'

Metcalf had a vendetta against Dr Monro but most of the incidents he cites against him are somewhat trivial:

'I well remember on Saturday, the day after Good Friday, a patient of the name of Lloyd, Dr Monro's patient, was in the Green Yard, no other patient being there, during two or three hours' excessive rain, Dr Monro going through the upper gallery with a friend with him, came to the window of the keeper's room, I was standing by, he observed to his friend that that was the airing yard, I opened the window hoping that he would see Lloyd in the green yard but he took no notice of him although he, Lloyd, appeared to me to stand in full view.'[210]

Metcalf took the trouble to send copies of his leaflet to some of Bethlem's Governors, which, in the post-1815 climate, ensured that action would be taken. The criticisms of Edward Monro were of a relatively minor nature and, while revealing a certain lack of bedside manner, did not amount to actual cruelty. They were dismissed, but Metcalf's accusation that the Apothecary and Steward were guilty of extortion and embezzlement were taken more seriously.

A Governors' inquiry into Metcalf's allegations revealed that Wallett had been charging the relations of a wealthy inmate several guineas a week for a private room when in fact the patient was being housed inside the criminal block at the Government's expense. The Steward, a man named Humby, had discovered this impropriety but, instead of reporting it, had agreed to take a cut of the cash from Wallett. When confronted, the pair admitted to taking the money and put the affair down to 'an error of judgement'. Aware that they were fighting for their jobs, the two men wrote a letter to the Governors that consisted mostly of pathetic pleading.

'We commit our case to you,' wrote Wallett and Humby, 'confiding in your avowal that there is no person at all times so entirely himself, nor any man so perfect in his judgement, but that error will sometimes steal his best ideas, and place him on a basis of fragile composition.'[211]

This verbal self-flagellation cut no ice with the Governors, who summarily dismissed the errant officers in March 1819. Fortunately for the hospital, Metcalf's leaflet did not get distributed widely, sparing Bethlem's staff the embarrassment of yet another public scandal. The vacant positions were quickly filled by Edward Wright, who became resident Apothecary, and Nathaniel Nicholls, who became the Steward. During his three decades at Bethlem Nicholls did not engender much complaint; Wright's time there was less harmonious.

Like many of Bethlem's newly appointed staff, Wright was sympathetic to the reform movement and was even personally acquainted with Edward

Wakefield. When appointing Wright, the Governors at last recognised the importance of the Apothecary to the overall medical regime at Bethlem by giving him the title Superintendent, in return for which he had to make daily tours of the hospital.

Edward Wright was a well-qualified medic and a strong advocate of the new 'science' of phrenology, which held that the shape of a person's head could be used to diagnose his or her character, personality traits, and criminality. (This is where the expression 'having your bumps felt' probably originates, referring to the manner in which phrenologists would use their hands to feel for the shape of a patient's head.) He was deemed suitable for the post of Apothecary and began his career at Bethlem with some promising innovations, the most notable of which was the establishment of a free consultancy service for ex-patients; there were also occasions when Wright would travel, free of charge, to the houses of old patients. This was in marked contrast to not only his predecessors but also to Edward Monro and Tuthill, both of whom continued to charge exorbitantly for private consultations.

During his first few years as Apothecary, Wright seems to have enjoyed his job and to have developed a good working relationship with both Monro and Tuthill. In fact, things were looking up for Bethlem in general when in July 1823 an anonymous book, entitled *Sketches in Bedlam*, was published, which strove to end some of the rumours that still persisted about the hospital.

The tone of *Sketches in Bedlam* is not dissimilar to that of the promotional pamphlet produced by Thomas Bowen in 1783 in that it offers an entirely optimistic and glowing account of day-to-day life inside the hospital. The level of detail and comments about individual patients meant that the anonymous author was either a member of staff or had recently been so. The prospect of publications by staff members disturbed the Governors, who began a hunt to unmask the mysterious writer, who had simply signed himself 'A Constant Observer'.

Two Special Committees met on 16 and 19 July during which a shortlist of prime suspects was drawn up. Many considered John Haslam to be a strong candidate as author, as did a majority of Bethlem's staff, but much of the detail provided in the book concerned patients, events and routines that had arrived long after the disgraced Apothecary's departure. A much better candidate was the current Apothecary, Edward Wright, whose name occurs continually throughout the book, usually in very favourable terms. He is, for example, observed to have performed 'the duties of his situation, arduous as they are, with diligence and regularity, highly to his honour: ever attentive and humane towards the unhappy patients and kind and considerate to all acting under his authority.'[212]

As the prime suspect, Wright was hauled before the Special Committee and challenged on the issue, but he denied all knowledge of the book. In his defence, Wright claimed that an ex-keeper from the Hospital, James Smyth, had admitted in writing to being the author. Naturally the Committee members asked to see Smyth's written confession but Wright refused, claiming that he had not kept it. The Governors were less than convinced by this and tried to secure a meeting with Smyth, but the former member of staff 'respectfully declined to attend'. As a consequence, Wright remained at the top of their list of suspects but, with no positive proof, he was not reprimanded.

Sketches in Bedlam proved to be popular and was to provide the world with its first view of the inside of the hospital since the dark days of the 1816 Select Committee. The book's outline of daily life in Bethlem showed the advances that had been made following the move to St George's Fields. The most obvious difference was the application of regular and rigorous care routines for the inmates. No longer were the Bedlamites left semi-naked, chained to walls in cells coated in festering straw; instead they were housed individually in cells that had iron beds with flock mattresses, pillows, blankets and linen, all of which were laundered weekly (although some of the 'disorderly patients' in the basement were still sleeping on straw). Inmates were given regular food, medical treatment, exercise and baths, while the use of restraint was minimised only to the most disruptive cases. In place of chains, it was claimed that unruly inmates would be confined 'to their rooms for an hour or two, until they become cool and orderly.' The book also describes Bethlem's twice-weekly church services, which had been introduced in 1816 against the wishes of Monro and Tuthill, both of whom believed that it would disrupt the inmates. These fears proved to be unfounded.

Despite its obsequiousness, much of what is described in *Sketches* was based on fact (other inspections confirm it), but with an added dose of positive spin and fanciful thinking. For example, patients receiving outside visitors (a practice that was banned in Moorfields) are alleged to 'come up [from their rooms] cheerfully, receive with ecstasy the hopes their friends give them, and depart from the meeting generally gratified.'

Following some forty pages of fawning over Bethlem's management ('unparalleled in any other part of the world') the remainder of *Sketches* goes on to outline the individual cases of 140 patients then resident, including famous names such as James Hadfield, Margaret Nicholson and Bannister Truelock.

Most of these descriptions are short and take the form of general notes about their behaviour. George Watson, for example, is described as being 'very much disordered in the mind, highly irritable, and will strike furiously at any one on the slightest offence. He speaks very seldom, and is in general quiet and inoffensive.' Some of the more sensationalist cases receive longer write-ups, including many of those confined in the criminal department for offences such as murder. The insight *Sketches* provides into Bethlem's intake of patients is remarkable and indicates that, while the majority of patients came in as charity cases, there were still a fair few people from educated and wealthy backgrounds among its number. It is noticeable that even in the nineteenth century 'religious exuberance' remained a prominent cause of referral to Bethlem, as did delusions of the individual being a member of the Royal Family (this is especially true of the female patients). The descriptions of each person's background, behaviour and prognosis suggests not only that the author of *Sketches* had an intimate knowledge of the patients, but also that the medical staff were now looking to treat each case individually rather than by the universal application of bleeding and vomits as was the case until 1816.[213]

It was, however, this naming of patients and description of their condition that had so infuriated Bethlem's Governors. The entire book was deemed to have been a breach of trust between the patient and the hospital, and led to the Governors issuing a furious public denouncement:

'The committee is of the opinion, on the whole, that the work in question is disgraceful to the writer, and disgusting to the reader, displaying an inexcusable violation of the confidences of the Governors in some person, who is, or has been, under their employ, and manifesting the most unkind and improper feeling towards the unhappy patients and their friends in making the public parties to their private history, their mental affliction, and their personal infirmities.'[214]

The Governors were right to be concerned at the publication of personal case notes, but the glowing picture of Bethlem presented by *Sketches* did convince many people that Bethlem had changed for the better. The new regime had learned much from the mistakes of the past and outside visitors were once again welcomed into the hospital, provided they were accompanied by a Governor. Many chose to leave comments of their visit in a guest book, which contained remarks from physicians, surgeons, politicians and the landed gentry, all of whom seem to have found Bethlem to their liking. On 19 May 1820, for example, Dr Charles Pennington recorded that: 'I have this day visited every part of this establishment, and have great pleasure in testifying to the excellent management of all its parts.'

A more impressive view was given by John Capper, a member of the Home Secretary's staff, who had been despatched to check out the hospital's criminal wing in June 1818. He writes that:

'The prisoners appear clean, amply supplied with wholesome provisions, and well clothed; and when I view the nature of the crimes which many of these unfortunates had committed, and the terror which had been created in the minds of those persons who formerly had custody of them, prior to their removal to this establishment, I cannot refrain from noticing, that I did not find one of these prisoners under restraint of either handcuffs or fetters.'[215]

With such positive testimonies, it is surprising to find that at the time of the publication of *Sketches* there were vacancies for thirty-eight male and twelve female inmates. Given that the old Bethlem had a waiting list with dozens of names on it, this might suggest that the reputation afforded to the hospital by the 1815 Select Committee was dissuading admissions. In this respect the positive descriptions in *Sketches* in Bedlam may have been of some help as only a short while later Bethlem once more found itself with a full complement of patients.[216]

21

A Reformed Hospital?

In the years following the failure of Rose's reforming Madhouse Bill of 1819 there had been occasional talk of trying to bring Bethlem under the umbrella of the 1774 Madhouse Act, but nothing came of this. It was not until 1827 that the campaigners started to stir themselves again after Garrett Dillon uncovered instances of physical abuse at a private madhouse in Hoxton. The resultant outcry brought the matter of madhouse reform back before Parliament and, following yet another Select Committee inquiry, led to the passing of the 1828 Madhouse Act. At the heart of this new legislation was the establishment of a Metropolitan Lunacy Commission, a body that covered only London asylums but which had the added ability for its inspectors to revoke the licences of individual madhouses and to free individual patients (county commissioners were also given these new powers). The Act also required that all asylums containing more than 100 inmates had to have a residential medic and that a religious service should be conducted once a week.

Improvements did follow, especially in the private madhouses, two of which were immediately shut down, but the widespread use of magistrates as lay inspectors led to problems as many of them proved unable or unwilling to take on the role afforded to them. This issue, and several other amendments, was dealt with in 1832 when MPs passed the Act for the Care and Treatment of Insane Persons, which had been sponsored by the Lord Chancellor.

Many private madhouse owners fought tooth and nail against both these Bills, but to no effect. The same was not true of Bethlem Hospital, whose

Governors are estimated to have spent several hundred pounds on campaigns to exclude the hospital's inclusion in these Madhouse Bills. Their campaigning was successful and by 1832 Bethlem was the only asylum to be specifically excluded from outside inspection. Given past ferocity over this issue, there seems to have been remarkably little fuss over Bethlem's exclusion, but the decision was later questioned when a whiff of scandal again pervaded the hospital's corridors.[217]

The first predicament concerned the Apothecary Edward Wright, whose opening years of employment were generally adjudged to have been successful and productive. However, following the publication of Sketches in Bedlam (which Wright was widely believed to have written) the relationship between the Apothecary and other members of staff became somewhat more strained. A particular bone of contention was Wright's professional interest in phrenology and the physical workings of the human brain. It was Wright's belief that the origins of madness lay in physical defects within the brain, which suggested to him that some forms of madness were ultimately incurable; this view was against prevailing thought, which suggested that the correct management of all lunatics could eventually bring about a cure. To prove his point Wright took advantage of his position as the senior residential medical officer to perform autopsies on those patients who were unfortunate enough to die while staying in Bethlem.

Wright spent increasing amounts of time in the hospital mortuary where he would indulge his passion for post-mortem phrenology, a practice that some on the staff found distasteful. At the same time he began to display signs of instability and was frequently observed to be in a drunken state while on hospital premises. This behaviour took a turn for the worse when, on the night of 25 August 1830, Wright was discovered 'in a very intoxicated state' inside the female galleries. His clothes were reported to have been dishevelled and he was said to have been 'associating' with a woman at the time. Although Wright contrived to hush up this matter, somebody tipped off one of Bethlem's reformist-minded Governors, Colonel James Clitherow, who immediately advised the Apothecary that he should resign his position so as to avoid bringing the hospital into disrepute again. Wright refused, so Clitherow placed him on suspension, pending an inquiry into his behaviour.

On 28 September 1830 a special Court of Governors met to investigate Wright's recent record at Bethlem. Although he had initially been charged with being drunk on duty (the alleged incident of sexual misconduct was ignored), the investigation revealed other indiscretions. One of these was Wright's failure to keep proper case notes, which was serious enough, but it was the discovery that he had routinely been removing the heads of dead patients and keeping them that proved to be his undoing. The Governors discovered this after interviewing one of the keepers, who was asked why Wright spent such long periods of time in the mortuary:

'Smoking,' replied the keeper, 'and opening and taking off the heads of the dead patients occasionally.'

The Governors were shocked and asked the keeper what Wright did with the heads, thinking that they might form part of a medical study.

'They are frequently put into pans,' said the keeper, 'and allowed to lie there till the skin or flesh got off; and I suppose they were taken away after that.'

Wright was hauled before his inquisitors and asked to explain his fascination with his patients' skulls. Like his predecessors, Wright argued that his mortuary research was perfectly normal and that, furthermore, it had the blessing of the rest of the medical staff. As proof Wright summoned and cross-examined Edward Monro and George Tuthill in front of the Governors.

'In your opinion, as a medical man of many years standing, is it good and profitable to inspect the heads and bodies of the dead?' asked Wright of Tuthill.

'Certainly it is,' replied the Physician.

'Did you, of your own knowledge, ever know that any inconvenience arose from that practice in Bethlem Hospital?'

'Certainly not.'

'Do you not believe that it is one of the grand means, by a sedulous prosecution of which we can, and can alone, expect to better our knowledge of insanity?'

'I do.'

'Did it ever come to your knowledge that I had made such dissections?'

'Certainly.'

Even with Tuthill's backing, Wright was deemed to have 'forfeited the confidence of the Governors' and in November 1830 he was sacked, albeit with a £200 pay-off. According to Clitherow, Wright was 'a degraded character, unfit for the association of gentlemen'. Wright was incensed and, like Haslam before him, fought his dismissal tooth and nail but to no effect. With his reputation tarnished, he worked abroad periodically before permanently moving to Australia in 1836. His problems with alcoholism continued and culminated in 1845 with his trial for the manslaughter of a patient owing to negligence and drunkenness: he was acquitted on a technicality.[218]

Bethlem's Governors experienced a lucky escape with Wright, whose behaviour and dismissal failed to attract much public attention. The same would not be true of their next bête noire, Bolton Hudson, who had been the receiver and accountant to Bridewell and Bethlem since 1820. Given that both institutions had previously suffered greatly at the hands of embezzlers, it might be expected that the move to St George's Fields would have engendered a culture of better financial management. This had certainly been the Governors' intention, but their planned annual close audit of the accounts never materialised, leaving Hudson free to pocket large sums of money that were being paid to the hospital in rent.

The situation continued for years until April 1835 when one of the Governors became suspicious and asked that the annual accounts be given to an independent auditor to check. Although some impropriety had been suspected, the true scale of Hudson's fraud was mind-blowing; it was calculated that in the course of a decade or so the accountant had managed to pocket £10,066 (around £800,000 today), of which almost £9,000 had come directly from Bethlem's coffers. With another financial disaster looming, the arrest of Hudson was ordered, but the accountant had by then fled to France with his family where he remained beyond the reach of the British law.

Legal proceedings within Britain recovered £3,000 from Hudson's estate, but worse news was to come as the accountants found evidence of a further financial fraud, this time by Thomas Coles, Bridewell and Bethlem's Treasurer, who had been suspected of keeping some of the charitable donations for himself. Coles was forced to resign in December 1835 and a few months later it was estimated that he had taken £5,000, but by this time he too was living in France with his family. Bethlem received a net loss of £12,000, a sum that represented nearly an entire year's income; more than half a century earlier an equivalent fraud by William Kinleside had caused years of financial turmoil, but this time there was no follow-up crisis.

How this loss was made good is not known, but embarrassment over the fraud caused the Governors to cover up the affair, ensuring that neither Hudson nor Coles would be prosecuted for their crimes; indeed, Hudson is alleged to have qualified for a pension from Bethlem in his later years. A new Treasurer and accountant were appointed and, as usual after such a scandal, accountancy procedures were tightened, but several years later an audit revealed that embezzlement was still a problem among the staff.[219]

The financial scandal involving Hudson and Coles did not draw much adverse publicity towards Bethlem and Bridewell, but news of it did circulate and was to have other unforeseen consequences. In some reformist circles there was still much anger that Bethlem had managed to exempt itself from the 1828 and 1832 Madhouse Acts (and thus also from the need for mandatory inspections), but news of the embezzlement provided them with another route by which an official inspection could be obtained.

In 1818 concerns over the financial practices of charitable organisations led the British Government to launch a wide-ranging investigation into the activities of all such bodies operating within England and Wales. The resultant investigative body was the Charity Commission, an institution that had the power to make inquiries into the assets, financial affairs and management of any charitable institution. The Charity Commission had twenty permanent Commissioners, any two of whom could come together to initiate an inquiry. With around 30,000 charities to examine, the Charity Commission was struggling to cope with its task, so much so that by 1835 there was a great desire to speed up the process; accordingly, the number of Commissioners needed to undertake an inquiry was dropped from two to just one. This decision coincided with the revelation of the fraud inside Bethlem and Bridewell, an event that appears to have caught the attention of a Charity Commissioner named Francis Offley Martin, a man who had links with many radical reformers including 'Honest Tom' Duncombe, a vigorous campaigner for the regulation of all madhouses.

Bethlem Hospital might have been operating outside the reach of London's Metropolitan Lunacy Commission but, as a charitable institution, it was subject to the will of the Charity Commission, which was at liberty to make a detailed inspection whenever it suited. It was Francis Martin who, in 1836, took advantage of the situation by empowering himself to make an official inspection into the hospital's affairs.

The Charity Commission was by and large concerned with investigating individual charities with the purpose of listing and auditing their assets (especially property), their income and expenditure (including the manner in which money was spent), and who was responsible for the general management. However, Commissioner Martin was to broaden the scope of his inquiry into Bethlem considerably so that it would include not just financial details but every aspect of the hospital's organisation, including the manner in which it was treating its inmates. It is questionable as to whether Martin had the power to do this, but by order of the Government Francis Martin claimed he was free to examine whatever paperwork he wanted and to look in any part of the hospital at any time of day or night, and the Governors did not challenge this. After twenty years on the St George's Fields site, Bedlam was to receive its first all encompassing inspection.220

Martin busied himself in Bethlem during the latter part of 1836, minutely examining its accounts, title deeds, rents, Committee minutes, etc, as well as making lengthy tours of the hospital building making note of its general condition and suitability for the task of housing lunatics. He also inspected its staff, officers and even Governors, observing them at work, questioning them about their routines and the effectiveness of their procedures. No stone was left unturned and, given Martin's radical connections and Bethlem's historical reputation for cruelty, it might have been expected that the resultant report would be damning. However, Martin was an experienced Commissioner who was not prone to exaggerate the truth to suit his political feelings; his final report, published in 1837, was fair and balanced and revealed to the world just how much Bethlem had changed during the previous two decades.

In common with its primary objective, Martin's report devotes much space to looking at the hospital's accounts. Despite the 1835 fraud, Martin reveals

that the finances were sound, with the annual income hovering at around
£16,000, a figure that did not include a small profit obtained from the
Government funding of the Criminal Department. However, problems still
remained with paying for the incurable lunatics who on average cost three
times more than their curable counterparts and whose average stay in
Bethlem was twelve years. To compensate for this, the Governors had been
'borrowing' large sums from the hospital's general fund to pay for the
shortfall in the incurable fund, something of which Martin disapproved.
Beyond this, and the regrettable frauds, Bethlem's finances were generally
thought to be on a fairly sound footing, which was in great contrast to the dire
financial crisis of a few decades previously.

The finances dealt with, Martin moved on to the issue of medical
treatment, which, again, proved to be much to the Commissioner's liking.
Dr Edward Monro was deemed to have departed from the bad habits of his
father and was observed to attend the hospital regularly and his patients
diligently. The other joint Physician was no longer George Tuthill, who had
died a year previously, but instead Dr Alexander Morison, a thirty-six-year-
old medic who had been studying mental health for more than a decade and
had even authored two books on the subject. Morison ran a successful
independent practice with many wealthy clients, yet during Martin's visits
the new Physician was spending up to four hours at a time in the hospital.
'The patients are visited by him individually, every one of them, being
considered under his own peculiar care,' wrote Martin, who made no
reference to the use of bleeding, vomits, laxatives, caustics or any of the other
physical treatments that had been in use under Thomas Monro.

With the medical regime generally to his liking, Martin examined the
treatment of the inmates, of which again he seemed to broadly approve.
Certainly the conditions in which they were being kept was vastly different
from that seen in the old Moorfields building:

'Few sights can be more gratifying than the present condition of the
interior of Bethlem. The scrupulous cleanliness which prevails
throughout the house, the decent attire of the patients, and the
unexpectedly small number of those under restraint (sometimes not

one person throughout the building)… The galleries and sleeping-rooms being swept out every morning, and scoured all over at least twice a week. On the basement the floors are of stone, and in the sleeping-rooms slope towards a grate for purposes of drainage. When used by dirty patients they are scrubbed daily, and on the female side are also washed over with a solution of lime and water, by which a cheerful appearance is preserved.'[221]

The patients were observed to be properly fed, washed and shaved regularly, to have decent clothes and bedding and to be kept warm and dry during the winter months. This was all to Bethlem's credit, but Martin did have some reservations about the hospital, the most serious of which was the lack of occupational therapy for inmates.

For some years George Tuthill had tried to effect an employment regime for the inmates but with only limited success. The arrival of Morison, who was a moderate supporter of Tuke's moral management ideas, had seen the expansion of this programme, allowing Martin to report that able-bodied patients 'are set to work as soon as possible about the ordinary business of the house, in assisting the nurses and keepers in making the beds, washing and cleaning the wooden bowls and trenchers used at meal times, scouring, washing and sweeping the galleries.' Others were employed to knit, mend or wash clothes.

Bethlem had also introduced some leisure facilities. 'In the airing ground some of the men play at ball, trap-ball, leap-frog, cricket and other games. The patients also amuse themselves with cards and dominoes and the women are encouraged to dance together in the evenings.' Martin noted, however, that there were only sixty-two books available for the patients to read.

Despite this Martin declared that there was often the 'want of sufficient occupation of the men, the greater number of whom may be seen sauntering about the galleries in listless and hopeless indifference.' He believed that as well as knitting and cleaning, some men could be employed to do physical tasks such as gardening, shoemaking and metalworking. According to Martin this situation was compounded by the small size of Bethlem's airing grounds, which were greatly reduced by the presence of the Criminal Buildings.

Martin's greatest criticism was, however, a familiar one: 'It may be questioned whether the exemption of Bethlem from visitation under the Acts [of Parliament] is in any way beneficial.' Bethlem, he argued, still suffered from a culture of secrecy that dissuaded outsiders from taking an active interest in what occurred there, but there was an easy solution: allow the Physicians to take on students. 'This has no small effect in promoting the advancement of medicine and surgery, and in securing the good treatment of patients. At Bethlem there is no such stimulus to exertion, and but for the inquiry of the committee of 1814-15, the horrors which then existed unknown in the heart of the metropolis might, it is possible, have still prevailed.'

The overall conclusion of the Charity Commission's report was that in most respects Bethlem was little different from the many other charitable asylums operating in England and Wales. The Governors were told that they were presiding over a clean, efficient and generally humane institution, but that 'much yet remains to be accomplished'.[222]

As the new boy and an avowed reformer, Alexander Morison took many of Martin's criticisms to heart and tried both to widen the scope of the patient's employment and to introduce pupils into the medical system. On both accounts the Governors proved to be awkward and only made a limited provision. Monro and Morison were permitted to take on two pupils each, but a lack of financial and logistical support meant that much of the time all four places lay vacant. The Governors also failed to act on some of the more minor points raised by Martin, including the lack of a public annual report that provided details of any changes in staff and management and statistics associated with the patients. Such a document had been promised for decades but was not forthcoming, yet, ironically, it would have been easy to compile as there was a wealth of statistical data being recorded by staff at all levels.

The secrecy culture thus prevailed but, as Queen Victoria took the throne, so the madhouse reform movement began to gain a new momentum that included a desire for Bethlem to be brought in line with the rest of the country's asylums.

It was the reformist-minded medical newspaper *The Lancet* that, in November 1840, chose to launch the first serious public attack against

Bethlem since 1828. Under the editorship of Thomas Wakley, a campaigning MP and surgeon, *The Lancet* alleged that Bethlem was once again abusing its patients by the routine use of restraints such as chains and fetters. Evidence of this was provided by, among others, Charles Tulk, who described a visit he made to Bethlem on 31 October 1840 to see a man named Fransome:

> 'Upon opening the door [to his cell] the stench was loathsome in the extreme. I could scarcely enter it; for it was as bad as the filthiest dog-kennel. This patient was in a maniacal state but with occasional, though rare, glimpses of coherency ... He frequently said that he was shamefully used, and he offered us some pieces of wool, which he had torn off his dress, for us to smell, in proof of his dirty condition. His hands were manacled, and he was chained to the bed. This patient had been subject to restraint for, I believe, sixteen weeks.'[223]

Such allegations produced a flood of correspondence within *The Lancet*, much of it highlighting problems not just with Bethlem but with the asylum inspection regime in general. In September 1841 Thomas Wakley drew on his readers' complaints to register his opposition to the mandatory three-year renewal of the 1832 Madhouse Act. 'The treatment of lunatics had been much discussed of late,' said Wakley within the House of Commons, 'and it seemed to be a general impression that some alteration should be made in the existing law, and that without delay.'[224]

The attempt at preventing the Act's renewal failed and inspired Wakley and other like-minded MPs to put forward a Bill that would widen the Metropolitan Commissioners' geographical coverage. This had hitherto been limited to Greater London, but the reformers proposed extending their powers to asylums across the whole of England and Wales. This extension was needed because, according to some sources, many local magistrates had been issuing licences to asylums without having ever set foot inside them. The Bill's passage through Parliament was far from easy, with Wakley and others continually trying to alter its content to suit their purposes, but in May 1842 the Lunacy Inquiry Bill became law.

The Bill's chief aim was to ensure that all asylums would be inspected but, much to the outrage of Wakley, there was one institution that had been specifically excluded from inspection: 'The Lord Chancellor and/or Home Secretary may, if he or they think fit, require (in writing) the metropolitan commissioners to visit any such hospital or asylum (except Bethlem) and to report as to the state and condition thereof respectively and the system of treatment therein adopted, in such manner as they or he shall think fit.'[225]

Yet again pressure from Bethlem's Governors ensured that their hospital could remain outside the attention of the madhouse inspectors, but Wakley and *The Lancet* had rattled them. As madhouses around England and Wales spruced themselves up in preparation for the arrival of inspectors, so Bethlem made efforts to improve its public image also. In 1843 the Governors published their first ever annual report, something that had first been promised back in 1816. In response to some of Martin's earlier criticisms, the report agreed to make improvements to the range of employments undertaken by patients and to make proper provision for medical students at Bethlem. These small efforts were doubtless welcome but did little to deflect the approaching storm, for within the country at large the issue of lunacy and lunatic asylums was growing in prominence.[226]

By widening the Metropolitan Commissioners' sphere of influence, the Lunacy Inquiry Bill of 1842 revealed that many of the provincial madhouses were in a very poor state and that there was no central Government plan to deal with the nationwide issue of lunacy. The public's attention was sharpened when Daniel McNaughton, an alleged lunatic, stabbed to death the Prime Minister Robert Peel's secretary; the thought that there might be hundreds of dangerous lunatics wandering the streets inspired the Lord Chancellor to order the Metropolitan Commissioners to compile a report that listed all the asylums in England and Wales and detailed their physical condition, capacity, admission procedures, medical and other regimes.

The resultant report, published in 1844, revealed that the asylum system was in a state of chaos. Institutions showed themselves to be clogged with incurable patients, which was forcing potentially curable lunatics to be placed in workhouses where a good many of them quickly degenerated into an incurable state. It was estimated that, while there were approximately 17,000 pauper lunatics in England and Wales, there was only space for 4,500 in the public asylums.

Furthermore, for those lunatics that managed to find an asylum place, there was a wide variation in the quality of the institution and the treatment they experienced. Some were well run and did not restrain any of their patients; others were crumbling, brutal places with high death rates and violent medical treatments. In Durham, for example, the West Auckland Asylum was found to have 'a small, cheerless day-room of the males, with only one unglazed window; five men were restrained, by leg-locks, called hobbles, and two were wearing, in addition, iron-handcuffs and fetters from the wrist to the ankle: they were all tranquil. The reason assigned for this coercion was, that without it they would escape.'[227]

From the mass of data presented one fact was obvious: those asylums that were regularly visited by the Commissioners were much better run and had a higher cure rate than those that had received little or no attention from the inspectors. The Lunacy Inquiry Act revealed that the Acts of 1828 and 1832 were not working as intended and that further legislation was needed. In 1845, and following a series of impassioned speeches by Lord Ashley (a key promoter of lunacy reform), Parliament passed not one but two new Lunatic Acts.

The net effect of these two Acts was first to establish the Lunacy Commission, a permanent inspectorate that had the power to visit any and every the lunatic asylum in England and Wales, and second to make the building of county asylums compulsory. The new Lunacy Commission, which consisted of six inspectors, had the power to order changes to the institutions it visited, which included the ability to change aspects of patients' care and even to regulate their diet.

It was a great step forward, but there was again one great exception: at every stage Bethlem Hospital was specifically excluded from the new commissioners' remit. Some seasoned campaigners, such as Thomas Wakley and Thomas Duncombe, were absolutely furious. Duncombe fought tooth and nail to have Bethlem placed under the power of the Lunacy Commission, only to be defeated in the House of Lords, many of whose number served in the hospital's Court of Governors. He received just one compromise on this matter, a clause that held that the Lord Chancellor or Home Secretary could order an inspection of Bethlem if he felt there was a need for it. With feelings over Bethlem starting to run extremely high, the inclusion of this clause was to spark a prolonged battle between reformers within the new Lunacy Commission and Bethlem's Governors. After nearly a century of head-to-head confrontation with the madhouse reform movement, the final battle to bring Bethlem under the influence of official inspectors was about to begin.

22

The Battle for Bethlem

The 1845 Lunacy Act fulfilled many of the demands that had been made of Parliament by the madhouse reformers. It did not, however, give them their ultimate prize, the inclusion of Bethlem Hospital in the Lunacy Commission's general remit. To many this specific exclusion was illogical and perplexing. If, the reformers complained, the hospital was being run in a humane and efficient manner, as its Governors claimed, why did it insist on operating behind closed doors? This suggested to some that Bedlam was still hiding some terrible secrets in its wards, although there was little hard evidence to support this idea. However, facts were considered to be of lesser importance than the principle of inspection, so Bethlem found itself a cause célèbre for the madhouse reformers. An active search began for ways in which the hospital could be forced to surrender itself to the Lunacy Commission.

The campaigners quickly fixed their sights on the provision made in the 1845 Act for the Lord Chancellor or Home Secretary to order the Lunacy Commission to make an investigation should the need warrant it. To enact this clause would, however, require campaigners to supply proof of serious abuse or malpractice in Bethlem, but this was no easy thing. Since the notorious days of James Norris, Bethlem had been reformed and allegations of untoward behaviour toward patients were few and far between. Furthermore, many of those who had visited the hospital were happy with what they had witnessed, including an annual visit made to the Criminal Department by an envoy from the Home Office.

Finding an equivalent to the James Norris case was a tall task, but it did not stop the campaigners from trying. In 1847 and 1848 two alleged cases of abuse at Bethlem were drawn to the attention of the Lunacy Commission, which duly applied to the Lord Chancellor for the right to inspect the hospital under the 1845 Act. On both occasions permission was not forthcoming, it being adjudged that there was not enough proof of malpractice to warrant further action. The resistance exhibited by the Government to Bethlem's detractors, which included important figures such as Thomas Wakley, Lord Ashley and Thomas Duncombe, made it abundantly clear that the clause in the 1845 Act could only be used in the most extreme of circumstances, but the reformers did not have long to wait for this.[228]

In April 1851 Thomas Hyson, a newspaper proofreader from Lambeth, received news that his twenty-year-old daughter (and only child) Hannah was perilously ill following her admittance to Bethlem a few weeks earlier. Thomas and his wife went to see Hannah and were appalled at what they saw:

> 'What our feelings were I can hardly tell,' wrote Hyson to Bethlem's Governors, 'my Poor Girl could not stand, and was a complete idiot. But, sir, what was my horror when called up stairs by her Mother and others, when they had undressed her to put her to bed, her body, her legs, and her arms has above twenty wounds and lacerations on them, two also on her face; her bones ready to start through the skin, how caused or inflicted no one who has seen her but wish and desire to know.'[229]

Hannah Hyson died shortly afterwards and, following a series of complaints made by her father, a post-mortem was performed in front of him and all of Bethlem's medical officers together with several independent witnesses. The cause of death was deemed to be general paralysis, the girl's many wounds being diagnosed as self-inflicted following days of violent convulsion. Thomas Hyson was unhappy with the verdict and said so to the Governors; this inspired the Treasurer to make his own investigation into the state of the hospital, which, perhaps unsurprisingly, gave it a clean bill of health.

News of Hannah Hyson's alleged mistreatment soon found its way to the Lunacy Commissioners who, as luck would have it, were already investigating the case of Ann Morley, a former Bethlem patient who had been discharged a few months earlier in December 1850. On her release Morley had been examined by Dr Pearce Nesbitt at Northampton County Asylum, who was appalled to report that her 'system was so enfeebled that she was unable to sit up, she had a prolapsus of the uterus and anus with great mucous discharges and suffered severely from tenesmus [a feeling of incomplete defecation]. Her lower extremities were livid and oedematous and their motions paralysed.'[230]

Ann Morley was more fortunate that Hannah Hyson in that she was alive when she left Bethlem and, on recovering her health and senses, she began to accuse some of Bethlem's nurses of subjecting her to random acts of violence and cruelty. Nesbitt was appalled at what he heard and, even though there was little medical evidence to back up Morley's claims of violence, he reported the matter to the Lunacy Commission. The Commissioners took Morley's and Hyson's cases to the Home Secretary and again asked for his consent to conduct a full inspection of Bethlem. This time the evidence for abuse and medical malpractice appeared strong, allowing the Home Secretary to grant permission for an inspection. The Lunacy Commissioners wasted no time and, even though the official letter granting them an inspection had yet to be posted, on 28 June 1851 four Lunacy Commissioners arrived at the gates of Bethlem, demanding to be let in.

That four senior Commissioners should have volunteered to undertake the inspection (usually only one or two were required) suggests that the Lunacy Commission and its supporters were taking the opportunity offered to them very seriously indeed. This is further underlined by the choice of Commissioners, all of whom had connections with the asylum reform movement. Samuel Gaskell, for example, was an experienced mental health physician who had been in charge of Lancaster County Asylum, during which time he introduced many reforms. He was joined by his friends Bryan Procter, a solicitor with a brilliant literary mind, and William Campbell, a lawyer and promoter of madhouse reform, together with the surgeon Dr John Hume, who had been the Duke of Wellington's personal physician.[231]

This overwhelming collection of legal and medical firepower was an indication that Bethlem could yet again expect to have every aspect of its management examined and questioned in minute detail. The style of the inspection was particularly associated with Samuel Gaskell, the nominal head of the four Commissioners, who was once described as being 'very good tempered, accommodating, and unselfish … His only fault is that he is too minute and occasionally rather exacting.'

There was justifiable concern among the Governors and staff that the Commissioners had already decided that Bethlem was operating an abusive regime long before they had set foot inside the building. This sense of a fait accompli was probably heightened when it was discovered that the Home Secretary had not given the Commissioners permission to undertake a wide-ranging inquiry but had instead limited them to making a preliminary visit to the hospital. However, by the time this was discovered it was too late to stop the process: the Commissioners were already inside the building and were insistent on 'examining everyone and everything'.

The process lasted for months, during which time every member of staff was interviewed at least once, as were a number of the Governors, inmates and their relations. All recent paperwork was inspected, especially that relating to the medical officers, and the general condition of the galleries, cells, kitchens and other facilities observed. On a number of occasions the Commissioners left Bethlem for what appeared to be the last time only to return again a few days or weeks later claiming that they had uncovered new evidence that warranted required further exploration.

The Governors repeatedly asked the Commissioners to provide them with feedback from their inquiry and to discuss the nature of any complaints against the hospital, but they would not. It was a very trying time and there was every sign that the Commissioners were bending their operational rules in order to obtain an outcome that suited them. The Governors would later claim that witnesses were not allowed to check transcripts of interviews for accuracy, that the Commissioners had discarded positive evidence in favour of complaints from disgruntled staff members and ex-patients, and that, while every effort had been made to accommodate the many demands made of them, the inspectors had behaved in an aggressive and secretive manner. The Commissioners were also accused of having used poor interviewing tactics, which, as the following exchange demonstrates, included the use of leading questions.

Q: Where is the fault found?

A: The fault is to be found with Dr Wood.

Q: You think he is indolent and careless?

A: Yes.

Q: And he does not take sufficient trouble, you think?

A: No.[232]

In February 1852, and following eight months of turmoil, the completed Commissioners' report was delivered to Bethlem's President. Neither he nor the Governors had been given any idea as to what might be said about Bethlem, but they must have suspected that the Commissioners' tone would be critical. Even so, on reading the report they were shocked by its contents and at its central allegation of systematic neglect and abuse for which there was only a small amount of first-hand evidence. Instead, the Commissioners were apt to use hearsay accounts relating to incidents where patients had been left naked on wet and dirty straw or had been mopped down with cold water. It was alleged that the use of unnecessary restraint was rife throughout the wards and that medical staff were guilty of slack procedure, absenteeism and malpractice: it did not make for comfortable reading.

The ferocity of the Commissioners' conclusions took the President by surprise but he was not given long to digest the allegations when, after only a few days, the Home Secretary asked for an official response. The President argued that he would need to consult with many of those named as witnesses and to make enquires into some of the specific allegations of abuse. This, he argued, would be best achieved by printing further copies of the Commissioners' report and distributing it to all the Governors and staff for their individual comment. This process was in hand when the Commissioners intervened and persuaded the Home Secretary to prohibit the distribution of the report to the Governors until April (it was then February) and to Bethlem's officers (most of whom had been subject to severe criticism) until late June. Furthermore, the Governors were told that each recipient of the report was to be bound by confidentiality not to reveal any of the contents or discuss them with a third party.

Even *The Lancet*, which had been campaigning heavily against Bethlem since learning of the Lunacy Commission's interest, expressed doubts about this behaviour. 'It is to be regretted that neither the Governors nor the medical officers were permitted to be present, in person, or by counsel, during the inquiry; they ought to have had the opportunity of cross-examining the witnesses.'[233]

It took the Governors several months to compile and print their response to the accusations made against them and their staff. The resultant document was published in November 1852 and made evident the Governors' displeasure at the means and methods adopted by the Lunacy Commission. It was implied that Bethlem and its associated staff had been the subject of a deliberate smear campaign. 'Few things are more easy than to excite a cry of cruelty against the management of a lunatic asylum, and few more difficult to disprove,' wrote the Governors in the opening section of their response. They, and the medical staff, then refuted the allegations made against them in the strongest possible terms:

> 'The cures during the last seven years have not only equalled, but exceeded those of any corresponding period since the hospital was founded; mechanical restraint had been gradually diminished and at last altogether discontinued. Upon these grounds we earnestly appeal to the Committee, whether changes must necessarily degrade us all, and should be thus hastily made, without giving us the opportunity of defending ourselves against any charges which may have been made against us.'[234]

The directly contrasting views of the Commissioners and the Governors were difficult for many to fathom. Where did the truth lie, if anywhere? Naturally, *The Lancet* chose to believe the Commissioners' version of events and argued strongly that the only means of rectifying the issue was to bring Bethlem under the jurisdiction of the 1845 Lunacy Act. 'The most reprehensible, the most unconstitutional, the most pregnant with dangerous abuses, was the surreptitious exemption of Bethlem from the operation of the [1845] Act.'[235]

Others felt that the truth lay probably somewhere in between the picture of neglect painted by the Commissioners and the point-blank denials provided by the Governors and officers. Half a century later one of the hospital's biographers, Geoffrey O'Donoghue, puzzled over this issue and read and re-read all the reports and correspondence associated with it. 'Bewilderment only increased with each reading,' he commented, 'but if I had to give judgment on appeal I should admit that the [Commissioners'] report justly condemned some features in the system under which the hospital had been – conscientiously enough – administered up to this period.'[236]

As in 1815, the bulk of Bethlem's problems were laid at the feet of its medical officers and in particular the Apothecary, William Wood, who was adjudged to have allowed the Matron to have a free rein over conditions in the female wards, where the majority of abusive cases were said to have occurred. Wood defended himself in a letter to the Governors, claiming that for years he had been overworked and disempowered. 'I have been oppressed with an amount of labour, and ceaseless anxiety, and overwhelming responsibility to the very verge of human endurance. With a limited authority and no assistance I have struggled to promote the welfare of those committed to my charge.'

His protests were ignored and, as with Haslam before him, the Apothecary found himself made a scapegoat, not just by the Lunacy Commissioners, but also by his colleagues Edward Monro and Alexander Morison. Having been resident Apothecary since 1845, Wood resigned after being demoted beneath a newly appointed (and much younger) resident Apothecary; his departure left Monro and Morison fighting to save their skins.[237]

The joint Physicians attempted to deflect criticism away from themselves and onto Wood, but with only limited success. Both were accused of devoting too little time to their Bethlem duties, an accusation that was possibly true of Edward Monro (who had even been known to poach Bethlem's apprentices to work in his own madhouse), but it was certainly not the case with Alexander Morison, a man who was devoted to his work. Morison refuted the charges against him by providing the Governors with a detailed timetable of his hours of attendance, which were greatly in excess of his agreed schedule; Monro, on the other hand, attempted to dismiss the charges against him using only vague examples.

Public outrage at the allegations made by the Lunacy Commissioners was great and led to further calls for Bethlem to be placed under government regulation. 'The Governors of Bethlem have to vindicate themselves from the charge of supineness or incompetence,' wrote the editor of *The Lancet*. 'The medical officers have to defend their professional reputation from aspirations, implied or expressed, of neglect or incapacity; the public have the right to demand and to insist upon a public investigation into the past management of this asylum.'[238]

Shortly after receiving the Commissioner's report, the Governors chose to act on one of its recommendations and employed a residential Physician-Superintendent. The post was not only residential but full-time, which meant that a Physician would not only be available for consultation day and night, but would be in direct charge of all Bethlem's medical staff. It was hoped that this would prevent some of the confusion that had arisen between the responsibilities of the joint Physicians and the Apothecary. To allow this change to take place, Monro's and Morison's roles were downgraded to that of consultants. Monro chose to ride the storm and accepted the new terms, but Alexander Morison took this as a snub to his reputation and in April 1853 tendered his resignation in return for an annual pension of £150.

The changes to the medical staff were only a part of the Lunacy Commission's demands; the real aim of its investigation had been to persuade the Government that Bethlem ought to be brought under its control and thus be open to regular outside inspection. The Governors had devoted a great deal of time and money to ensuring that successive Lunacy Bills either failed in Parliament or specifically excluded the hospital from inspection, but this time they admitted defeat. After enduring almost half a century of assaults from various reformers, it was evident that the only means of obtaining some peace and quiet was to submit to their key demand. Shortly after Morison's resignation it was announced that 'the Hospital should be visited as other places of confinement were, if it were for no other reason than that of preventing the repetition of such calumnies as had been vented against them'. This was seen as being a somewhat grudging acceptance, but it did have the effect of calming down the heated accusations that had been levelled against Bethlem and was even greeted joyously by some. 'So the farce has been played out to the last act,' opined *The Lancet*. 'After a long course of mismanagement; their establishment has fallen under official censure.'[239]

In the spring of 1853 the Government passed a new Asylum Act whose chief function was to tidy up some loose ends associated with the 1845 Act including a clause that revoked Bethlem's exception from outside inspection. Accordingly, on 1 November that year, six centuries of self-regulation at Bethlem came to an end when, in accordance with the Act, Bethlem's Governors registered the hospital with the Lunacy Commission, agreeing to be subject to its terms and conditions.

The significance of all this change was underlined when, two years later, Edward Monro chose to retire from his perfunctory role as consulting Physician. Monro had three sons, one of whom, Henry, was a physician working with mental health patients at St Luke's Hospital, but he did not choose (nor would he probably have been allowed) to follow his father's footsteps into Bethlem. For the first time in a century and a quarter, and much to the relief of some outside observers, Bethlem Hospital found itself without a member of the Monro family on its staff.

For some while Edward Monro had not enjoyed good health and within months of retiring he was dead. One of his obituaries noted that much of his wealth was derived from his having been a paid expert witness at more than 400 trials, making him a 'favourite with the lawyers'. Having shed the baggage of its past, Bethlem Hospital was about to enter a new and better phase in its history.

The departures of Alexander Morison and Edward Monro coincided with many managerial reforms within Bethlem, but probably the most important appointment was that of Dr Charles Hood as the new residential Physician-Superintendent. Hood is credited by many as the man responsible for ensuring that Bethlem's standards and treatments not only matched those of other asylums but exceeded them. He was also responsible for steering the hospital away from its reliance on poor patients, which were increasingly being housed in the new county asylums, towards a hospital that catered mostly for private patients.

During the 1850s and '60s Bethlem was still subject to occasional acts of hostility by the Charity Commission, which included attempts to turn it into a county asylum and remove it from central London. Hood opposed these ideas and for the most part was able to defend Bethlem's corner, although his successor was unable to prevent the transference of its Criminal Department to the purpose-built Broadmoor Hospital in 1864.[240]

The stability associated with the Hood era continued forward into later Victorian times, so that by the turn of the twentieth century Bethlem was no longer popularly viewed as being an abusive asylum but was instead thought of as a psychiatric hospital. By the time of the First World War the St George's Fields building was considered to be unsuitable for the needs of psychiatric patients and it was thought desirable to move the hospital away from London and into the countryside (an idea that Charles Hood had fought back in 1856). As on previous occasions, organising the move took time, but in 1930 the entire facility was transferred to a grand purpose-built red-brick building in Monks Orchard House in Beckenham, Kent. The St George's Fields building, which was deemed unsuitable for human habitation, soon afterwards became home to the Imperial War Museum, which still occupies it to this day.

The Monks Orchard Bethlem Hospital received some handsome financial endowments and, although still a charity, it mostly catered for better-off middle-class patients, including many who had been traumatised by their war experiences. Its interior was notably plush, with pictures, soft furnishings and the latest medical facilities including an X-ray department and surgical theatre. The only complaints were minor and were mostly concerned with petty theft or the quality of food.

The Governors remained in charge at Bethlem and by all accounts managed to run it efficiently, although there were many times when money was tight. This was especially true near the end of the Second World War when Bethlem sustained severe damage from three German rockets. Finding the money to put right the damage proved to be problematic and was swiftly followed by another dilemma.

The creation of the National Health Service (NHS) in 1948 presented the Governors with the threat that Bethlem might cease to be independent and would instead become part of a Government-run health service. To avoid this Bethlem merged with Maudsley Hospital, an acute-care psychiatric hospital and teaching centre in South London that received independent funding and management from the then London County Council.

The merger effectively saw the end of Bethlem's Court of Governors, a body that had presided over it for centuries and which in its time had seen fit to oppose monarchs, medics and any number of politicians. In its place came a Board of Governors that covered both Bethlem and Maudsley Hospitals; this was in theory supposed to be independent, but in practice the new board quickly became filled with appointees from regional health authorities, universities and other interested bodies. The joint administration procedure proved to be fraught with problems, many of which are alleged to have been generated by Maudsley Hospital's desire to take advantage of their junior partner's endowments, spacious buildings and grounds. In some respects it was a throw-back to the time when Bethlem had to live under the shadow of Bridewell, but the excellence of Maudsley as a psychiatric research institute led to the addition of many specialist facilities that Bethlem would not otherwise have received, including departments for child psychiatry, addiction studies, eating disorders and neurological sciences.

As a major provider of mental health services to the NHS, the Bethlem and Maudsley Hospitals became a Special Health Authority (SHA) in 1982. Although technically independent of the NHS, the Bethlem and Maudsley SHA was subject to many of the philosophical and managerial ideas emanating from central Government. This led to a series of wide-ranging financial reforms and cost-cutting exercises that were designed to make the NHS and its service providers act in a more market-like fashion. Many of these reforms are thought not to have greatly benefited the Bethlem and Maudsley SHA, which, during the 1980s and '90s, lurched from one financial crisis to the next. Some of these problems were eased in 1994 with the formation of the Bethlem and Maudsley NHS Trust, which saw the SHA become a public sector corporation complete with executive and non-executive directors.

More reorganisation followed when, in 1999, the Bethlem and Maudsley NHS Trust merged with two other local NHS Trusts to form the South London and Maudsley NHS Foundation Trust. With several specialist centres across South London and its suburbs, it is the largest mental health trust in the country, and provides mental health care to patients on both a local and national level.[241]

Bethlem Hospital still exists at its Monks Orchard site, where it provides the South London and Maudsley Trust with a wide variety of specialist psychiatric services including units for substance abuse, eating disorders and anxiety. Although now enveloped within a much larger administrative structure, Bethlem Royal Hospital, as it is currently called, is nonetheless a direct descendant of the small religious institution that was founded in the City of London more than 750 years ago. Furthermore, the modern Bethlem routinely works with adolescents, mothers and other vulnerable people from South London and across the country, making its current practices entirely relevant to the original aims of its founder, Simon FitzMary, who wanted to found a charitable hospital for the benefit of disadvantaged people. As the cultural memories of the old Bedlam slowly fade into history, it is to be hoped that modern Bethlem Royal Hospital will be around for many more centuries to come.

Bibliography

Listed below is a selection of the more useful books and papers that formed a part of my research for this book. Those who are seeking a more academic and in-depth treatment of Bethlem and the history of mental health issues should first look at the works of Andrews, Porter and Scull. Especially recommended is Andrews et al, *The History of Bethlem*, and the more popular (but out-of-date) account given by O'Donoghue in *The Story of Bethlehem Hospital*.

Anon, *A Letter from a Subscriber to the York Lunatic Asylum to the Governors of that Charity* (York: Wilson, Spence and Mawman, 1788)

Anon, *A Report from the Committee, Appointed ... to Enquire into the State of the Private Madhouses in this Kingdom ...* (London: J. Whiston, 1763)

Anon, *Five Letters on Important Subjects. First Printed in a Public Paper, now Collected and Revised* (London: W. Owen, 1772)

Anon, *General Observations and Prescriptions in the Practice of Physick on Several Persons of Quality* (London: W. Mearsat, 1715)

Anon, *Letters Written to and for Particular Friends, on the Most Important Occasions* (London: J. Osborn, 1750)

Anon, *Mrs Clerke's Case* (London: J. Morphew, 1718)

Anon, *Reasons for the Establishing and further Encouragement of St Luke's Hospital for Lunaticks* (London: Teape and Son, 1751)

Anon, *Report from the Select Committee Appointed to Enquire into the State of Lunatics* (Shannon: Irish University Press, 1968; originally published 1807)

Anon, *Report of the Metropolitan Commissioners in Lunacy to the Lord Chancellor 1844* (London: Bradbury and Evans, 1844)

Anon, *Sketches in Bedlam* (London: Sherwood, 1823)

Anon, *Standing Rules of Orders for the Governors of the Royal Hospitals of Bridewell and Bethlem with the Duties of the Governors and of the Several Officers and Servants* (London: Thomas Parker, 1792; H. Bryer, 1802)

Anon, *State of an Institution near York, called the Retreat for Persons afflicted with Disorders of the Mind* (York: The Governors, 1796)

Anon, *The Annual Report of the Lunatic Asylum erected at York with a Short History of its Rise and Progress* (York, 1785)

Anon, *The Curiosities of London and Westminster*, 4 Vols (London: E. Newbery, 1786)

Anon, *The History, Debates, and Proceedings of Both Houses of Parliament of Great Britain from the Year 1743 to the Year 1774* (London: Debrett, 1792)

Anon, *The Plot Investigated* (London: Macklew, 1786)

Anon, 'Thoughts on Private Mad-houses, or A Case Humbly Offered to the Consideration of Parliament', *Royal Magazine*, 8 January 1762, pp27-9

Aleph, *London Scenes and London People* (London: City Press, 1863)

Allen, T., 'An Exact Narrative of an Hermaphrodite now in London', *Philosophical Transactions*, ii (10 February 1668), p624

Alleridge, P. H., *Catalogue to Bethlem Royal Hospital Museum* (London: Bethlem Royal Hospital, 1976)

Bethlem Royal Hospital (Bethlem & Maudsley NHS Trust, 1996)
        The Bethlem Hospital 1247-1997: A Pictorial Record (Chichester: Phillimore, 1997)

Andrews, J., 'The Lot of the "Incurably" Insane in Enlightened England', *Eighteenth Century Life*, xii (1988), pp1-18

'In her Vapours [or] indeed in her Madness? Mrs Clerke's Case: An Early Eighteenth Century Psychiatric Controversy', *History of Psychiatry*, Vol 1, 1990, pp125-43

Bedlam Revisited: A History of Bethlem Hospital c1634-1770 (University of London, 1991)
        'A Respectable Mad-Doctor? Dr Richard Hale, FRS (1670-1728)', *Notes and Records of the Royal Society of London*, Vol 44(2), 1990, pp169-204
        Customers and Patrons of the Mad-trade: The Management of Lunacy in Eighteenth-century London with the Complete Text of John Monro's 1766 Case Book (California: University of California Press, 2003)

Andrews, J., Briggs, A., Porter, R., Tucker, P. and Waddington, K., *The History of Bethlem* (London: Routledge, 1997)

Andrews, J. and Scull, A., *Undertaker of the Mind: John Monro and Mad-doctoring in Eighteenth-century England* (University of California Press, 2001)

Arnold, T., *Observations on the Nature, Kinds, Causes, and Preservation of Insanity* (London: Philips, 1806)

Baker, F. (ed), *The Works of John Wesley: Letters 1721-1755* (Oxford: Clarendon Press, 1980-82)

Bakewell, T., *The Domestic Guide in Cases of Insanity* (London: T. Allbut, 1805)
        A Letter to the Chairman of the Select Committee on the State of Madhouses, to which is Subjoined Remarks on the Nature, Causes, and Cure of Mental Derangement (Stafford: The Author, 1815)

Barry, J., *Medicine and Charity before the Welfare State* (London: Routledge, 1994)

Battie, W., *De Principiis Animalibus Exercitationes Viginti Quattuor* (London: J. Whiston, 1757)

    A Treatise on Madness (London: Whiston and White, 1758)

Belcher, W., *An Address to Humanity: Containing, a Letter to Dr Thomas Monro; a Receipt to make a Lunatic, and Seize his Estate; and a Sketch of a True Smiling Hyena* (London: The Author, 1796)

Black, W., *A Dissertation on Insanity* (London: Ridgway, 1810)

Blackmore, R., *Treatise of the Spleen or Vapours* (London: J. Pemberton, 1724)

Boswell, J., *Life of Johnson* (Oxford: Oxford University Press, 1953)

Bowen, T., *An Historical Account of the Origin, Progress, and Present State of Bethlem Hospital* (London: For the Governors, 1783)

    Extracts from the Records and Court Books of Bridewell Hospital: Arranged in Chronological Order, with Remarks (London: The Hospital, 1798)

    Remarks upon the Report of a Select Committee of Governors of Bridewell Hospital, appointed the first of March, 1798, etc (London: W. Wilson, 1799)

Bridewell Hospital, *A Statement of the Amount of the Accumulating Fund for rebuilding Bethlem Hospital* (London: H. Bryer, 1805)

Brown, M., 'Rethinking Early Nineteenth Century Asylum Reform', *The Historical Journal*, Vol 49(2), 2006, pp425-252

Browne, W. A. F., *What Asylums Were, Are and Ought to Be* (Edinburgh: Black, 1847)

Brydall, J., *Non Compos Mentis: or, the Law relating to Natural Fools, Mad Folks, and Lunatic Persons* (London: Cleave, 1700)

Bucknill, C., *The care of the Insane and their Legal Control* (London: Macmillan, 1880)

Burrows, G. M., *Commentaries on the Causes, Forms and Symptoms, and Treatment, Moral and Medical, of Insanity* (London: Underwood, 1828)

Byrd, M., *Visits to Bedlam: Madness and Literature in the Eighteenth Century* (Columbia: University of South Carolina Press, 1974)

Byrne, J. C., *Undercurrents Overlooked* (London: Richard Bently, 1860)

Carkesse, J., *Lucida Intervalla: Containing Divers Miscellaneous Poems*, M. V. De Porte (ed), (Los Angeles: University of California Press, 1979)

Cheyne, G., *The English Malady: or, a Treatise of Nervous Diseases of all Kinds* (London: Wisk, Ewing and Smith, 1733)

Cibber, C., *An Apology for the Life of Mr Colley Cibber* (London: Robert Lowe, 1889; originally published 1740)

Cobbett, W., *Cobbett's Parliamentary History of England: from the Norman Conquest in 1066 to the year 1803* (London: T. C. Hansard, 1806-20)

Codrington, T., 'London South of the Thames', *Surrey Archaeological Collections*, Vol 28, 1915 pp11-163

Connolly, J., *The Treatment of the Insane without Mechanical Restraints* (London: Smith and Elder, 1856)

Cox, J. M., *Practical Observations on Insanity* (London: Baldwin, 1806, 2nd edition)

Crowther, B., *Practical Remarks on Insanity; to Which is Added a Commentary on the Dissection of the Brains of Maniacs; with some Account of Diseases Incident to the Insane* (London: G. Hayden, 1811)

Cruden, A., *The London Citizen Exceedingly Injur'd: or a British Inquisition Display'd* (London: The Author, 2nd edn, 1739)

Mr Cruden Greatly Injured: an Account of a Trial between Mr. Alexander Cruden, Bookseller to the Late Queen, Plaintiff, and Dr Monro (London: The Author, 1740)

The Adventures of Mr Cruden the Corrector (London, The Author, 1754)

Cunningham, P., *The Letters of Horace Walpole: Earl of Orford* (London: R. Bentley, 1857)

Curnock, N. (ed), *The Journal of the Rev John Wesley* (London: Kelly, 1909; Epworth Press, 1938)

Currie, J., *Medical Reports on the Effects of Water, Cold and Warm, as a remedy in Fevers and other Diseases* (Liverpool: M'Crery, 1797)

Deane, P. and Cole, W. A., *British Economic Growth, 1688-1959: Trends and Structure* (Cambridge: Cambridge University Press, 1962)

Defoe, D., *Augusta Triumphans* (London: Roberts, 1728)

de Porte, M. V., *Nightmares and Hobbyhorses: Swift, Stern and Augustan Ideas of Madness* (San Marino: The Huntingdon Library, 1974)

Digby, A., 'Changes in the Asylum: The Case of York, 1777-1815', *The Economic History Review*, Vol 36(2), 1983, pp218-39

Madness, Morality and Medicine: A Study of the York Retreat, 1796-1914 (Cambridge: Cambridge University Press, 1985)

D'Israeli, I., *Curiosities of Literature* (Boston: Lilly, Wait, Colman and Holden, 1834)

Dudley, J. W., *Letters of the Earl of Dudley to the Bishop of Llandaff* (London: J. Murray)

Dyce, A., *The Collected Works of Thomas Middleton* (London: Edward Lumley, 1840)

Falconer, W., *A Dissertation on the Influence of the Passions upon Disorders of the Body* (London: Dilly, 1788)

Fallowes, T., *The Best Method for the Cure of Lunatics* (London: For the Author, 1705)

Faulker, B., *Observations on the General and Proper Treatment of Insanity* (London: Reynell, 1789)

Fiske, J., *The Life and Transactions of Margaret Nicholson; Containing not Only ... her Attempt to Assassinate his most Gracious Majesty; but also Memoirs of her Remarkable Life ...* (London: J. Fiske, 1786)

Floyer, J., *IvxpoXovoLa, or the History of Cold Bathing, both Ancient and Modern* (London: S. Smith and B. Walford, 1702)

Foucault, M., *Madness and Civilisation* (New York, Mentor Books, 1965)

French, C. N., *The Story of St Luke's Hospital* (London: Heinemann, 1951)

Frings, P., *A Treatise on Phrenzy* (London: T. Gardener, 1746)

Gandon, J. and Mulvany, T., *The life of James Gandon* (London: Cornmarket Press, 1969; originally published 1846)

Glover, M. R., *The Retreat, York: An Early Quaker Experiment in the Treatment of Mental Illness* (York: W. Sessions, 1984)

Hahn, J. S., *On the Healing Virtues of Cold Water, Inwardly and Outwardly applied, as proved by Experience* (London, 1738)

Hallaran, W. S., *An Inquiry into the causes producing the Extraordinary Addition to the Number of Insane* (Cork: Edwards and Savage, 1810)
Practical Observations on the Causes and Cure of Insanity (Cork: Hodges and MacArthur, 1818)

Harcourt, L. V. (ed), *The Diaries and Correspondence of the Right Hon George Rose: Containing Original Letters of the most Distinguished Statesmen of his Day* (London: Richard Bentley, 1860)

Harrison, J. F. C., *The Second Coming: Popular Millenarianism, 1780-1850* (London: Routledge and Kegan Paul, 1979)

Haslam, J., *Observations on Madness and Melancholy; Including Practical Remarks on those Diseases, Together with Cases, and an Account of the Morbid Appearances on Dissection* (London: Callow, 1809)
Medical Jurisprudence (London: Hunter, 1817)
A Letter to the Governors of Bethlem (London: Taylor and Hessey, 1818)
Illustrations of Madness, Porter, R. (ed), (London: Routledge Kegan and Paul, 1988; originally published in 1809)

Haywood, E., *The Distress'd Orphan, or Love in a Madhouse* (London: J. Roberts, 1726)

Hervey, N., 'Advocacy or folly: the Alleged Lunatics' Friend Society, 1845-63', *Medical History*, Vol 30(3), 1986, pp245-75
The Lunacy Commission 1845-60, with special reference to the implementation of policy in Kent and Surrey (Unpublished PhD, University of Bristol, 1987)

'A Slavish Bowing Down: the Lunacy Commission and the Psychiatric Profession 1845-1860', in Bynum, W. F., Porter, R. and Shepherd, M., *The Anatomy of Madness*, Vol ii

Higgins, G., *A Letter to the Right Honourable Earl Fitzwilliam respecting the Investigation which has lately taken place into the Abuse at the York Lunatic Asylum* (Doncaster: Sheardown, 1814)

Hill, R. G., *A Lecture on the Management of Lunatic Asylums and the Treatment of the Insane* (London: Simpkin and Marshall, 1839)

House of Commons, *Select Committee on the State of Criminal and Pauper Lunatics* (London: House of Commons, 1807)

Howard, J., *The state of the prisons in England and Wales, with preliminary observations and an account of some foreign prisons and hospitals* (Warrington: Eyres, 1784)

An Account of the Principal Lazarettos of Europe (London: Cadell, 1789)

Hughson, D., *London, being an accurate History and Description of the British Metropolis and its Neighbourhood* (London: J. Stratford, 1808)

Hunter, R. and Macalpine, I. (eds), *A Treatise on Madness and Remarks on Dr Battie's Treatise on Madness: A Psychiatric Controversy of the Eighteenth Century* (London: Dawsons, 1963)

Three Hundred Years of Psychiatry: 1535-1860 (Oxford: Oxford University Press, 1963)

Ingram, A. (ed), *Voices of Madness: Four Pamphlets, 1683-1796* (Gloucestershire: Sutton, 1997)

(ed) *Patterns of Madness in the Eighteenth Century: A Reader* (Liverpool: Liverpool University Press, 1998)

The Madhouse Language (London: Routledge, 1992)

Jackson, K., *Separate Theaters: Bethlem ('Bedlam') Hospital and The Shakespearean Stage* (University of Delaware Press, 2005)

Jacobi, M., *On the Construction and Management of Hospitals for the Insane* (London: Churchill, 1841)

Jay, M., *The Air Loom Gang* (London: Bantam Books, 2004)

Johnson, A. H., *The History of the Worshipful Company of the Drapers of London* (Oxford: Clarendon Press, 1914-1922)

Johnstone, J., *Medical Jurisprudence: On Madness* (Birmingham: J. Belcher, 1800)

Knight, P. S., *Observations on the Causes, Symptoms, and Treatments of Derangement of the Mind* (London: Longman, 1827)

Laurie, P., *A narrative of the proceedings at the laying of the first stone of the new buildings at Bethlem Hospital, ... July 26, 1838* (London, 1838)

Lewis, J., *Report respecting the Present State and Condition of Bethlem Hospital* (London: For the Governors, 1800)

Luttrell, N., *A Brief Historical Relation of State Affairs from September 1678 to April 1714* (Oxford: Oxford University Press, 1857)

Macalpine, I. and Hunter, R., *George III and the Mad-Business* (London: Pimlico, 1993)

MacBride, D., *A Methodical Introduction to the Theory and Practice of Physick* (London: Strahan, 1772)

MacDonald, M., *Mystical Bedlam: Madness, Anxiety and Healing in Seventeenth Century England* (Cambridge: Cambridge University Press, 1981)
   'Insanity and the Realities of History in Early Modern England', *Psychological Medicine*, Vol 11, 1981, pp11-25

Mackenzie, H., *The Man of Feeling* (London: Cassell and Co, 1886; originally published 1771)

Malley, C. D., 'Helhiah Crooke, MD, FRCP, 1576-1648', *Bulletin of the History of Medicine*, Vol 42(1), 1968, p4

Martin, F. O., *The Report of the Commissioners for Enquiry into Charities for 1837* (London, 1837)
   An Account of Bethlem Hospital: Abridged from the Report of the Late Charity Commissioners (London: William Pickering, 1853)

Mason, W., *Animadversions on the Present Government of the York Lunatic Asylum, in which the case of Parish Paupers is distinctly considered in a Series of Propositions* (York: The Author, 1778)
   Animadversions on the Present Government of the York Lunatic Asylum, in which the case of Parish Paupers is distinctly considered in a Series of Propositions (York: The Author, 1778)

Matthew, H. C. G. and Harrison, B. H. (eds), *Oxford Dictionary of National Biography* (Oxford: Oxford University Press, 2004)

Mayne, Z., *Two Dissertations concerning Sense, and the Imagination* (London: J. Tonson, 1728)

Mead, R., *Medical Precepts and Cautions* (London: Brindley, 1751)

Metcalf, U., *The Interior of Bethlem Hospital* (London: The Author, 1818)

Monro, J., *Oratio anniversaria* (London: G. Russel, 1757) *Remarks on Dr Battie's Treatise on Madness* (London: John Clarke, 1758)

Monro, T., *Observations of the Physician (Dr. Monro) and Apothecary (Mr. Haslam) of Bethlem Hospital, upon the evidence taken before the Committee of the House of Commons for regulating madhouses* (London: H. Bryer, 1816)

Montagu, M. F. A., *Edward Tyson, 1650-1708* (American Philosophical Society, 1943)

Moran, R., 'The Origin of Insanity as a Special Verdict: The Trial for Treason of James Hadfield', *Law and Society Review*, Vol 19, 1985, pp487-519

Morison, A., *Cases of Mental Disease* (London: Longman and Highly, 1828)

Munk, W., *The Roll of the Royal College of Physicians* (London: Longman, Green, Longman and Roberts, 1861)

Nicholson, M., *Authentic Memoirs of the Life of Margaret Nicholson, who attempted to Stab his Most Gracious Majesty* (London: J. Ridgeway, 1786)

O'Donoghue, E. G., *The Story of Bethlehem Hospital from its Founding in 1247* (London, Unwin, 1914)

Bridewell Hospital: Palace, Prison, Schools (London: John Lane the Bodley Head Ltd, 1923)

Oliver, E., *The Eccentric Life of Alexander Cruden* (London: Faber and Faber, 1934)

Pargeter, W., *Observations on Maniacal Disorders* (Reading: The Author, 1792)

Payne, T., *A Description of Bedlam with an Account of its Present Inhabitants, both Male and Female* (London: T. Payne, 1722)

Peers, E. A., *Elizabethan Drama and its Mad Folk* (Cambridge: Cambridge University Press, 1914)

Percival, T., *Medical Ethics* (Manchester: Johnson and Bickerstaff, 1803)

Poole, S., *The Politics of Regicide in England, 1760-1850: Troublesome Subjects* (Manchester: Manchester University Press, 2001)

Porter, G. R., *The Nation in its Various Social and Economical Relations* (London: Charles Knight, 1843)

Porter, R., 'The Rage of Party: a Glorious Revolution in English Psychiatry?', *Medical History*, Vol 27, 1983, pp35-50

Mind-Forg'd Manacles: A History of Madness in England from the Restoration to the Regency (London: Penguin, 1990)

Pote, J., *The Foreigner's Guide: or, a Necessary and Instructive Companion both for the Foreigner and Native: In Their Tour Through the Cities of London and Westminster* (London: H. Kent, 1763; originally published in 1729)

Reed, R. R., *Bedlam on the Jacobean Stage* (Cambridge, MA: Harvard University Press, 1952)

Richardson, S., *Familiar Letters on Important Occasions* (London: Routledge, 1938; originally published in 1741)

Robinson, N., *A New System of the Spleen, Vapours, and Hypochondriack Melancholy* (London: Bettesworth, Innys and Rivington, 1729)

Rose, G. R., *The Diaries and Correspondence of the Right Hon George Rose* (London: R. Bentley, 1860)

Rowley, W., *A Treatise on Female, Nervous, Hysterical, Hypochondriacal, Bilious, Convulsive Diseases with Thoughts on Madness, Suicide, etc* (London: Nourse, 1788)

Russell, D., *Scenes from Bedlam* (London: Baillière Tindall, 1996)

Salmon, W., *A Compleat System of Physick, Theoretical and Practical* (London: T. Passinger, 1686)

Sawrey, S. (ed), *The Morbid Anatomy of the Brain, in Mania and Hydrophobia; with the Pathology of these two Diseases, as Collected from the papers of the Late Andrew Marshal* (London: Longman, Hurst, Rees, Orme and Brown, 1815)

Scull, A., *Museums of Madness* (London: Allen Lane, 1979)

The Most Solitary of Afflictions: Madness and Society in Britain, 1700-1900 (New Haven, Conn: Yale University Press, 1993)

'Museums of Madness Revisited', *Social History of Medicine*, Vol 6(1), 1993, pp3-23

Scull, A., MacKenzie, C. and Hervey, N., *Masters of Bedlam: the Transformation of the Mad-Doctoring Trade* (Princeton: Princeton University Press, 1996)

Seymour, R., *A Survey of the Cities of London and Westminster* (London: J. Read, 1734)

Sharpe, J. B., *Report together with the Minutes of Evidence, and an Appendix of Papers, from the Committee appointed to consider of Provision being made for the better Regulation of Madhouses in England* (London: Baldwin and Co, 1815)

Shorter, E., *A History of Psychiatry* (Chichester: J. Wiley & Sons, 1997)

Smith, L. D., 'Behind Closed Doors; Lunatic Asylum Keepers, 1800-60', *Social History of Medicine*, Vol 1(3), 1988, pp301-7

Smollett, T., *Sir Launcelot Greaves* (London: J. Cochrane, 1736)

Southcomb, L., *Peace of Mind and Health of Body United* (London: M. Cooper, 1750)

Stafford, R., *A Clear Apology and just Defence for Himself* (London: Andrew Sowle and Abel Roper, 1690)

Stevenson, C., 'Robert Hooke's Bethlem', *Journal of the Society of Architectural Historians*, Vol 55 (3), 1996, pp254-75

Stevenson, C., 'The Architecture of Bethlem at Moorfields', in Andrews, J., Briggs, A., Porter, R., Tucker, P. and Waddington, K., *The History of Bethlem* (London: Routledge, 1997

Stow, J., *A Survey of London* (London: Whittaker and Co, 1842; originally published in 1598)

Strype, J., *Survey of the Cities of London and Westminster* (London: A. Churchill, 1720; updated from the 1598 edition by John Stow)

Symonds, C., 'Thomas Willis, FRS (1621-1675)', *Notes and Records of the Royal Society of London*, Vol 15, 1960, pp91-7

Tate, W. E., *The Parish Chest* (Cambridge University Press, 1969)

Telford, John, *The letters of the Rev John Wesley* (London: Epworth, 1931)

Thornbury, W. and Walford, E., *Old and New London* (London, 1878)

Thorne, R. G., *The History of Parliament: The Commons, 1790-1820* (London: Secker and Warburg, 1986)

Timbs, J., *Curiosities of London* (London: Virtue & Co, 1876)

Tompson, Richard, *The Charity Commission and the Age of Reform* (London: Routledge and Kegan Paul, 1979)

Tuke, S., *Description of the Retreat: An Institution near York for Insane Persons of the Society of Friends, containing an Account of its Origin and Progress, the Modes of Treatment, and a Statement of Cases* (London: Dawsons, 1964; originally published in 1813)

Practical Hints on the Construction and Economy of Pauper Lunatic Asylums (York, 1816)

Tuke, T. H., 'On Warm and Cold Baths in the Treatment of Insanity', *Journal of Mental Science*, Vol 5, 1858, p102

Turnor, E. and Turnor, A., *The True Case of Mrs. Clerke: set Forth by her Brothers, Sir Edward and Mr. Arthur Turnor. to which are added, all the Depositions on that Occasion. In Answer to a Scandalous Pamphlet, lately Publish'd, call'd, Mrs. Clerke's Case* (London: John Morphew, 1718)

Wale, W. (ed), *George Whitefield's Journals: To Which is Prefixed his 'Short Account' and 'Further Account'* (London: H. J. Drane, 1905)

(ed), *George Whitefield's Letters. For the Period 1734-42* (Edinburgh: The Banner of Truth Trust, 1976)

Wallis, P. J., Wallis, R. V., Whittet, T. D., Burnby, J. G. L., *Eighteenth Century Medics (Subscriptions, Licenses, Apprenticeships)* (London: Project for Historical Bibliography, 1988)

Ward, E., *The London Spy* (London: Folio Society, 1955; originally published in 1700)

Ward, R. W., and Heitzenrater, R. P. (eds), *The Works of John Wesley: Journal and Diaries (1735-75)* (Nashville, Tenn: Abingdon Press, 1993)

Webster, J., *Observations on the Admission of Medical Pupils to the Wards of Bethlem Hospital, for the Purpose of Studying Mental Diseases* (London: The Author, 1842)

Weiner, D. B., 'Book Review: Undertaker of the Mind', *The Journal of Modern History*, Vol 75, 2003, pp406-7

Wesley, J., *The Works of John Wesley* (Grand Rapids, Michigan: Zondervan Publishing House, 1958-59)

West, D. J. and Walk, A. (eds), *Daniel McNaughton: His Trial and the Aftermath* (Ashford, Kent: Headley, 1977)

Williams, C. (ed), *Sophie in London, 1786, Being a Diary of Sophie v. La Roche* (London: Jonathan Cape, 1933)

Williams, D., 'The Missions of David Williams and James Tilly Matthews, 1793', *English Historical Review*, Vol 53, 1938, pp651-68)

Willis, T., *The Practice of Physick: Two Discourses concerning the Soul of Brutes* (London: Dring, Harper and Leigh, 1684)

Windle, B. C. A. (ed), *A Philological Essay Concerning the Pygmies of the Ancients by Edward Tyson* (London: D. Nutt, 1894)

Wright, E., *Bethlem Hospital Minutes of Evidence taken by the Committee Appointed to Inquire into the Charges inferred against Dr. Wright and his Answer* (London: Mills, Jowett, and Mill, 1830)

Wynter, A., *On the Construction and Government of Lunatic Asylums* (London: Churchill, 1847)

Endnotes

Abbreviations

DNB   Matthew, H. C. G. and Harrison, B. H. (eds), *Oxford Dictionary of National Biography* (Oxford: Oxford University Press, 2004)

TNA: PRO   The National Archives: Public Record Office, Kew, Richmond, Surrey, TW9 4DU

1   Ward's description is given in Ward, E., *The London Spy* (London: Folio Society, 1955; originally published in monthly instalments between 1698 and 1700), pp47-52. I have edited some of the quotes. The anti-monarchist was probably Richard Stafford; see Chapter One of this book for further details.

2   The first used of the word 'Bedlem' to refer to the hospital occurs in 1418; the first written recording of 'Bedlam' as a euphemism for a chaotic scene is in 1667, but its origins are thought to be much earlier. Barnhart, R. K. (ed), *Dictionary of Etymology* (London: Chambers, 1988), p85.

3   Rumour concerning Bethlem's origins: Timbs, J., *Curiosities of London* (London: Virtue & Co, 1876), p51. The 1403 visitation: TNA: PRO C 270/22.

4   *The Honest Whore*: see Dyce, A., *The Collected Works of Thomas Middleton* (London: Edward Lumley, 1840), Vol 3, p122. For further information on Bethlem's place in seventeenth-century theatre see Jackson, K., *Separate Theaters: Bethlem ('Bedlam') Hospital and The Shakespearean Stage* (University of Delaware Press, 2005); Pepys's Diary: entry for 19 Feb 1669.

5   Andrews, J., Briggs, A., Porter, R., Tucker, P. and Waddington, K., *The History of Bethlem* (London: Routledge, 1997), p111.

6   Anon, *General Observations and Prescriptions in the Practice of Physick on Several Persons of Quality* (London: W. Mearsat, 1715), p9.

7   For a discussion and history of Tom O'Bedlams see D'Israeli, I., *Curiosities of Literature* (Boston: Lilly, Wait, Colman and Holden, 1834), Vol 3, pp286-94.

8   Seymour, R., *A Survey of the Cities of London and Westminster* (London: J. Read, 1734), p187.

9   DNB, Vol 52, p63; Stafford, R., *A Clear Apology and just Defence for Himself* (London: Andrew Sowle and Abel Roper, 1690); Luttrell, N., *A Brief Historical Relation of State Affairs from September 1678 to April 1714* (Oxford: Oxford University Press, 1857), Vol 2, p27.

10   Andrews et al, *The History of Bethlem*, p124.

11   Seymour, *Survey of the Cities ...*, Vol 1, p187.

12   *Report of the Charity Commissioners* (London: W. Clowes, 1840), Vol 32(4), p506; Andrews et al, *The History of Bethlem*, pp113-14.

13   O'Malley, C. D., 'Helhiah Crooke, MD, FRCP, 1576-1648', *Bulletin of the History of Medicine*, Vol 42(1), 1968, p4.

14   The 1633 Royal Commission is published in Hunter, R. and Macalpine, I., *Three Hundred Years of Psychiatry: 1535-1860* (Oxford: Oxford University Press, 1963), pp106-8.

15   For biographical information on Crooke see O'Malley, 'Helkiah Crooke ...'; Andrews et al, *The History of Bethlem ...*, pp63-65, 87-9. The 1633 Royal Commission is published in Hunter and Macalpine, *Three Hundred Years ...*, pp106-8.

16   D'Israeli, I., *Curiosities of Literature*, pp286-4; for information on poor laws and settlement acts see Tate, W. E., *The Parish Chest* (Cambridge University Press, 1969).

17   Willis, T., *The Practice of Physick: Two Discourses concerning the Soul of Brutes* (London: Dring, Harper and Leigh, 1684); a translation of earlier works produced between 1659 and 1669. For further information on Willis see Symonds, C., 'Thomas Willis, FRS (1621-1675)', *Notes and Records of the Royal Society of London*, Vol 15, 1960, pp91-7.

18   Stevenson, C., 'The Architecture of Bethlem at Moorfields', in Andrews et al, *The History of Bethlem*, p233. Some of the original words were written as abbreviations; I have expanded these.

19   Stevenson, 'The Architecture of Bethlem ...', p234.

20   Strype, J., *Survey of the Cities of London and Westminster* (London: A. Churchill, 1720; originally published in 1598 by John Stow).

21   Bowen, T., *An Historical Account of the Origin, Progress, and Present State of Bethlem Hospital* (London, 1783), p5.

22   Ward, *The London Spy*, p48.

23   Stevenson, C., 'Robert Hooke's Bethlem', *Journal of the Society of Architectural Historians*, Vol 55(3), 1996, pp254-75; Andrews et al, *The History of Bethlem*, pp219-20, 246-8.

24   Stevenson, 'The Architecture of Bethlem ...', p231.

25   Anon, *The Curiosities of London and Westminster* 4 Vols (London: E. Newbery, 1786), Vol 1, pp90-1. Many aspects of this description are drawn from the one given in Seymour, *Survey of the Cities ...*, Vol 1, p186-9.

26   Seymour, *Survey of the Cities ...*, Vol 1, p186; Bowen, *An Historical Account ...*, p5. Cibber's son, Colley Cibber, says of his father: 'My Father, Caius Gabriel Cibber, was a Native of Holstein, who came into England some time before the Restoration of King Charles II to follow his Profession, which was that of a Statuary, etc. The Basso Relievo on the Pedestal of the Great Column in the City, and the two Figures of the Lunaticks, the Raving and the Melancholy, over the Gates of Bethlehem-Hospital, are no ill Monuments of his Fame as an artist.' Cibber, C., *An Apology for the Life of Mr. Colley Cibber*, Vol 1 (London: Robert Lowe, 1889). The statues are now on permanent display in the Bethlem Royal Hospital Museum, Beckenham, Kent.

27   Cruden, A., *The London Citizen Exceedingly Injur'd: or a British Inquisition Display'd* (London: The Author, 1739, 2nd edn), p5.

28   For further biographical information on Meveral and Allen, see Munk, W., *The Roll of the Royal College of Physicians* (London: Longman, Green, Longman and Roberts, 1861), Vol 1, pp172 and 361; Andrews et al, *The History of Bethlem*, p269.

29   For further information on Tyson, see Montagu, M. F. A., *Edward Tyson, 1650-1708* (American Philosophical Society, 1943); Munk, W., *The Roll of the Royal College ...*, Vol 1, pp399-400. Also DNB, Vol 55, pp818-9; Windle, B. C. A. (ed), *A Philological Essay Concerning the Pygmies of the Ancients by Edward Tyson* (London: D. Nutt, 1894).

30   Floyer, J., *IvxpoXovoLa, or the History of Cold Bathing, both Ancient and Modern* (London: S. Smith and B. Walford, 1702), pp15-16.

31   Seymour, *Survey of the Cities ...*, p187. Floyer's work is thought to have been influential on the German mania for hydrotherapy that started in the early nineteenth century. For further historical works on cold bathing see: Hahn, J. S., *On the Healing Virtues of Cold Water, Inwardly and Outwardly applied, as proved by Experience* (London, 1738); Currie, J., *Medical Reports on the Effects of Water, Cold and Warm, as a remedy in Fevers and other Diseases* (Liverpool: M'Crery, 1797).

32   See *Memoirs of the American Philosophical Society*, Vol 479, 1935, p327; Montagu, *Edward Tyson ...*

33   For biographical information on Branthwait and Woodward see Munk, *The Roll of the Royal College ...*, Vol 2, pp1-4.

34   Biographical information on Richard Hale can be found in Andrews, J., 'A Respectable Mad-Doctor? Dr Richard Hale, FRS (1670-1728)', *Notes and Records of the Royal Society of London*, Vol. 44(2), 1990, pp169-204; Munk, *The Roll of the Royal College* ... Vol 2, pp43-4.

35   Andrews, 'A Respectable ...', pp175-6. Will: TNA: PRO PROB 11/625, proved on 1 October 1728.

36   Turnor, E. and Turnor, A., *The True Case of Mrs Clerke* (London, J. Morphew, 1718), pp20-4.

37   Turnor, E. and Turnor, A., *The True Case* ..., p44.

38   Turnor, E. and Turnor, A., *The True Cas e...*, p56; Anon, 'Mrs Clerke's Case' (London: J. Morphew, 1718).

39   From Andrews, 'A Respectable ...', p180. The original source is cited as *Lloyd's Evening Post*, 26-28 September 1728.

40   An increase in patients had led Bridewell and Bethlem's Governors to consider the idea of employing two Physicians in place of Richard Hale, but this division of power did not appeal to those medics who applied to be Hale's replacement. The idea was dropped, leaving Dr Monro as sole Physician.

41   For biographies of Richard Tyson and the other candidates from 1728, see Munk, *The Roll of the Royal College* ..., Vol 2, pp53, 61, 66, 67. One of Sir Richard Manningham's exploits is highlighted in the extraordinary tale of Mary Toft, the so-called 'rabbit woman' of Surrey; see Douglas, J., 'An Advertisement occasioned by some passages in Sir R. Manningham's Diary, lately published, 1727', *Medical History*, Vol 5, 1961, pp349-60; DNB, Vol 54, 2004, pp891-3.

42   The patient that Monro inherited with the post was Lady Frances Erskine Mar, whose case shows remarkable similarities to that of Mrs Clerke. See Andrews, 'A Respectable...', pp178-80.

43   Barry, J., *Medicine and Charity before the Welfare State* (London: Routledge, 1994), p79.

44   Curnock, N. (ed), *The Journal of the Rev John Wesley* (London: Kelly, 1909), Vol 2, pp385-6.

45   Anon, *General Observations and Prescriptions* ..., p9.

46   All quotes are taken from Payne, T., *A Description of Bedlam with an Account of its Present Inhabitants, both Male and Female* (London: T. Payne, 1722).

47   Andrews et al, *The History of Bethlem* ..., pp316-20.

48   DNB, Vol 24, p656.

49   Oliver, Edith, *The Eccentric Life of Alexander Cruden* (London: Faber and

Faber, 1934); Cruden, A., *The London Citizen Exceedingly Injur'd: or a British Inquisition Display'd* (London: The Author, 2nd edition 1739).

50   Cunningham, P., *The Letters of Horace Walpole: Earl of Orford* (London: R. Bentley, 1857), Vol ii, p6.

51   James Monro's will: TNA: PRO PROB 11/798; proved 5 December 1752.

52   Frings, P., *A Treatise on Phrenzy* (London: T. Gardener, 1746). For a brief discussion on this see Hunter and Macalpine, *Three Hundred Years ...*, pp371-2; Southcomb, L., *Peace of Mind and Health of Body United* (London: M. Cooper, 1750).

53   British Library SLOANE MSS 4055 f.37. Battie's surname is alleged to be the origin of the term 'batty' when used to describe someone who is silly or mad.

54   French, C. N., *The Story of St Luke's Hospital* (London: Heinemann, 1951), pp7-8. The original founders were Thomas Crowe, a physician; Richard Speed, a druggist; William Prowing, an apothecary; James Sperling, merchant; Thomas Light, merchant; and Francis Magnus.

55   The appeal for money for the new hospital came shortly after the establishment of St Patrick's Hospital for 'idiots and lunatics' in Dublin, the building of which had largely been funded by a legacy from Dean Swift. It was perhaps a desire to outdo Dublin that caused Londoners to rally to the proposed new hospital's cause; they dug deep into their pockets and provided the necessary subscriptions to get the project off the ground.

56   Anon, *The Curiosities of London*, Vol 1, p94.

57   French, *The Story of St Luke's ...*, pp17-21; Hunter, R. and Macalpine, I. (eds), *A Treatise on Madness and Remarks on Dr Battie's Treatise on Madness: A Psychiatric Controversy of the Eighteenth Century* (London: Dawsons, 1962), p10.

58   Battie's private madhouse: Hunter and Macalpine, *Three Hundred Years ...*, pp200-1 and 402-3. Battie's lectures: Battie, W., *De Principiis Animalibus Exercitationes Viginti Quattuor* (London: J. Whiston, 1757).

59   Battie, W., *A Treatise on Madness* (London: Whiston and White, 1758), p2.

60   Battie, *A Treatise ...*, p4. I have edited the first sentence to make it less verbose.

61   Battie, *A Treatise ...*, p68

62   Battie, *A Treatise ...*, pp93-4; French, *The Story of St Luke's ...*, pp17-18. Original spellings have been retained.

63   Anon, *Reasons for the Establishing and further Encouragement of St Luke's Hospital for Lunaticks* (London: Teape and Son, 1751); Monro, J., *Oratio*

anniversaria (London: G. Russel, 1757); Andrews, J. and Scull, A., *Undertaker of the Mind: John Monro and Mad-doctoring in Eighteenth-century England* (University of California Press, 2001), p54.

64   Monro, J., *Remarks on Dr Battie's Treatise on Madness* (London: John Clarke, 1758).

65   Quotes from Monro, J., *Remarks* ..., pp3, 15, 18-19. The italics are in the original and indicate passages that are lifted from Battie's work.

66   Monro, J., *Remarks* ..., pp35-36.

67   Monro, J., *Remarks* ..., p50.

68   *Biographia Medica*, Vol 1, p51.

69   *Critical Review*, Vol 4, 1757, pp509-16; *Literary Review*, Vol 5, 1758, pp224-8.

70   Haller's quote taken from Andrews and Scull, *Undertaker of the Mind*, p63. They acknowledge their source as *Albrecht von Haller's Briefe an August Tissot* (Bern: Huber, 1977), p87.

71   Quote taken from Hunter and Macalpine, *A Treatise* ..., p17.

72   For a view of Battie and Monro as ideological rivals, see Hunter and Macalpine, *A Treatise* ..., pp13-19; for a more sympathetic analysis see Andrews and Scull, *Undertaker of the Mind*, pp59-70. Shorter, E., *A History of Psychiatry* (Chichester: J. Wiley & Sons, 1997) describes Battie as a founder of modern psychiatry: 'It was with Battie that the birth of psychiatry commenced' (p10).

73   Hunter and Macalpine, *Three Hundred Years* ..., p297; Defoe, D., *Augusta Triumphans* (London: Roberts, 1728), pp30-2.

74   Anon, *The History, Debates and Proceedings of Both Houses of Parliament of Great Britain from the Year 1743 to the Year 1774*, Vol 4 (London: J. Debrett, 1792), pp123-4. This case is provided in summary notes; I have adjusted this to make it read smoothly.

75   Anon, *The History, Debates* ..., pp123-8.

76   Views on the failure of the 1763 legislation can be found in Porter, R., *Mind-Forg'd Manacles: A History of Madness in England from the Restoration to the Regency* (London: Penguin, 1990), p151; Andrews and Scull, *Undertaker of the Mind*, pp155-9; Hunter and Macalpine, *A Treatise* ..., p20.

77   Howell, T. B., *A Complete Collection of State Trials And Proceedings for High Treason and Other Crimes* (London: T. C. Hansard, 1816-28), Vol 27, pp1282-356. Wood was returned to the madhouse but initiated another a trial against Monro shortly afterwards. At this the defence tried in vain to get him to talk about the Princess in the boat again but he refused to mention

the subject. 'Such is the extraordinary subtlety and cunning of madmen,' remarked Mansfield later. Monro was again acquitted.

78 Boswell, J., *Life of Johnson* (Oxford: Oxford University Press, 1953), p635.

79 The figure of 96,000 is from Macdonald, M., *Mystical Bedlam: Madness, Anxiety and Healing in Seventeenth Century England* (Cambridge: Cambridge University Press , 1981), p122; *The World*, 7 June 1753, p138. For an analysis and discussion of visitor numbers see Andrews et al, *The History of Bethlem*, pp178-82.

80 Admission figures are taken from Andrews et al, *The History of Bethlem*, pp178-9. Charles Savage's will may be found at TNA: PRO PROB 11/892, 19 October 1763; Jeremiah Marlow: *Annual Register*, 1765, p141.

81 Anon, *Letters Written to and for Particular Friends, on the Most Important Occasions* (London: J. Osborn, 1750), pp221-2.

82 Battie, *A Treatise ...*, pp68-9.

83 O'Donoghue, E. G., *The Story of Bethlehem Hospital from its Founding in 1247* (London: Unwin, 1914), pp234-5. It should be noted that Andrews, in 'A Respectable ...', p177, casts doubt on the attribution of this quote to Richard Hale. Monro, J., *Remarks ...*, p39. In 1722 T. Payne paid the Keeper to gain private access to the galleries.

84 Ward, *The London Spy*; Anon, *Letters Written to ...*, p222.

85 Hunter and Macalpine, *Three Hundred Years ...*, p427; Andrews, J., *Customers and Patrons of the Mad-trade* (California: University of California Press, 2003); Andrews and Scull, *Undertaker of the Mind*, pp26-7; Andrews et al, *The History of Bethlem*, p191.

86 This law was originally passed on 11 August 1699; Seymour, *Survey of the Cities...*, p187.

87 O'Donoghue, *The Story of Bethlehem ...*, pp281-3; Andrews and Scull, *Undertaker of the Mind*, pp26, 274.

88 Anon, *Standing Rules and Orders for the Governing of the Royal Hospitals of Bridewell and Bethlem* (London: Thomas Parker, 1792), p23; Hunter and Macalpine, *Three Hundred Years ...*, pp428-9.

89 The trial is summarised in *Annual Register*, 1771, pp78-9. The fate of Mrs Leggatt's husband, who was responsible for delivering her to the madhouse in the first place, is not known.

90 Anon, *Five Letters on Important Subjects. First Printed in a Public Paper, now Collected and Revised* (London: W. Owen, 1772), pp21-7.

91 *Hansard*, 11 February 1773, col 696. 'Gentlemen of the long robe' is slang for lawyers, solicitors and other members of the legal profession. However,

it is not known how they could have disrupted the bill, except through their presence in the House of Lords, which is a distinct possibility.

92   *Commons Journal*, Vol 34, 1774, pp492, 526, 546, 563, 564, 588, 593, 605, 726, 733-4.

93   *Hansard*, 11 February 1773, col 697; 22 April 1773, col 837-8; Hunter and Macalpine, *Three Hundred Years ...*, p452.

94   William Kinleside was the son of William, also an apothecary who worked in Bridge Street between 1694 and 1744. William junior operated from the same premises between 1719 and 1783. Wallis, P. J., Wallis, R. V., Whittet, T. D. and Burnby, J. G. L., *Eighteenth Century Medics (Subscriptions, Licenses, Apprenticeships)* (London: Project for Historical Bibliography, 1988). William Kinleside senior's will: TNA: PRO PROB 11/739, 8 May 1745.

95   *St James's Chronicle*, 5-7 March 1775.

96   *The Gentleman's Magazine*, Vol 45, 1775, p207; O'Donoghue, *Bridewell Hospital: Palace, Prison, Schools* (London: John Lane the Bodley Head Ltd, 1923), pp201-3; William Kinleside's will: TNA: PRO PROB 11/1216, 28 March 1792.

97   Bowen, *An Historical Account ...*, p16.

98   Martin, F. O., *An Account of Bethlem Hospital* (London: William Pickering, 1853), p9.

99   Bowen, *An Historical Account ...*, dedication.

100   Bowen, *An Historical Account ...*, p8.

101   O'Donoghue, *The Story of Bethlehem ...*, p278.

102   French, *The Story of St Luke's ...*, p23.

103   *Biographia Medica*, Vol 1, p52; DNB, Vol 4, p380; *London Magazine*, Vol 45, 1776, p392.

104   Bowen, *An Historical Account ...*, p8. I have edited the quote.

105   Anon, *The Plot Investigated* (London: Macklew, 1786), pp4, 15; *Annual Register*, 1786, pp233-4; *The Times*, 11 August 1786.

106   In 1786 the Board of Green Cloth consisted of the Lord Steward; the Treasurer of the Household; the Comptroller of the Household; Masters of the Household; Clerks of the Household; and the Chief Metropolitan Magistrate. The Board still exists but it only regulates liquor, betting and gaming licences attached to the Royal palaces.

107   Anon, *The Plot Investigated*, pp49-50.

108   Margaret Nicholson's case is given in Anon, *The Plot Investigated*; *Annual Register*, 1786, pp233-4; *The Times*, 10 August 1786.

109   *The Times*, 10 August 1786.

110   Anon, *Sketches in Bedlam* (London: Sherwood, 1823), pp253-8.

111   *Biographia Medica*, Vol 2, pp155-6.

112   Howard, J., *An Account of the Principal Lazarettos in Europe* (London: Cadell, 1789), pp139-141. Howard's patient numbers broadly agree with the totals given for 1787, which were: 'Admitted into the Hospital of Bethlem Last Year [1787] = 219; Cured of their Lunacy and discharged from thence = 205; Buried = 12; Remaining in the said Hospital under cure = 282. There are generally more than 270 distracted persons in the Hospital, exclusive of those who have been discharged, and are supplied with physic at the expense of this hospital, and advice to prevent a return of their lunacy.' *The Times*, 26 March 1788.

113   Gandon, J. and Mulvany, T., *The life of James Gandon* (London: Cornmarket Press, 1969; originally published 1846). There is no historical record of the competition that Gandon entered. This caused O'Donoghue (*The Story of Bethlehem* ..., p312) to suggest that Mulvany had confused Gandon with the architect Gandy, who won a similar competition held in 1811. This, however, seems somewhat unlikely as Mulvany quotes from Gandon's actual reminiscences on the subject. See also *Civil Engineer's and Architect's Journal*, February 1847, p48.

114   Seymour, *Survey of the Cities* ..., pp186-7.

115   Anon, *Standing Rules and Orders of the Royal Hospitals of Bridewell and Bethlem*, pp5-6.

116   O'Donoghue, *Bridewell Hospital*, pp202-3; Andrews et al, *The History of Bethlem*, p382.

117   Crosby's will: TNA: PRO PROB 11/1229, 3 March 1793; I have searched *The Times* for the advertisements; the earliest I could find was 20 January 1800.

118   Scull, A., MacKenzie, C. and Hervey, N., *Masters of Bedlam: the Transformation of the Mad-Doctoring Trade* (Princeton: Princeton University Press, 1996).

119   Biographical notes on John Haslam: DNB, Vol 25, pp709-11; *Medical History*, Vol 6, 1962, pp22-6.

120   Haslam, J., *Observations on Madness and Melancholy; Including Practical Remarks on those Diseases, Together with Cases, and an Account of the Morbid Appearances on Dissection* (London: Callow, 1809), p133.

121   From Scull, 'The Domestication of Madness', p241; the original reference is given as Pargeter, W., *Observations on Maniacal Disorders* (Reading: The Author, 1792), pp50-51.

122   Haslam, *Observations on Madness* ..., p276.

123   Crowther, B., *Practical Remarks on Insanity, to Which is Added a Commentary on the Dissection of the Brains of Maniacs, with some Account of Diseases Incident to the Insane* (London: G. Hayden, 1811); *The Times*, 26 August 1815.

124   *The Edinburgh Medical and Surgical Journal*, Vol 8, 1812, pp96-9. Given the praise that is heaped on Haslam in this review, it is conceivable that the reviewer was in fact the Bethlem Apothecary himself.

125   For details of Matthews's time in France see Williams, D., 'The Missions of David Williams and James Tilly Matthews, 1793', *English Historical Review*, Vol 53, 1938, pp651-68. For a biography of Matthews's life see Jay, M., *The Air Loom Gang* (London: Bantam Books, 2004).

126   Quotes from Haslam, J., *Illustrations of Madness*, Porter, R. (ed) (London: Routledge Kegan and Paul, 1988; originally published in 1809), pp lii, 19.

127   Haslam, *Illustrations of Madness*, p liii.

128   Haslam, *Illustrations of Madness*, pp80-1.

129   Bowen, T., *Remarks upon the Report of a Select Committee of the Governors of Bridewell Hospital* (London: W. Wilson, 1799), p15.

130   O'Donoghue, *The Story of Bethlehem* ..., p287.

131   O'Donoghue, *The Story of Bethlehem* ..., pp286-7; Andrews et al, *The History of Bethlem*, pp398-9.

132   Aleph, *London Scenes and London People* (London: City Press, 1863); Thornbury, W. and Walford, E., *Old and New London* (London, 1878), Vol 2, p200.

133   Andrews et al, *The History of Bethlem*, p400.

134   Gossey Field is now beneath the western portion of Barnsbury Street in Islington, where, by coincidence, the author happened to live for several years. The connection to the Drapers' Company is commemorated by The Drapers Arms public house on Barnsbury Street. Johnson, A. H., *The History of the Worshipful Company of the Drapers of London* (Oxford: Clarendon Press, 1914-22); O'Donoghue, *The Story of Bethlehem* ..., pp289-90; Andrews et al, *The History of Bethlem*, pp400-2.

135   Codrington, T., 'London South of the Thames', *Surrey Archaeological Collections*, Vol 28, 1915, pp11-163.

136   Hughson, D., *London, being an accurate History and Description of the British Metropolis and its Neighbourhood* (London: J. Stratford, 1808), Vol 5, p 34.

137   *The Gentleman's Magazine* (January 1824, p34) notes that the 'purgative spring' was discovered in 1660 and was 'held in considerable esteem'. Porter, G. R., *The Nation in its Various Social and Economical Relations* (London:

Charles Knight, 1843), p243; O'Donoghue, *The Story of Bethlehem* ...,
pp297-300; *Annual Register*, 1788, p206.

138   *The Times*, 28 August 1815.

139   Andrews et al, *The History of Bethlem*, pp405-8; O'Donoghue, *The Story of Bethlehem* ..., pp309-14.

140   Jay, *The Air Loom Gang*, pp264-5.

141   Jay, *The Air Loom Gang*, p265.

142   Hadfield's discharge papers indicate that he was born in Aldersgate, London (TNA: PRO WO 121/25/271). For Hadfield's life before 1800 see Howell, *A Complete Collection of State Trials* ..., Vol 27, p1282.

143   Descriptions of the attempted assassination may be found in several contemporary sources, including *The Times* (London), 16 & 17 May 1800, and *Bell's Weekly Messenger*, 18 May 1800; TNA: PRO KB 33/8/3; TS 11/223; PC 1/3490. A full summary of original sources may be found in Moran, R., 'The Origin of Insanity as a Special Verdict: The Trial for Treason of James Hadfield', *Law and Society Review*, Vol 19, 1985, pp487-519; see also DNB, Vol 24, pp422-3.

144   A transcript of Hadfield's case may be found in Howell, *A Complete Collection of State Trials* ..., Vol 27, pp1282-356. An excellent summary of the case together with its aftermath and implications may be found in *Law and Society Review*, Vol 19, 1985, pp487-519.

145   Details of the Treasury Solicitor's dealings with Hadfield can be found in TNA: PRO 11/223 and also in *Law and Society Review*, Vol 19, 1985, p510.

146   *The Times*, 3 April 1802; Moran, 'The Origin of Insanity...', p516; Anon, *Sketches in Bedlam*, pp14-27; DNB, Vol 24, p423.

147   Howard, J., *The state of the Prisons in England and Wales, with preliminary observations and an account of some foreign prisons and hospitals* (Warrington: Eyres, 1784).

148   Anon, *Report from the Select Committee Appointed to Enquire into the State of Lunatics* (Shannon: Irish University Press, 1968; originally published 1807).

149   *Journal of the House of Commons*, 20 January 1807, p72; 23 January 1807, p76; 15 July 1807, p715; 6 April 1808; 23 June 1808; Anon, *Report from the Select Committee* ....

150   O'Donoghue, *The Story of Bethlehem* ..., pp339, 342-3; Hunter and Macalpine, *Three Hundred Years* ..., p10.

151   See Walker and McCabe, *Criminal Insanity in England*, Vol 2, pp2-5; Andrews et al, *The History of Bethlem*, pp404-5; O'Donoghue, *The Story of Bethlehem* ..., pp342-3.

152   The final cost was £122,572, of which the hospital itself provided £38,369. Andrews et al, *The History of Bethlem*, p409; Timbs, *Curiosities of London*, p52.

153   Anon, *The Annual Report of the Lunatic Asylum erected at York with a Short History of its Rise and Progress* (York, 1785).

154   Mason, W., *Animadversions on the Present Government of the York Lunatic Asylum, in which the case of Parish Paupers is distinctly considered in a Series of Propositions* (York: The Author, 1778); Anon, *A Letter from a Subscriber to the York Lunatic Asylum to the Governors of that Charity* (York: Wilson, Spence and Mawman, 1788).

155   The story of Hannah Mills and the founding of the York Retreat are to be found in Anon, *State of an Institution near York, called the Retreat for Persons afflicted with Disorders of the Mind* (York: The Governors, 1796); Digby, A., *Madness, Morality and Medicine: A Study of the York Retreat, 1796-1914* (Cambridge: Cambridge University Press, 1985); Digby, A., 'Changes in the Asylum: The Case of York, 1777-1815', *The Economic History Review*, Vol 36 (2), 1983, pp218-39; Andrews et al, *The History of Bethlem ...*, pp419-20.

156   Details on the building of the Retreat from Digby, *Madness, Morality ...*, pp18-20. Quote from ibid, p33.

157   Tuke, S., *Description of the Retreat: An Institution near York for Insane Persons of the Society of Friends, containing an Account of its Origin and Progress, the Modes of Treatment, and a Statement of Cases* (London: Dawsons, 1964; originally published in 1813), p223. Also in Digby, *Madness, Morality ...*, p58. The humanitarian treatment of the insane adopted by the Retreat was Britain's first example of European 'moral therapy'. Although Philippe Pinel was best known for such practices, there were others in Europe who had come to a similar conclusion. In Italy, for example, the physician Vincenzo Chiarugi had advocated the establishment of 'therapeutic asylums' in his voluminous 1793 book entitled *On Insanity*. Although Pinel dismissed Chiarugi's works, both men shared a basic belief that the patient was an individual whose mind could be regenerated by the application of kindness, reason and humanity. This was in stark contrast to the segregation, chains, purges and bleeding used by Bedlam and almost every other madhouse.

158   Digby, *Madness, Morality ...*, p238. Original quote cited as being from Tuke, *Memoirs*, entry for 3 January 1811.

159   *York Chronicle*, 25 September 1813.

160   *York Herald*, 23 October 1813; quoted in Digby, 'Changes in the Asylum ...', p226.

161 Godfrey Higgins (1772-1833) was an eccentric man who is best known for his esoteric writings and for his claim to be a 'chosen chief' for an ancient order of British druids. He campaigned for many causes and was described by his parish as being a 'political radical, reforming county magistrate and idiosyncratic historian of religions'.

162 Anon, *State of an Institution* ..., p5.

163 Anon, *A Vindication of Mr Higgins* (York, 1814), p9. Quotes in Digby, 'Changes in the Asylum ...', p226.

164 Scull, A., *The Most Solitary of Afflictions: Madness and Society in Britain, 1700-1900* (New Haven, Conn: Yale University Press, 1993), p111.

165 Descriptions of York Asylum come from Digby, 'Changes in the Asylum ...'; Digby, *Madness, Morality* ...; Hansard, T. C., *The Parliamentary Debates from the Year 1803* ..., p1128; Byrne, J. C., *Undercurrents Overlooked* (London: Richard Bently, 1860), p210.

166 *The Times*, 25 August 1815; Andrews et al, *The History of Bethlem* ..., pp421-2.

167 This patient was named Mrs Fenwick, a former governess to a Mr William Fry. *The Times*, 25 August 1815.

168 *The Times*, 25 August 1815.

169 Haslam, J., *A Letter to the Governors of Bethlem* (London: Taylor and Hessey, 1818), pp2-15; *The Times*, 31 August 1815, 2 September 1815.

170 Haslam, *A Letter to the Governors* ..., pp12-14; see also Scull, A., MacKenzie, C. and Hervey, N., *Masters of Bedlam: the Transformation of the Mad-Doctoring Trade* (Princeton: Princeton University Press, 1996), p32.

171 Rose, G. R., *The Diaries and Correspondence of the Right Hon George Rose* (London: R. Bentley, 1860), Vol 1, p32; Dudley, J. W., *Letters of the Earl of Dudley to the Bishop of Llandaff* (London: J. Murray), p197. For a full biography of Rose, see Thorne, R. G., *The History of Parliament: The Commons, 1790-1820* (London: Secker and Warburg, 1986), Vol 5, pp45-53.

172 Wallett took up his position on 18 February 1815, Forbes on 15 February 1815. *The Times*, 28 August 1815, 29 August 1815.

173 *The Times*, 28 August 1815.

174 *The Times*, 29 August 1815.

175 *The Times*, 25 August 1815.

176 The full Committee consisted of Rose, Wynn, W. Smith, Samuel Whitbread, Robert Seymour, Sir Thomas Baring, Robert Peel, Curtis, Tierney, Shaw, Mr Vessey Fitzgerald, Mr Lockhart, Lord Advocate for Scotland (Archibald Colquhoun), Mr Thompson, Sumner, Mr Hart Davis,

Sir John Newport, Manning, Bennet, Levevre, Mr Frankland Lewis, Mr Tomline, Sturges Bourne. *Journal of the House of Commons*, 1815, p253.

177   *The Times*, 26 August 1815.

178   *The Gentleman's Magazine*, May 1815, p473.

179   *The Times*, 28 August 1815.

180   *The Times*, 28 August 1815.

181   *The Times*, 29 August 1815.

182   *The Times*, 31 August 1815.

183   *The Times*, 4 September 1815. See also Haslam's version of Norris's confinement in Haslam, J., '*A Letter to the Governors ...*'

184   *The Times*, 12 September 1815.

185   *The Times*, 12 September 1815.

186   Anon, *Sketches in Bedlam*, p xiv.

187   Tuke, S., *Practical Hints on the Construction and Economy of Pauper Lunatic Asylums* (York, 1816).

188   See *The Times*, 25, 26, 28, 29, 31 August 1815; 2, 4, 7, 28 September 1815; 4, 12, 26 October 1815; Sharpe, J. B., *Report together with the Minutes of Evidence, and an Appendix of Papers, from the Committee appointed to consider of Provision being made for the better Regulation of Madhouses in England* (London: Baldwin and Co, 1815).

189   Haslam, '*A Letter to the Governors ...*', pp27-8; Monro, T., *Observations of the Physician (Dr. Monro) and Apothecary (Mr. Haslam) of Bethlem Hospital, upon the evidence taken before the Committee of the House of Commons for regulating madhouses* (London: H. Bryer, 1816).

190   Martin, F. O., *The Report of the Commissioners for Enquiry into Charities for 1837* (London, 1837), p518.

191   *The Times*, 15 April 1816.

192   Hansard, *The Parliamentary Debates ...*, pp426-7.

193   Monro, T., *Observations of the Physician ...*

194   *The Times*, 13 May 1816.

195   Haslam, *Illustrations of Madness*, p xxxix; Haslam, '*A Letter to the Governors ...*', pp30-1; Jay, *The Air Loom Gang*, pp305-6.

196   *The Times*, 16 May 1816.

197   DNB, Vol 38, pp664-5; *The Times*, 9 November 1816.

198   John Lumsden Propert was born near Cardigan on 19 July 1793. He was educated at Cardigan Grammar School but left at the age of fifteen to become an ensign in a militia regiment. He left the service in 1809 and qualified as a naval surgeon, after which he obtained the diploma of Member

of the Royal College of Surgeons. In 1851 he founded the Royal Medical Benevolent College (now Epsom College), a foundation that would benefit members of the medical profession and their families if they fell on hard times. Propert died of cerebral apoplexy on 9 September 1867, aged 74.

199   *The Times*, 21 June 1816; 28 August 1815.

200   Haslam, '*A Letter to the Governors ...*', pp56-7.

201   Haslam, '*A Letter to the Governors ...*', pp17-18.

202   DNB, Vol 25, pp710-11; Scull et al, *Masters of Bedlam ...*, pp37-8; *Annual Register*, 1844, p254.

203   Hansard, *The Parliamentary Debates ...*, pp1126-7.

204   Hansard, *The Parliamentary Debates ...*, p860.

205   *Lords' Calendar*, p120 (26 June 1816); *Journal of the House of Commons*, p31 (5 February 1817); *Lords' Calendar*, p122 (21 March 1817); Hansard, *The Parliamentary Debates...*, pp142-143 (3 February 1818); pp971-974 (10 March 1819); *Journal of the House of Commons*, p210 (10 February 1819); Hansard, *House of Lords*, pp1344-1348 (26 June 1819).

206   *The Times*, 13 May 1816; 12 June 1816.

207   Hansard, *The Parliamentary Debates ...*, col 1126 (17 June 1816).

208   Munk, *The Roll of the Royal Colleg e...*, Vol iii, pp153-4, 171-2; DNB, Vol 55, p710. Tuthill received a knighthood in 1820.

209   Martin, F. O., *The Report of the Commissioners for Enquiry*, p525.

210   Poole, S., *The Politics of Regicide in England, 1760-1850: Troublesome Subjects* (Manchester: Manchester University Press, 2001), p133; Ingram, I., *The Madhouse Language* (London: Routledge, 1992), p153; Metcalf, U., *The Interior of Bethlehem Hospital* (London: The Author, 1818).

211   O'Donoghue, *The Story of Bethlehem ...*, p329.

212   Anon, *Sketches in Bedlam*, p xxx.

213   The above information comes from Anon, *Sketches in Bedlam*.

214   O'Donoghue, *The Story of Bethlehem ...*, pp346-7.

215   Anon, *Sketches in Bedlam*, p 297.

216   Martin, F. O., *An Account of Bethlem Hospital: Abridged from the Report of the Late Charity Commissioners* (London: William Pickering, 1853).

217   Martin, *An Account ...*, p8.

218   Wright, E., *Bethlem Hospital Minutes of Evidence taken by the Committee, Appointed to Inquire into the Charges inferred against Dr Wright and his Answer* (London: Mills, Jowett, and Mill, 1830); O'Donoghue, *The Story of Bethlehem ...*, p330; Andrews et al, *The History of Bethlem*, pp442-3

219   Martin, *The Report...*, pp8-9; O'Donoghue, *The Story of Bethlehem* ...,
       pp330-1.
220   Tompson, R., *The Charity Commission and the Age of Reform* (London:
       Routledge and Kegan Paul, 1979); Martin, *An Account* ....
221   Martin, *An Account...*, p29; Andrews et al, *The History of Bethlem*, p436.
222   Martin, *An Account...*, pp29-40.
223   *The Lancet*, 21 November 1840, p296.
224   *Hansard*, 21 September 1841, col 693.
225   *Hansard*, 3 May 1842; *Bills Public*, 1842, Vol 3, pp113-26. My italics.
226   Webster, J., *Observations on the Admission of Medical Pupils to the Wards of
       Bethlem Hospital, for the Purpose of Studying Mental Diseases* (London: The
       Author, 1842).
227   Anon, *Report of the Metropolitan Commissioners in Lunacy to the Lord Chancellor
       1844* (London: Bradbury and Evans, 1844), p54.
228   Hervey, N., 'A Slavish Bowing Down: the Lunacy Commission and the
       Psychiatric Profession 1845-1860', in Bynum, W. F., Porter, R. and
       Shepherd, M., *The Anatomy of Madness*, Vol ii, p124; Hervey, N., 'Advocacy
       or folly: the Alleged Lunatics' Friend Society, 1845-63', *Medical History*, Vol
       30(3), 1986, pp245-75.
229   *The Lancet*, 15 May 1852, p483; Andrews et al, *The History of Bethlem* ...,
       p467
230   Andrews et al, *The History of Bethlem* ..., p468.
231   *Report of the Commissioners*, Vol i, pp421-30, Vol ii, pp125-7; *Journal of Mental
       Science*, Vol 32, 1886, pp235-6; *The Times*, 14 June 1881; *Journal of the Royal
       College of Surgeons Edinburgh*, Vol 25(4), 1980, pp219-32.
232   Hervey, N., *The Lunacy Commission 1845-60, with Special Reference to the
       Implementation of Policy in Kent and Surrey* (Unpublished PhD, University of
       Bristol, 1987), Vol 1, pp426-7; O'Donoghue, *The Story of Bethlem* ..., pp332-
       3.
233   Hervey, *The Lunacy Commission* ..., Vol i, pp421-30; *The Lancet*, 23 April
       1853, p396.
234   *The Lancet*, 22 May 1852, pp499-500 (edited).
235   *The Lancet*, 5 June 1852, pp546-7.
236   O'Donoghue, *The Story of Bethlem* ..., pp332.
237   For Wood's resignation letter see *The Lancet*, 17 July 1852, pp66-7.
238   *The Lancet*, 5 June 1852, pp546-7.
239   *The Lancet*, 23 April 1853, p396; Andrews et al, *The History of Bethlem*, p480;
       The Lancet, 17 July 1852, p60.

240   Hervey, *The Lunacy Commission* ..., Vol i, pp427-8.

241   Information from Alleridge, P. H., *Bethlem Royal Hospital* (Bethlem & Maudsley NHS Trust, 1996) and annual reports of the South London and Maudsley NHS Foundation Trust.

Index